The Drama's Patrons

THE DRAMA'S PATRONS

A STUDY OF THE EIGHTEENTH-
CENTURY LONDON AUDIENCE

by Leo Hughes

UNIVERSITY OF TEXAS PRESS
AUSTIN & LONDON

International Standard Book Number 0–292–70091–1
Library of Congress Catalog Card Number 74–146971
Copyright © 1971 by Leo Hughes

Printed by The University of Texas Printing Division, Austin
Bound by Universal Bookbindery, Inc., San Antonio

The drama's laws, the drama's patrons give,
For we that live to please, must please to live.

*Samuel Johnson's Prologue for the opening
of Drury Lane, September 1747.*

PREFACE

The following study represents almost a quarter century of accumulating materials on the theatrical public in London from the days of Dryden to those of Sheridan. It attempts to show the complex interrelationship between playgoer and performer and, somewhat more incidentally, playwright. It tries to discover how an increasingly self-conscious public thought of itself, of its newly realized privileges and powers. Further, it attempts to describe, hopefully without distortion, what the leading poet of the age called "the many-headed monster of the pit," to show in some detail audience behavior, which, though not actually monstrous, was by no means uniformly placid. Finally, it tries to analyze the principal changes in taste, in manners, and in moral attitudes.

Since my aim has been to gather evidence from contemporary newspapers, pamphlets, plays, criticisms, diaries, letters—all of which exist in profusion in our great libraries and private collections—my principal indebtedness is to institutions, especially to libraries and foundations, rather than to individuals. Grants from the Guggenheim Foundation, from the Folger Shakespeare Library, and from The University of Texas Research Institute have enabled me to carry this work to its completion. My one extensive debt to fellow scholars is a complex one to acknowledge, yet very real. Since I had completed most of my collecting before the first volumes of *The London Stage* appeared, I am not actually in debt to its editors for many details, and those few I have borrowed I have been careful to acknowledge in the notes. I have, however, relied heavily upon *The London Stage* in the writing of this book, principally in my dependence on its full calendar and repertory. Perhaps the best way to state the case would be to say that if this splendid work had been available twenty years ago my own labors would have been reduced appreciably.

CONTENTS

The Drama's Patrons

1. Role and Rights

IN THE PAST GENERATION or so the significance of analogical or metaphorical expression has become increasingly apparent, not merely for its rhetorical usefulness but even more for the wealth of suggestion such expression can convey, sometimes without the speaker's awareness. England in the critical period following the Revolutionary Settlement of 1689 was becoming more conscious of the problems of self-government, especially of the overriding problem of equilibrium between the demands of the many and the demands of the one, between maintaining public peace and security and affording a maximum of individual liberty. From this search for the precise point of equilibrium—a search we now know to be endless yet ever necessary—grew something of an obsession with government, an obsession revealed in the recurrence of symbols involving affairs of state.

The theatre of the day provides ample illustration of this stress on government—on the struggle for power—and of the extension of the power base as people became increasingly jealous of their new-found rights. In the third number of his *Theatre* (9 January 1720) Richard Steele playfully proposed, as a means of suiting public taste better than the former practice, a form of governing board to be "stil'd auditors of the drama." Combining as usual pleasantry and serious purpose, Steele set forth in some detail the manner of election and representation: the various parts of the house would be represented by ladies, by cits, by gentlemen of wit and pleasure, even by a footman who "can write and read [and who] shall be Mercury to the board."[1]

In the famous prologue from which I take the title for this study, Samuel Johnson touches more fleetingly on the same kind of analogue. "The drama's laws the drama's patrons give" suggests a representative body with the full force of the electorate behind it. And Johnson's friend and former pupil David Garrick chose the same metaphor for more detailed elaboration a generation later in his epilogue to John Burgoyne's *Maid of the Oaks* (1774).

> With more than pow'r of parliament you sit,
> Despotic representatives of wit!
> For in a moment, and without much pother,
> You can dissolve this piece, and call another!
> As 'tis no treason, let us frankly see,
> In what they differ, and in what agree,
> The said supreme assembly of the nation,
> With this our great Dramatic Convocation!
> Business in both oft meets with interruption:
> In both, we trust, no brib'ry or corruption;
> Both proud of freedom, have a turn to riot,
> And the best Speaker cannot keep you quiet.

In another prologue by Johnson, this one for his friend Oliver Goldsmith's *Good-Natured Man* (1768), further parallels with government are employed. This time the audience represents not the chosen representatives who make the laws but the even more powerful body politic to which the lawmakers are responsible for their very offices.

---

[1] Richard Steele, *The Theatre, 1720*, edited by John Loftis, p. 10.

> Distrest alike, the statesman and the wit,
> When one a borough courts, and one the pit,
> The busy candidates for pow'r and fame
> Have hopes and fears and wishes just the same.

A whole florilegium of examples might easily be gathered from contemporary commentaries, examples in which the audience is seen as resembling a legislature, a judiciary, the whole electorate.[2] Common to all are the concepts of power, of right, of authority, with scarcely more than a hint of responsibility, for this was an age in which the English people led the world in a realization of emerging power and right vested in the people.

With the growing realization of power came, inevitably, a growing self-awareness, a search for terms with which to describe both role and identity. The problem of role, or the function of the whole audience, not the role-playing of individual spectators, can be far more briefly stated than the problem of identity or definition of that audience. Meyer Howard Abrams has provided an incisive account of the role of the audience in an age dominated by a "pragmatic" view of literary aims.

To Sidney, poetry, by definition, has a purpose—to achieve certain

[2] "As they [the public] are the sole judges of what is transacted before the curtain they are (when the director can't put an end to such disputes) to judge of the follies behind it; and whatever right an actress or a manager may claim, there is some right in an audience" (letter signed "Coke upon Littleton," *London Daily Post and General Advertiser*, 4 December 1736).

"If the Publick is the sole Judge of Theatrical Performances; if the Approbation or Dislike of an Actor depends upon them, and the Manager regulates his Conduct accordingly: He is in fact no more than Agent for the Publick, and stands accountable to them for the Disposal of that Money they so liberally bestow" (*The Disputes between the Managers of the Theatres and Their Actors Adjusted*, pp. 8–9).

"As I address this letter to you in the spirit of the public, I expect to be attended to; for though an histrionic monarchy, you hold your empire on their opinion" (*Bingley's Journal*, 29 September 1770).

"The public is the only jury before whom the merits of an actor or actress are to be tried, and when the endeavors of a performer are stampt by them with the seal of sanction and applause, from that there should be no appeal" (*Theatrical Guardian*, 5 March 1791).

effects in an audience. It imitates only as a means to the proximate end of pleasing, and pleases, it turn out, only as a means to the ultimate end of teaching; for "right poets" are those who "imitate both to delight and teach, and delight to move men to take that goodnes in hande, which without delight they would flye as from a stranger. . . ." As a result, throughout this essay the needs of the audience become the fertile grounds for critical distinctions and standards.[3]

Abrams is well aware that the pragmatic critic of the eighteenth century was, like Sir Philip Sidney, quick to use the magic name of Aristotle to lend weight to his demand for a kind of literature that would both delight and teach. In placing the emphasis on this combination, the pragmatic critic was, however, using not Aristotle but Horace—and even adding an emphasis foreign to the Roman. There were adequate indications, even here and there a frank admission, that edification was no real concern of many playgoers. Horace had provided an alternative as well as a combination of entertainment and edification: "Poets aim either to benefit, or to delight, or to unite what will give pleasure with what is serviceable for life."[4] Harry Bailly doubtless represents the common demand of the audience when, having "stynted" Chaucer in his burlesque romance, he suggests a fresh start.

> Lat se wher thou kanst tellen aught in geeste,
> Or telle in prose somwhat, at the leeste,
> In which there be som murthe or som doctryne.[5]

By Sidney's time, as Abrams indicates, it seemed unwise, particularly with the puritanical Stephen Gosson about, to admit the possibility of aiming at "murthe" alone.

Other Gossons arose in time, named William Prynne or Jeremy Collier or William Law, so that by the end of the seventeenth century even a writer like William Congreve, badly miscast as moral reformer, defends his work in the same familiar terms. A passage

---

[3] Meyer Howard Abrams, *The Mirror and the Lamp*, pp. 14–15.

[4] Horace, *The Art of Poetry*, ll. 334–335.

[5] Geoffrey Chaucer, *The Canterbury Tales*, edited by F. N. Robinson, p. 167.

from William Shenstone, a man of uncommon sense, confirms that edification, not mirth alone, is a prerequisite.

Notwithstanding all that Rousseau has advanced so very ingeniously upon plays and players, their profession is, like that of a painter, one of the imitative arts, whose means are pleasure, and whose end is virtue. They both alike, for a subsistence, submit themselves to public opinion; and the dishonour that has attended the last profession seems not easily accountable.[6]

Clearly the audience assumed an important role in determining the content of eighteenth-century plays,[7] and the playgoers were quick to accept it. The importance of audience acceptance forces the crucial question of identity: Who were the critics? At first glimpse there may seem to be no mystery at all. The critics are the audience, the auditors and viewers who, to borrow modern terminology, sit out there beyond the footlights. They are "the town" to whom Theophilus Cibber addresses himself in his *Epistle . . . to David Garrick* (1755). Cibber acknowledges the existence of the problem of definition, though he disposes of it with deceptive ease.

This phrase [the town] has been made frequent use of, without any determinate meaning. . . . I think, the town may be supposed to include all degrees of persons, from the highest nobleman, to the lowly artizan, &c. who, in their different stations, are encouragers of dramatic performances:—Thus all persons, who pay for their places, whether noble, gentle, or simple, who fill the boxes, pit, and galleries, in a theatrical

---

[6] William Shenstone, "Essays on Men, Manners and Things," in *The Works in Verse and Prose*, II, 269.

[7] Just how "pragmatic" a view this is in the case of the theatre may be seen in its wide acceptance today: "The drama is unique among the arts in its dependence upon the immediate reactions of a large audience. . . . Every dramatist in a secular society must compromise with the demands of the mummers and the tastes of the crowd" (Richard Findlater, *The Unholy Trade*, p. 18). "Of all literary kinds, drama, in the success of which collective appreciation and the taste of the average man count for so much, offered the most stubborn resistance to the declared and open change" (Louis Cazamian, *A History of French Literature*, p. 367). "Drama, more than other arts, is responsive to the society which produces it; being so public in both its essence and its limitation" (Laurence Kitchin, *Mid-Century Drama*, p. 28).

sense, form the town; as k——g, l——rds and commons, in a constitutional one, make that great body, the nation.[8]

Of all persons, "young" Cibber, as he was called to distinguish him from his more famous father, must have been aware of the folly of treating as one and the same group those who "are encouragers of dramatic performances" and those who simply "pay for their places."[9] There are frequent occasions on which claimants to the title of audience would appear to be identified not with Cibber's encouragers of dramatic performances or with those who pay for their places but quite precisely with the minority that comes resolved to hiss—or to applaud.[10] Over the long period treated here, however, we cannot afford to accept anything so narrow. We must account for the disapprovers, though not for the Gossons who only disapprove from a distance. We must even account for the non-payers, especially for the many in a "papered" house[11] who come with orders in hand and their prejudices already well fixed. In short, what I am intent upon here might better be labeled caveat

---

[8] Theophilus Cibber, *An Epistle from Theophilus Cibber to David Garrick Esq.*, p. 2.

[9] For a fictitious but nonetheless plausible scene of both Cibbers and their easy acceptance of the jeers of an audience, see Henry Fielding's picture of them as Marplay Senior and Junior in the revised *Author's Farce* (1734). For an account of young Cibber in an actual encounter with concerted opposition, when "his old friend impudence kept him from being either out of his countenance or in the least disturb'd at the noise," see *The Wentworth Papers, 1705–1739*, edited by James Joel Cartwright, p. 541.

[10] The question "who speaks for the town?" which goes directly to the point at issue, was asked at some of the most crucial points in the history of occasional violence in the theatre: (1) on 8 December 1743 when "Bystander" asks it in the *London Daily Post*; (2) in January–February 1763 when the author of *Theatrical Disquisitions* asks it; (3) in 1773 in connection with the Macklin riots.

[11] This still current phrase appeared two centuries ago in an anonymous attack on George Colman, in *The Spleen: or, The Offspring of Folly* (1776). It is glossed as referring to "not a house built of cards, or paper'd, instead of being wainscoted; but a theatre filled with written orders, to prevent the success of good writers, support the dullness of bad ones, and enforce the villainous impositions of managers."

rather than definition, for precise definition applicable night after night for the long period involved is not easy to come by.

As the audience became more aware of its political powers, it sought parallels with state affairs in the theatre. These parallels permit close examination of the various claims of *rights, powers, privileges*, and *authority*. Easily the most significant document produced by the Revolutionary Settlement of 1689 was the first Bill of Rights. "Rights" became the by-word, as may be observed in the final, climactic provision for Steele's proposed board of governors, the only one of the eleven provisions requiring an elaboration, which was designed for emphasis:

This Body so chosen, shall have full Power, in the Right of the Audiences *of Great Britain*, to approve, condemn, or rectify whatever shall be exhibited on the *English* Theatre.

And the Players guiding themselves by their Laws, shall not be accountable to, or controlled by any other Opinions or Suggestions whatever, nor ever appeal from the Judgments of these duly elected *Auditors*. Provided notwithstanding, that any daily Spectators shall have reserv'd to them, and their Successors for ever, their full Right of Applauding, or Disliking the Performance of any particular Actor, whenever his Care, or Negligence, shall appear to deserve either the one, or the other: But in Matters merely relating to the Conduct of the Theatre, the said elected *Auditors*, from time to time, shall be deemed able, and to have Right, to give Laws for ever.[12]

Just how seriously Steele meant this sweeping claim to be taken is hard to say. His own awareness of the shadow of power under which he was then operating as a sharer in the management of Drury Lane doubtless contributed something. Watson Nicholson has briefly sketched the lord chamberlain's involvement in theatrical affairs.[13] More recently, John Loftis has supplied a full account of Steele's own share in these events.[14] Steele was to die before the

---

[12] Steele, *Theatre, 1720*, p. 10.

[13] See Watson Nicholson, *The Struggle for a Free Stage in London*, pp. 16–19.

[14] Details of the story can be found in Nicholson, *Struggle*; and John Loftis, *Steele at Drury Lane*, especially pp. 121–149.

more significant struggle with the full power of the national government began. The greater struggle was caused by a combination of loosely related events—the production of some plays by John Gay and Henry Fielding, especially, which seemed to subvert both authority and morality, and the increase in the number of unlicensed theatres, especially one in the East End. Those in charge of state affairs eventually felt obliged to reassert the authority of the state.[15] After two abortive attempts in 1733 and 1735, the Licensing Act was passed in 1737;[16] the act limited severely the number of theatres and required all plays to be submitted to a state licenser.

This law, while curbing sharply the powers Steele had proposed for his imaginary board of auditors,[17] still left a great deal of authority to the English audience. The state licenser might have the power to say what plays were *not* to be played; he had none over what was to be played and, more important, none over how these plays were to be received. The power and right to approve or disapprove a licensed play was reserved to the audience, almost without limit.

Since the two concepts of power or authority and rights or privileges are not precisely synonymous, though often overlapping, it may be more practical to treat them separately. Already asserted are the extent of the power or authority of an audience, chiefly in the form of claim—"sole judge," "only jury," "no appeal"—and at least one concession from the traditionally rival claimant, the man-

[15] Nicholson, *Struggle*, pp. 46–71; P. J. Crean, "The Stage Licensing Act of 1737," *Modern Philology*, 35 (August 1937–May 1938), 239–255.

[16] See Nicholson, *Struggle*, pp. 55–59, 63–71. The attempt in 1733 came to nothing. The one in 1735 was led by the City. Sir John Barnard and his colleagues were motivated by a concern over morality and economics but hastily withdrew their bill when they discovered their Court allies intent only upon strengthening the powers of the Lord Chamberlain.

[17] The Licensing Act provided another important curb, as an objector to the raising of prices late in the century was to recall. When told that he had an alternative to paying the higher price, he pointed out the emptiness of the alternative: "This could only be true if the stage were left unshackled by charters and if it were left open to any man to build a theatre" (item from unidentified newsclipping, 17 September 1792, British Museum, London).

ager—Garrick's "with more than power of parliament you sit." To these can be added many more instances and the even more forceful evidence of behavior motivated by an assumption of power conferred by right.

Assertions of power form a leitmotiv throughout the century. Sometimes they appear as straightforward statements.

This point . . . I reduce to one general head: an audience, which may be justly look'd upon as the *primum mobile* of all diversions, by whose generosity they are supported and by whose smiles or frowns they flourish or languish.[18]

. . . I believe we shall find the town in general to be justly and actually the governor of the stage, as it now stands: for tho' it be in the power of a manager to produce what actors and what pieces he pleases, yet the town, if they differ from him in opinion, will immediately bring him over to theirs.[19]

A public performer is so much in the power of spectators that all unnecessary severity is restrained by that general law of humanity which forbids us to be cruel where there is nothing to be feared.[20]

The power of an audience is well known, and, too often, wantonly, and absurdly asserted.[21]

The *public* is their *critic*—without whose fair approbation they know no play can rest on the stage, and with whose applause they welcome such attacks as yours.[22]

Sometimes the assertions appear in the less direct form of a suggestion of master-servant relationship. The age-old formulation remained unchanged but it no longer matched the facts: the theatrical companies still labeled themselves in playbills as Their Majesties Servants, but everyone was aware of the shift in power, and there were occasions when the actual master-servant relationship was asserted, for the guidance of actors or managers who showed any disposition to forget.[23]

[18] James Ralph, *The Touch-Stone* (1728), p. 136.
[19] "Occasional Prompter," No. 19, in *Daily Journal*, 25 March 1737.
[20] *Idler*, No. 25, 7 October 1758.
[21] *Theatrical Disquisitions*, p. 12.
[22] Richard Brinsley Sheridan, *Critic* (1779), I, i.
[23] The samples given here by no means exhaust the supply. Others appear in

The servants of the public ought certainly to live by the public. . . . It is impudent in a servant [the theatrical manager] to talk thus to his masters. . . . For the public strictly and truly speaking are the player's masters and his [the manager's] too.[24]

. . . for as they are servants to the publick, and afford at a very considerable price, no inconsiderable part of their entertainment, I shall never see them either unjust or ungrateful to the publick without speaking.[25] Whatever notions modern performers may have imbibed, by inflated applause and profuse recompence, actors are neither more or less than the servants of the public. 'Tis the public that gives them countenance; 'tis the public that supports the theatre; 'tis the public that pays them their wages; and whenever they are disobedient, refractory or insolent, 'tis the public that must correct them.[26]

Tho' I am sensible my affairs are too inconsiderable to be laid before the publick, yet as I am their servant, and have been so much favour'd with their indulgence I thought it my duty to [do] my utmost to contribute to their entertainment.[27]

The company of comedians may still be *called* the servants of the public, but how empty and ridiculous will appear this nominal compliment, when the public are become the servants of the managers.[28]

Even where the power of the audience is not stated explicity it is often conceded in a variety of ways. Following George Farquhar's *Discourse* (1702), with its suggestion that "the rules of English comedy don't lie in the compass of Aristotle or his followers but in the pit, box, and galleries," are repeated suggestions on the part of playwright and actor that the audience should determine the plays

---

D–ry-L–ne P–yh–se broke open (1748), *Morning Chronicle* (24 November 1773), *Critical Review* (November 1773), *Town and Country Magazine* (April 1775), and *The Playhouse Pocket-companion, or Theatrical Vade-mecum* (1779). An equally long list of comments by actors who themselves accepted the servant role might be drawn up. Instead of providing such a list, I cite as conclusive a trio of statements by David Garrick: *London Daily Post* (2 and 3 December 1743); *Letters*, edited by David Mason Little and George Morrow Kahrl, II, 429–431, No. 341 (10 November 1764) and No. 1309 (*post* 1766).

[24] *The Case of Our Present Theatrical Disputes*, pp. 4, 47.

[25] *The Inspector*, No. 530 (21 November 1752).

[26] *A Dialogue in the Green-room upon a Disturbance in the Pit* (1763), p. vii.

[27] *General Advertiser*, 2 December 1743.

[28] *The Monthly Mirror*, I (1795–1796), 182.

to be given. The same advice is offered, in even bolder terms, by Charles Molloy in the preface to his three-act *Half-Pay Officers* (1720), which he presents as a mere sample, with more to come if this pleases. And, to cite just one more instance, the official pronouncement of the Drury Lane management in September 1774 little more than echoes this view. Their plan for the season is to offer their best actors in their best plays and "in selecting these they will be guided by *the received estimation* of the pieces" (emphasis supplied), by which they quite clearly mean not critical acclaim but public applause.

Another kind of evidence, that supplied by actions rather than words, would be even more convincing if only there were proof that the audience was in every case speaking in unison. Occasions in which only a comparatively small segment could bring proceedings to a halt unless and until their wishes were complied with are legion. Still, there are numerous occasions when the "town" acted with something approaching unanimity to make its wishes known and to exert its considerable power.

Two accounts in the *Daily Journal* for 5 and 8 January 1722 leave little room for doubt concerning the reception of Colley Cibber's *Rival Fools*. The first performance met with such violence that a more diffident actor-playwright-manager than Cibber would have withdrawn the play. The second night it was not allowed to go beyond the end of the third act and was never again attempted.

A less negative action was taken a few years later at the rival theatre in Lincoln's Inn Fields. In a letter to Jonathan Swift dated 20 March 1728 John Gay tells the story.

On the benefit day of one of the actresses last week one of the players falling sick they were oblig'd to give out another play or dismiss the audience; a play was given out, but the people call'd out for the Beggar's Opera, & they were forc'd to play it, or the audience would not have stayed.[29]

Other examples involving support for or opposition to specific plays

[29] Alexander Pope, *Correspondence*, edited by George Sherburn, II, 478–479.

or performers could be cited, but perhaps one more, this involving a quite different matter, will suffice. An entry in the diary of William Hopkins, prompter at Drury Lane, for 5–6 October 1768 reads:

This morning a printed paper was handed about requesting the lovers of theatrical Performances to meet this evening at the theatre to insist upon the doors not being opened till five o'clock.—As soon as the curtain was up, they called for Mr. Garrick, and would not suffer the play to begin. Mr. King went on and told the audience, "that he was desired by the managers to tell them the doors for the future should not be opened till Five," A great Clap,—He added, "that the managers was always willing to oblige the publick in everything that was in their power; but they thought that on very full nights it would be attended with some inconvenience." They would not hear of any alteration,—he then told them, "the doors should always for the future be opened at five, unless the publick applyed to have it altered."[30]

2

A possibly more significant—certainly a more excitingly dramatic—manifestation of the new obsession with power taken over by the people is observable in the repeated assertion of rights. A sage remark by Alexis de Tocqueville, aimed at the new democracy in America but applicable here, emphasizes at once the advantages and the dangers of power newly transferred.

It cannot be doubted that the moment at which political rights are granted to a people that had before been without them is a very critical one, that the measure, though often necessary, is always dangerous. A child may kill before he is aware of the value of life; and he may deprive another person of his property before he is aware that his own may be taken from him. The lower orders, when they are first invested with political rights, stand in relation to those rights in the same position as the child does to the whole of nature; and the celebrated adage may then be applied to them: *Homo puer robustus.*[31]

The French observer had already been anticipated by Goldsmith in a strongly worded passage in *The Traveller* (1764):

[30] William Hopkins, MS Diary, Folger Shakespeare Library, Washington, D.C.
[31] Alexis de Tocqueville, *Democracy in America,* I, 246.

That independence Britons prize too high
Keeps man from man, and breaks the social tie;
The self-dependent lordlings stand alone,
All claims that bind and sweeten life unknown;
See, though by circling deeps together held,
Minds combat minds, repelling and repell'd.[32]

(ll. 339–344)

The histories of two widely separated segments of the audience, the footmen in the upper gallery and the beaux on the stage, aptly illustrate Tocqueville's analysis and demonstrate the problems of democracy. In France the story of the footmen provides a revealing contrast to the situation in England. Evidently the servants did not behave in a manner sufficiently respectful of their betters, the state intervened, and lackeys were banned from the Comédie Française.[33] In England such intervention would have seemed impolitic, not to say tyrannical. In the second number of his *Theatre* (5 January 1720), Steele published a letter ostensibly from an actor who professes to be alarmed by the appearance of a self-appointed censor of matters theatrical.

You cannot but be sensible, Sir, that the English Actors stand upon a more precarious foot, than persons of any other profession whatsoever; nay, than even actors themselves do in any other country: Our neigh-

[32] The right to approve or disapprove of a performer or performance had been asserted well before the Bill of Rights. Twenty-one years earlier the poor clerk in Thomas Shadwell's *Sullen Lovers* (1668) protests because Sir Positive will not concede his right to protest, once he has paid his eighteen pence (III, i, 424–426). More seriously, John Dryden, who was no great admirer of the mob, conceded in his *Vindication of the Duke of Guise* (1683) that "To clap or hiss are the privileges of a freeborn subject in a playhouse" (p. 19). This sentiment is echoed on certain critical occasions when the state authorities indicated an intent to suppress free expression. See for example: *Common Sense* II, 218–219, involving the invasion of a French troupe in 1737; *Some Considerations on the Establishment of the French Strolers*, involving a second such invasion in 1749; *A Dialogue in the Green-room*, involving the riots over advanced prices in 1763.

[33] John Lough says that it is difficult to establish the date of the proclamation banning lackeys from the Comédie Française but quotes the *ordonnance* issued in 1716 when the Comédie Italienne reopened. The 1716 order bans "*tous domestiques portant livrées sans aucune réserve, exception, ni distinction*" (*Paris Theatre Audiences in the Seventeenth and Eighteenth Centuries*, pp. 77–78).

bours, the French, 'tis true, are under absolute power, but then they are under absolute protection: Here our audiences are often disturb'd by the caprice of two or three unruly people; nay, here the very footmen give laws to their masters, and will not suffer any one but themselves to be heard, till they are easy in their places, tho' they never pay for them. In France no one in a livery is admitted, even for his money; and all clamour, as hissings, and the like annoyance, is not only shameful, but criminal. But this particular happiness of our French brethren is owing to the same power that makes their fellow-subjects a miserable people: And while we are sure our defenceless condition is owing to that liberty, which makes every other English-man happy, it alleviates our distress.

Though footmen seem not to have commanded the attention of the observant Samuel Pepys in the first decade after the Restoration, a French visitor commented in 1676 that "*le paradis* [upper gallery] *est pour les lacquais qui entrent gratuitement*," an inaccurate statement if he means either that the gallery was reserved for them or that they were admitted free at the start of the play. Montague Summers, from whom I take the passage, observes that only the fifth act was free, but he quotes a rather late document, the opening lines of Thomas Southerne's *Wives Excuse* (1691), in support.[34] Possibly those responsible for collecting money had by this late in the play relaxed their vigilance so that liveried servants in attendance on their masters at the theatre had begun to crowd in toward the end of the play. Having established a precedent, they would doubtless have counted such admission a privilege and then a right.

Equally conjectural is the date at which Christopher Rich actually opened the gallery to the footmen for the entire play. Colley Cibber, looking back forty years later, recalls vividly the result of the manager's ruse to fill empty benches and curry favor with the footmen, but he does not attempt to fix the date.

This riotous privilege, so craftily given, and which from custom was at last ripened into right, became the most disgraceful nuisance that ever depreciated the theatre. How often have the most polite audiences, in

[34] Montague Summers, *The Restoration Theatre*, pp. 25–26.

the most affecting scenes of the best plays, been disturbed and insulted by the noise and clamour of these savage spectators![35]

Support for Cibber's strong language and the hazards of an insistence on ill-established rights are found in another passage from Southerne, which shows how far the liveried servants had advanced by 1691.

Act I, Scene i. *The outward room to the musick-meeting. Several footmen at hazard, some rising from play.*
1 Foot. A pox on these musick meetings; there's no fifth act
Here, a free cost, as we have at the play-houses,
To make gentlemen of us, and keep us out of
Harms way. [The printer evidently took this to be blank verse.][36]

Ten years later the impatience of these aspirants to gentility prompted them to attempt to extend their playhouse privilege by force. An item dated 27/30 December 1701 in the *New State of Europe* reports:

On Saturday night, there being a consort of Musick at the Theatre in Little Lincoln's Inn Fields, some of the footmen that were waiting, endeavouring to force into the house in opposition of the centinel, were all engag'd instantly in a bloody quarrel: whereupon the centinel firing upon 'em, kill'd one of 'em upon the spot, and several others were wounded in the scuffle.[37]

Numerous comments during the next generation and more testify to the impatience of both players and audiences with a kind of behavior that must have been intolerable. Passages from the *Female Tatler* and the *Touch-Stone* serve to represent public feeling in general.

Dropt near the play-house in the Haymarket, a bundle of horsewhips, design'd to belabor the footmen in the upper gallery, who almost every night this winter, have made such an intollerable disturbance that the

[35] Colley Cibber, *An Apology for the Life of Mr. Colley Cibber*, edited by Robert William Lowe, I, 233–234.
[36] Thomas Southerne, *The Wives Excuse: or, Cuckolds Make Themselves*, I, i, 1–4.
[37] The substance of this entry is reproduced by Avery in *The London Stage*, edited by William Van Lennep, et al., pt. 2, p. 17.

players could not be heard, and their masters forc'd to hiss 'em into silence. Whoever has taken up the said whips is desir'd to leave 'em with my Lord Rake's porter, several noblemen resolving to exercise 'em on their backs the next frosty morning.[38]

Our Servants (because not Slaves) are suffer'd to disturb at Will our politest Amusements: At an immense Sum we support these Entertainments, and they are allow'd gratis to put the Negative upon our hearing them: The Bread they eat, the Cloaths they wear are ours: yet, with one in their Belly, and the other on their Back, their Rudeness dare stand betwixt Us and our Pleasures; and the meanest Footman unpunished, fly in the Face of the whole Court.

'Tis well I write this, where the Truth from fatal Experience cannot be called in Question; for no such Liberties or Insolencies would be tolerated in any Part of the Globe, but Great Britain.[39]

It would be gratifying to report that the footmen eventually tired of making such utter nuisances of themselves and were tamed into something like genteel behavior. Unfortunately this part of the story has no such pleasant outcome. The heat generated between "repelling and repelled" finally reached the point of ignition, the footmen carried their arrogance beyond any tolerable bounds, and the rest of the audience revolted, their reaction taking a form quite different, it should be emphasized, from what it had been in France, where the government was called upon to intervene. I call attention to an ironic coincidence: during the very spring the audience was settling its own affairs concerning the obstreperous footmen, Sir Robert Walpole's government was preparing to assert, or establish, its authority over political satirists in the theatre.

On the night of Saturday 19 February 1737 the pit at Drury Lane led a revolt in which other members of the audience ardently joined and, even before the play began, evicted the noisemakers, meanwhile extracting from Charles Fleetwood a promise that he would no longer keep a "footmen's gallery." Before the first act was over the lackeys were back, having forced the door with a hatchet. Considering the well-tried patience of their opposition, it is con-

[38] *Female Tatler*, 9 December 1709.
[39] *The Touch-Stone* (1728), pp. 147–148.

ceivable that they might have been allowed to enjoy their triumph in peace—if they had only remained quiet. Instead they kept up a continuous gloating over their opponents until, after two more acts, the play was stopped, the riot act read, three or four leading noise-makers arrested, and the gallery more adequately secured.

Again the warning doubtless intended by the arrests was wasted. The following Monday night the footmen were back, prepared to storm the theatre.

Monday, 21 [February]. This Night a great Disturbance happened at Drury-Lane Play House, occasioned by a Great Number of Footmen, who assembled themselves there in a riotous Manner, with great Out-cries of burning the House and Audience together, unless they were immediately admitted into what they call their Gallery; and in order to strike a Terror, they began to hew down the Door of the Passage which leads to the said Gallery; of which Colonel De Veil, (who was in the House) had immediate Notice, and thereupon came out where they were thus assembled, and notwithstanding they threatened to knock his Brains out, he read the Proclamation to them, admonished them to retire and desist from so unlawful an Undertaking; for that he came as a Friend, and not as a Foe, to warn them of their Danger. This Proclamation, had its desired Effect, for they all went off in a few Minutes after the Proclamation was read.[40]

Colonel De Veil's sweet reasonableness, coupled with his firmness in the face of danger and the earlier arrests and releases un-doubtedly led the manager to hope for an end to hostilities. He was to be disappointed. After two weeks of comparative quiet the storm broke again.

Saturday, 5 [March]. This Night a great Number of Footmen as-sembled together with Sticks, Staves, and other offensive Weapons, in a tumultuous and riotous Manner, and broke open the Doors of *Drury-Lane* Play-house, for not being let into what they call their *Gallery*, and fought their Way in so desperate a Manner to the Stage Door (which they forced open) that 25 or 26 Persons were wounded in a very dan-gerous Manner, in the Fray; and Col. De Veil who was in the House, being thereupon applied to, and required to read the Proclamation, did accordingly attempt to do it, having a small Guard to support him; but

[40] *London Magazine*, February 1737, p. 107.

such was the Violence and Number of Footmen in this riotous Assembly, notwithstanding their Royal Highnesses the Prince and Princess of Wales, and others of the Royal Family were there, that it was impossible to appease their Fury, without coming to such Extremities as he thought very improper; and being thus obstructed, and hindered from reading the Proclamation, in the Execution of his Duty, and not knowing where this dangerous Attempt would end, he caused several of the Ring-leaders of this Disturbance and Riot to be taken into Custody.[41]

It is interesting to speculate on the "extremities" De Veil considered but rejected. London had no police force and no adequate technique for dealing with riots. Possibly the colonel thought of calling in the military and filling the neighborhood jails with prisoners in livery. Instead he had a few footmen arrested and somehow got them into an adjoining room, which by this time was also serving as a sort of field hospital. He left the remaining lackeys to expend their energies in fruitless violence. Remembering the "great outcries of burning the house" reported the preceding week, it is surprising that Drury Lane escaped with no real damage. Two of the footmen committed to Newgate were tried six weeks later and sentenced to six months of hard labor. With this demonstration of firmness the long war came to a halt, footmen no longer claimed "their gallery," and the public ceased to object to the behavior of footmen as a group.[42]

Asserting a right to make nuisances of themselves in the theatre was not the exclusive privilege of the footmen, as Colley Cibber's account shows. Without pausing for breath, Cibber turns at the end of his attack on the footmen to another offensive group.

From the same narrow way of thinking too, were so many ordinary people and unlicked cubs of condition admitted behind our scenes for money, and sometimes without it; the plagues and inconveniences of which custom we found so intolerable, when we afterwards had the stage in our hands, that at the hazard of our lives we were forced to get rid of them; and our only expedient was by refusing money from all

---

[41] *Ibid.*, March 1737, p. 163.

[42] I am not saying that there are no more complaints about the behavior of those who occupy the upper gallery. The next chapter will indicate a persistence of such complaints throughout the period.

persons without distinction at the stage-door. By this means we preserved to ourselves the right and liberty of choosing our own company there; and by a strict observance of this order, we brought what had been before debased into all the licenses of a lobby, into the decencies of a drawing-room.[43]

The only difficulty with the latter part of his account is that it gives a misleading picture of a stage free from fluttering exhibitionists whereas there is a wealth of evidence to show that none of the numerous attempts to drive them off had been successful.

The fact that there were spectators on the stage in France—Molière's *Facheux* (1661) provides an illustration—until they were driven off in 1759 may seem surprising in the light of what happened to the liveried servants, surprising until it is recalled that the offenders in this case were members of the gentry or nobility. In England the government tried to intervene but in a fashion so half-hearted that nothing actually came of it. On 17 January 1704 Queen Anne issued a proclamation providing, among other things, "that no person of what quality soever presume to go behind the scenes or come upon the stage, either before or during the acting of a play."[44] The fact that this provision was still being tacked onto bills ten years later indicates its scant effectiveness.

A chief difficulty was that the management and the actors, who derived a good share of their annual income from benefits, did not really wish to rid the stage of spectators. Considerable income was derived from selling space on the stage at these benefits, and as long as the practice continued there could be no hope of improvement. The swaggerers themselves, though not so organized as the footmen and not so vocal in asserting any "right" to get in everyone's way, acted as if such a right did exist. A much earlier comment by Cibber, in the dedication to his *Lady's Last Stake* (1708), gives a fair notion of their attitude.

As for those gentlemen that thrust themselves forward upon the stage

---

[43] Colley Cibber, *Apology*, I, 234.

[44] Copies of the proclamation appear in several places. I took this quote from the Winston Collection, British Museum.

before a crowded audience, as if they resolv'd to play themselves, and save the actors the trouble of presenting them, they indeed, as they are above instruction so they scorn to be diverted by it.

Even though these young incorrigibles were less organized than their footmen—they were motivated far more by a "desire of distinction" as *Spectator* 224 calls it[45] than by any zeal to maintain a fancied right—they could as readily be provoked into violence, as may be observed by an incident reported in the *Weekly Journal* for 11 October 1718.

Last Friday night as the play was acting, called the *Fair Quaker of Deal*, at the Theatre in Lincolns-Inn-Fields, three gentlemen demanded to go behind the scenes; but there being an order of the house made to the contrary, they were denied admittance; upon which they went into the pit, and with apples, &c. pelted the players in a shameful manner; after which they got upon the stage and drew their swords and broke down the sconces, lamps, &c. which put the house in an uproar, and 'twas an hour before the gentlemen could be brought to a civil behaviour.

Ten years later the *Touch-Stone* is even more caustic than Cibber had been but concludes with a revealing admission that no one would dare hope for a clear stage on benefit nights.

I cannot pass over in Silence, a Species of Animals belonging to this Order, whom I look upon as the Hermaphrodites of the Theatre; being neither Auditors nor Actors perfectly, and imperfectly both; I mean those Gentlemen who pass their Evenings behind the Scenes, and who are so busy in neglecting the Entertainment, that they obstruct the View of the Audience in the just Discernment of the Representation; and are a prodigious Hindrance to the Actors, in the Exactness of the Performance; the Beauty of which often depends upon a small Nicety....

This is not to be understood, as any Reflection upon that Part of an Audience, who are cramm'd behind the Scenes of a Benefit-Night: The Stage being for that Time for the Use of the House, and no body coming with a Design to be amus'd, there can be no Offence.[46]

---

[45] Steele also devotes part of *Spectator* No. 240 to describing one of these butterflies in action. The graphic picture is a little long to quote and much more readily accessible than the items I do give.

[46] James Ralph, *The Touch-Stone*, p. 55.

The champion who was eventually to rid his country of this pestilence was a long time about it. In his first stage offering, the satirical afterpiece *Lethe* (1740), David Garrick introduced a Beau whose chief traits are an airy manner, a desire to evade his creditors, and a love of quarreling without the courage to support it, in short a set of stereotypes.[47] In subsequent years Garrick tinkered with his satire, adding topical material from his later experience. In 1745 a version of *Lethe* was published, very likely without Garrick's authorization. Among the several changes, the additions to the Beau's character are most interesting. In the new version the Beau responds to Esop's question about his conduct by adding a report of his play-going.

Beau. No, no; the most heroic are to come; I generally stand upon the Stage at a Play; talk a-loud, confound the Actors, and disturb the Audience; at which they hiss, and cry, Off! Off! At which I take a Pinch of Snuff, and smile at 'em scornfully; upon which they attack us with whole Vollies of suck'd Oranges, and chew'd Apples.[48]

This exchange, retained and slightly expanded[49] in the first authorized edition published in 1749, anticipates what proved to be Garrick's first attempted reform when he assumed the management of Drury Lane in 1747. On opening night 15 September *The Merchant of Venice* was preceded by Samuel Johnson's prologue, spoken by Garrick himself, and followed by his own epilogue, spoken by Peg Woffington. The playbill carried a notice that no money was to be taken "for the future" for admission behind the scenes; the epilogue was designed to help enforce the rule and by its wit to forestall opposition.

> Sweet doings truly! we are finely fobb'd!
> And at one stroke of all our pleasures robb'd!
> *No beaux behind the scenes!* 'tis innovation!
> Under the specious name of reformation.

[47] This version is preserved in the Larpent MS play collection, Henry E. Huntington Library, San Marino, California.

[48] David Garrick, *Lethe: or, Esop in the Shades*, p. 5.

[49] Beau has become Fine Gentleman except in his exit, where the stage direction from the earlier versions is retained.

So begin the lines spoken by the charming actress. And they end with one of Garrick's favorite devices, an extended imitation of Shakespearean soliloquy, this one Othello's farewell to his profession. One couplet is enough to give the tone:

> "For ever now farewell the plumed beaux,
> Who make ambition—to consist in cloaths."[50]

Whatever success Garrick's efforts may have achieved was short-lived. In February a pamphlet entitled *D–ry–L–ne P–yh–se broke open* congratulated the new manager on his efforts and splendid results—while they lasted.

What an excellent design was this? And how decent and regular did your plays appear, while you persever'd in it? But on a sudden this seat of decorum is once more over-run by the Goths and Vandals: at present the beaux pop in and out with as little opposition as modesty; and have made so absolute a burrow of the stage, that unless they are *ferretted* out by some means or other, we may bid farewell to theatrical entertainments.[51]

An entry in prompter Richard Cross's notebook for 22 February 1748 suggests the kind of opposition Garrick faced, and very likely yielded to.

There was a report that my Lord Hubbard had made a party to hiss *The Foundling* [new play by Edward Moore] off the stage, that the reason was it ran too long, & they wanted variety of entertainments. . . . I believe the main cause of this anger, in spite of their excuses, was their being refus'd admittance behind the scenes.[52]

Despite an occasional bit of satire,[53] despite pleadings and bluster

---

[50] "Epilogue spoken by Miss Woffington, at the Opening of Drury-Lane Theatre, 1747," in David Garrick, *The Poetical Works of David Garrick, Esq.*, edited by George Kearsley, I, 96–98, ll. 1–4 and 36–37.

[51] *D–ry-L–ne P–yh–se broke open*, p. 18.

[52] Richard Cross, MS diary, Folger Shakespeare Library. Horace Walpole gives a slightly different version of their motives and indicates their mildness—compared at least to the footmen (Letter to Horace Mann, 11 March 1748, in Horace Walpole, *Horace Walpole's Correspondence*, edited by Wilmarth Sheldon Lewis, XIX, 469).

[53] *A Letter to Mr. G——k, Relative to His Treble Capacity of Manager, Actor,*

in the playbills, even despite the assistance rendered by the gods in the upper gallery,[54] the young gentry continued to exercise the privilege they had usurped. Finally it dawned upon Garrick that he could never rid the stage and greenroom of these pests as long as he continued to sell space on the stage.[55] In the summer of 1762 he therefore put a crew of carpenters to work enlarging the seating capacity, both in the boxes and in the galleries. By the time the first benefit of the season came, the management had already prepared the audience for the long-overdue reformation.

As frequenters of the theatre have often complained of the interruptions in the performance, occasioned by a crowded stage at the benefits—the performers will have no building on the stage, nor take any money behind the scenes, being willed to forego that advantage, for the sake of rendering the representation more agreeable to the public.[56]

History is discreetly silent on the actual sentiments of the performers. It is altogether possible that Mrs. Susanna Arne Cibber at Drury Lane and Henry Woodward at Covent Garden, who led off the benefit season on 15 March 1763, had other notions. Still, the managers of the two theatres remained firm—though customarily deferential—and the Covent Garden management began its 1763–1764 season with this obsequious note attached to the regular bills.

Whereas many complaints have been made of *interruptions* in the per-

---

and Author; with Some Remarks on Lethe (1749) quotes from the exchange between Beau and Esop, pretending to defend the former from Garrick's attack (pp. 11–12).

[54] See *A Lick at the Town* (Larpent MS play collection No. 92) or *Covent Garden Theatre* (Larpent No. 96) for actors' views of these annoying gentlemen and *Covent-Garden Journal* No. 27 for Fielding's tribute to "the mob" in the gallery who make them their favorite targets.

[55] From an entry in the 1751 diary of his French visit (*The Diary of David Garrick, Being a Record of His Memorable Trip to Paris in 1751*, p. 5) we might have expected Garrick to move faster. His first visit to the Parisian *comédie* (24 May 1751) impressed him with the "ten thousand absurdities" of the building on the stage.

[56] This and the next item I originally took from newsbills in the New York Public Library, Theatre Collection. Stone reproduces them also (*London Stage*, pt. 4, pp. 983, 1008).

formances of this theatre, occasioned by the admission of persons behind the scenes, in order to prevent the like for the future, it is humbly
hoped, no nobleman or gentlemen will insist on a privilege so dis-
pleasing to the audience in general; whose approbation it is the duty,
as well as the interest of the manager, to endeavor on all occasions to
deserve.

Coupling firmness with deference, the management did finally
terminate an objectionable practice, and virtually nothing concerning it is heard after 1763.

3

In more abstract terms the events just sketched represent one
episode in the ceaseless struggle over accommodation, over the ad-
justment of rights in conflict, the rights of individuals or minorities
to act as they chose in the theatre and the rights of the less vocifer-
ous majority to see and hear the play in peace. An even more significant case remains, significant in good part because the legal
guardians over rights, the judiciary, were forced to intervene.

No one would have contradicted John Dryden's statement that
clapping and hissing were "the privileges of a free-born subject,"
for everyone would grant that to disapprove of a play or player by
hissing came very close to being an inalienable right—as long as the
hiss or other sign of disapproval was occasional, in both senses of
the word; that is, if the sign of disapproval was given on the spot
while something considered intolerable was being presented and if
the disapproval was not so continuous as to seem interminable.
There were frequent opportunities to test this accepted principle,
for the English had developed a very generous tolerance of loud and
persistent clamor. What needed testing was a case in which opposition had become dangerously violent and obviously premeditated.
Such a case occurred just before midcentury. In briefest terms, two
rival factions, one favoring the new sensation David Garrick, the
other his close friend turned bitter enemy Charles Macklin, joined
in a quarrel in the fall of 1743 that finally led to a riot at Drury
Lane on the night of 6 December. On that occasion, according to
Benjamin Victor, "Lord Chief Justice Lee declared from the bench,

it was his opinion that a continual hissing was a manifest breach of the peace, as it was the beginning of a riot."[57]

While it is not easy to discern any immediate dampening effect of the ruling on the expression of opposition, the words of the Chief Justice did leave their mark. Twenty years later, at the time of the riots over prices at both theatres in the spring of 1763, the author of *Three Original Letters to a Friend in the Country* reminds the leaders of the disturbance of the ruling by Chief Justice Lee. Significantly he expresses misgivings over the severity of the ruling, but he is obviously not recalling it pointlessly. And one of the newspapers, the *Gazette and London Daily Advertiser* for 4 March 1763, reminds its readers of Justice Lee's curb on unrestrained hissing.

The most celebrated case of all, however, came in 1773 and by coincidence involved Charles Macklin, one of the principals of the 1743 riot, if I am warranted in assuming that Victor was referring to the Macklin-Garrick contest of December 1743. To give a full account of the whole story of Macklin's being forced out of his profession on 18 November 1773 is fortunately not necessary since a recent biography of the actor tells most of the essentials.[58] A sketch of the main events in the story, particularly of the judgments delivered by the courts, may, however, be useful because it lends further precision to the always vague limitations on an audience's expressing its opinion in terms at all violent.

In merest outline the story runs like this. At an age when most men would have been considering retirement, Macklin persuaded George Colman of Covent Garden to cast him in certain ambitious roles, principally Macbeth, long the near-monopoly of his old rival Garrick. Whatever his success—and in the hullabaloo that followed it is impossible to judge—Macklin drew certain opposition for which he was easily persuaded Garrick had been responsible. In no time, to use Goldsmith's phrase, "ferments arose," the disorganized opposition became a conspiracy, and Colman was required to dis-

---

[57] Benjamin Victor, *The History of the Theatres of London and Dublin*, I, 107.
[58] William Worthen Appleton, *Charles Macklin*, Chapter X.

charge Macklin from the company on a night when he was playing not a new role but his favorite of favorites, Shylock, a role he had played with enormous success for well over thirty years.

Though he seems to have been prompted more by motives of vengeance than by a desire to test any limitation of rights, Macklin's resolve to sue did have more significant and longer ranging effects.[59] A key document in this account, the report of the results of Macklin's motion in February 1774 to file an information, is not given by Macklin's recent biographer. Two points made in the report are well worth stressing:

(1) Mr. Dunning [Macklin's counsel] . . . observed that when what is called the public comes to be sifted it turns out to be a few idle 'squires, and a taylor at the head of his journeymen.

(2) [The judges of the Court of the King's Bench observed] that parties to hiss or to applaud were common, but this goes to deprive an actor of his bread, that there was no doubt but Mr. Macklin had been cruelly treated.[60]

Yet the justices seemed characteristically reluctant to proceed with the rigor Dunning was advocating, and they urged him to shift the charge from malicious conspiracy to a plea for damages. Dunning,

[59] His surliness and his indelible suspicion that Garrick was always conspiring against him made it hard not to be skeptical of Macklin and possibly unfair to him. A letter in the Folger Shakespeare Library addressed to his daughter Maria (14 March 1774) indicates that he had by that time at least understood the principles involved. Maria had asked him to come forward as he had done for years to help her in her benefit. He refused, with obviously great reluctance, on the grounds that he did not want to jeopardize his case by giving his opponents a weapon since it was clear they were interpreting the law as entitling "them at any time to hiss and explode, so as to drive whomsoever they please from the stage, by the law of custom." It is quite probable that Macklin's conduct was more courageous than most of his contemporaries could boast. According to the author of *Three Original Letters to a Friend in the Country* (1763), the mob, angered by Moody's refusal to kneel to them, would not let the play continue until the managers agreed to discharge the actor. See *London Stage*, pt. 4, p. 975 for a slightly different version, and pp. 977–978 for a sequel that would perhaps fit either version. At any rate, poor Moody was forced to give a public apology to which Macklin would never have stooped.

[60] These are from a clipping from an unidentified newspaper preserved in the R. J. Smith Collection of theatrical materials in the British Museum.

whatever his own feelings, represented a stubborn client and on 12 May 1774 was back with a demand for trial on the grounds of "riotous conspiracy," which the gentlemen of the bench granted. A month later the six defendants appeared before the redoubtable Lord Chief Justice Mansfield, who dismissed the charges against the one actor among them, James Sparks, but remanded the others for trial. The trial itself, in February 1775, resulted in conviction for all five, four on the double charge of riot and conspiracy, one on riot alone.[61]

When the guilty parties reappeared before Lord Mansfield in May, the Chief Justice was ready both to urge clemency on the now triumphant actor—Macklin was equally ready to prove that he was no Shylock in real life—and to draw from the case a guiding principle for the future. If the Chief Justice required prompting, which seems unlikely, he had already received it a year earlier, both in Dunning's comment and in a shrewd summation, *The Genuine Arguments of the Council, with the Opinion of the Court of King's Bench* (1774). His prefatory remarks close with this succinct statement of the issues.

The Town give out, that a player had dared to dispute the undoubted right of a British audience founded on immemorial custom, to approve or disapprove any actor or theatrical exhibition, by the usual mode of clapping or hissing. The charge is denied; and it is only humbly contended, that the meanest subject, even a player, a servant of the public, or a vagabond (who being liable to punishment, is also intitled to protection) hath a legal right to be heard against being for ever deprived of his livelihood; though such attempt were made by majesty itself (if that were possible) and that riots, conspiracies, and malice, are odious to, and punishable by the spirit, as well as the letter, of the laws of England.

Lord Mansfield's summation is even simpler and more forceful. He saw no reason to challenge the right so long exercised and asserted of showing approval or disapproval of any given performance since

[61] See Garrick, *Letters*, III, 994–996, Letter 896, for Garrick's severe reprimand and advice to Miles, one of the five.

The right of hissing or applauding was an unalterable right, but there was a wide distinction between expressing the natural sensations of the mind as they arose in what was seen and heard, and executing a pre-concerted design, not only to hiss an actor when he was playing a part in which he was universally allowed to be excellent, but also to drive him from the theatre, and effect his utter ruin.[62]

The Macklin case did not mark the end of theatrical controversy or even prove very effective in taming an audience that Joseph Palmer in the same month Lord Mansfield made his final pro-nouncement was finding, when compared with a Parisian audience, "little better than a bear-garden."[63] The latitude suggested was ac-tually more generous than in Justice Lee's pronouncement of 1743, for the earlier ruling, as the writer of *Three Original Letters* (1763) had objected, was sharply restrictive. Lord Mansfield, while stating the need of some limitation on the audience's right, had been care-ful to stress the fact that such a right did exist and furthermore was unalterable. Some, like Palmer, doubtless wished that the Lord Chief Justice had been less lenient, had used his considerable in-fluence to initiate reforms in the direction of curbing the free ex-pression of opinion. Others—and they must have constituted the greatest numbers—would have agreed with the author of *The Con-duct of the Four Managers* (1768), who thought the London audi-ence, especially the upper gallery, almost insufferably annoying at times but felt it was possible to endure a lot "for the sake of the in-valuable blessing of liberty." Colley Cibber's even more forceful statement must be taken as expressive of a widely held view. After

---

[62] From an unidentified clipping in the Folger Shakespeare Library extra-illustrated copy of F. A. Congreve, *Authentic Memoirs of the Late Mr. Charles Macklin, Comedian*, (London, 1798). Nearly twenty years later Lord Mans-field's ruling is cited in support of a manager. When on 17 September 1792 James Harris tried to start the season at the refurbished Covent Garden without an upper gallery he was faced with a near riot and finally obliged to provide a gallery. A writer in *The Diary: or, Woodfall's Register* for 20 September comes to Harris's support, citing the 1775 ruling as applicable to the management since "if any man, or set of men, attend a theatre *more than one night*, for the purpose of injuring the former [the actor] in his profession or the latter [the manager] in his property *an action would certainly lie*."

[63] Joseph Palmer, *A Four Months Tour through France*, pp. 76–77.

some stern comment on the increasing barbarity of the English audience, he resolves to endure the annoyance as a price for a unique blessing.

Now, though I grant that liberty is so precious a jewel that we ought not to suffer the least ray of its lustre to be diminished, yet methinks the liberty of seeing a play in quiet, has as laudable a claim to protection as the privilege of not suffering you to do it has to impunity. But since we are so happy as not to have a certain power among us which in another country is called the police, let us rather bear this insult than buy its remedy at too dear a rate.[64]

[64] Colley Cibber, *Apology*, I, 323–324.

2. A Varied Response

ON MONDAY 18 October 1779 the *Morning Chronicle* gave an account of a performance of *Othello* the preceding Saturday night at Drury Lane. A Mr. Henry had made his debut in the title role and, according to the reporter, had been visibly nervous, not to say frightened. Well he might have been, for "a London audience is at once, though the most candid of all others, the most difficult to satisfy, because the most competent to determine what is not real ability."[1]

That the superlatives used here were not empty, that the London audience was in fact the most generous—approximately the significance of "candid" two hundred years ago—and the most exigent in all Europe seems fairly clear. Possibly the closest parallel today would have to be sought in an opera house, that of Parma. Some

---

[1] James Jeremiah Lynch, (*Box, Pit, and Gallery*, p. 291) quotes an almost identical comment from Davies' *Dramatic Miscellanies*.

months ago a television program entitled *Bocca al lupo*[2] dramatized the adventures of a group of performers scheduled to appear before the notorious Parmegiani. In the early stages of the story the viewer was carried behind the scenes to share the apprehensions of the company in rehearsal as they prepared to thrust themselves into the jaws of that voracious yet discriminating monster. The outcome of the semi-documentary film was a happy one. The performers did even better than their best, better than was expected or demanded of them, and the audience showed by its loud and continued applause that it could be as generous as it had been exacting.

Evidence presented in the preceding chapter would support the claim that an English audience could be responsive, often violently so, especially when faced with something new. With material or performers they had grown accustomed to they could be equally apathetic. The stark lines in which the *Morning Chronicle* draws the audience represent an oversimplification to be sure, but it is not a dishonest appraisal done from chauvinistic motives. The commentator was addressing a London newspaper audience concerning a London theatrical audience. The two would not have been precisely coextensive but there was considerable overlapping. Any inadequacies lie in the fact that he was describing as typical a particular audience on a particular occasion in a particular mood. On another occasion in a different mood, without all of its members discarding their "candor" or their dissatisfaction with anything short of the best, the London audience could be maddeningly inattentive or touchingly generous, obstinately rigid or sweetly tractable.

If the operatic audience in Parma provides a parallel, the theatrical audiences of two major cities today provide a contrast. Kenneth Tynan sketches the reactions of a present-day German audience.

---

[2] By coincidence the *Newsweek* of 11 January 1965 carries two stories with some appositeness. One on Richard Tucker indicates the persistence of "*in bocca al lupo*" as a "time-honored operatic formula for averting the evil eye." The other gives a lively account of Cornell MacNeil's recent encounter with the violently responsive audience of Parma.

Whenever I go to a play in Germany, I am struck by the intense, appreciative calm of the audience. After a production that seems to them too pompously traditional or too offensively experimental, they may hoot a tentative protest; but they always enter the theater certain that they are about to see something worth the scrutiny of intelligent people. . . . Once in their seats, they listen with the kind of devout attention that you associate with a concert rather than a play. Coughing is rare and rapidly stifled.[3]

Even more striking is the contrast provided by an occurrence not on Russell or Hart Street in the eighteenth century but on Shaftesbury Avenue in the twentieth. An account from the *Manchester Guardian* of 21 February 1957 states that

An evening of acute embarrassment was spent at the Saville Theatre, London, on Tuesday, when an atrociously bad musical play "The Crystal Heart," moved the gallery to unmannerly but easily understandable displays of contempt. The ill-advised piece had had a rough opening in Scotland last month. Taking it down to London may have been gallant but ended in general distress for all: to hear and see an actress of the stature of Gladys Cooper "getting the bird" in line after line is an ordeal for anyone who cares for the lyric theatre or the public decencies.

Dramatic critics are reputed to be a hardy if not a hard-boiled breed. If the *Manchester Guardian*'s critic could suffer "acute embarrassment" over an audience's frank expression of disapproval by "barracking"—to use the more technical term found in another brief article in the same paper concerning the same play—how must he have suffered over the far more vigorous expression of two hundred years ago? Some suggestion of the lack of restraint in expressing feelings, particularly opposition, has already been made, but this particular side of the audience requires more detailed treatment.

A report published at the end of the Restoration period, *The Country Gentleman's Vade Mecum* (1699), supplies a description of the occupants of the pit,

Where sit the judges, wits, and censurers, or rather the censurers without either wit or judgment. These are the bully-judges that damn and

---

[3] Kenneth Tynan, "An Audience of Critics," *Holiday*, 36, no. 4 (October 1964), 111.

sink the play at a venture, 'tis no matter whether it be good or bad, but 'tis a play, and they are the judges, and so it must be damn'd, curs'd, and censur'd in course.[4]

Since the writer of this caustic description is unidentified there is no way of assessing possible bias. A clearer case from a later period is found in Henry Fielding's preface to his *Universal Gallant*, which had been roundly damned on its first appearance on 10 February 1735.

The cruel usage this poor play hath met with, may justly surprise the Author, who in his whole life never did an injury to any one person living. What could incense a number of people to attack it with such an inveterate prejudice, is not easy to determine; for prejudice must be allowed, be the play good or bad, when it is condemned unheard. I have heard that there are some young gentlemen about this town who make a jest of damning plays—but did they seriously consider the cruelty they are guilty of by such a practice, I believe it would prevent them.

After a generous discount because of the author's bias, Fielding still has a point. He makes it far better, however, in his first leading essay in the *Champion*, 15 November 1739. In introducing, *Spectator* fashion, the family of Vinegars, he comes to his young-man-about-town Tom Vinegar, the specialist in "modern poetry." Tom never misses a first night, where he invariably appears armed for damnation: "He frequently useth the words *damned stuff, that is low, etc.* in conversation, with which words alone, together with his cat-call, he often brags he can damn the best play in the universe."

There are several crucial words here, *low* being one of them; most important is the term "cat-call." This tiny instrument, long since condemned to oblivion, had a significance now largely obscured by the vague meaning of the term still in use.[5] For here was sufficient evidence of the soundness of the unhappy author's charge.

---

[4] *The Country Gentleman's Vade Mecum* (1699), reprinted in *Tricks of the Town*, edited by Ralph Strauss, p. 38.

[5] Though some dictionaries current today indicate that the term can apply, or did apply, to an instrument, the most widely used dictionary in this country gives no hint that it indicates anything more than a disapproving sound.

In his later role as Middlesex justice Fielding could justifiably take the carrying of weapons as evidence of malice prepense. Similarly, as harried playwright he could reasonably assume that when the Tom Vinegars of the town entered the playhouse armed with catcalls they were not disposed to judge calmly what was put before them.

There are dozens of allusions to this shrill instrument, especially in the first half of the eighteenth century. Led by Mr. Spectator himself, various writers of the familiar essay gave it their half-playful, half-serious attention. All of *Spectator* No. 361 is devoted to the subject. A country subscriber, Squire Shallow, writes in to inquire what has happened in the theatre, his own last visit having been accompanied by "a great concert of catcalls" at a performance of *The Humorous Lieutenant*. The editor obliges with a "dissertation upon the catcall," speculating on its origins, which some persons trace back to Orpheus though Mr. Spectator himself "cannot forbear thinking that the catcall is originally a piece of English music." Without abandoning the facetious tone he does insert a possibly more serious paragraph on the effects of the catcall, which has "struck a damp into generals and frightened heroes off the stage."[6]

Mr. Spectator's closing remarks, on a virtuoso artist who had developed the range and possibilities of the instrument, may well have prompted a similar response a generation later in *Common Sense* No. 69 (27 May 1738). In a long leading essay the journalist reports a visit to a Templar friend appropriately named Frank Townly. Young Townly had recently had his pocket picked and had lost, among other valuables, his catcall. At the time of the recorded visit he was looking over a selection of new instruments a manufacturer had brought in. A few sentences might profitably be reproduced to show how the author of the *Common Sense* essay

---

[6] *Parker's Penny Post*, No. 231 (24 October 1726), has a fairly close imitation of its distinguished predecessors, a Shoemaker who leads the critics in the theatre in the manner of Addison's famous Trunkmaker. When he "takes a little whistle and falls a whistling," he is joined by "a hundred whistles."

elaborated on his famous model, beginning with the last item of loss.

Two Catcals—the one a base, the other a treble. It was the last of these losses which my friend was about to supply.—There were a great many of them lying upon the table, some in *Pinchbeck*, some in silver. The artist had employ'd the utmost of his skill in adorning them:—On one side, you might see the comick Mask and tragick Buskin curiously engraved; on the other, a felonious critick snatching a laurel from a poor poet's brow:—The workmanship exceeded the materials.

While I was viewing all the wonders of this little tube, now become the terror of the poet and the player, a thousand reflections rose in my mind. I thought on the cruel palpitations it would cause in the hearts of many unfortunate adventurers for fame, as yet unborn.

Having wrung most of the humor from his subject, *Common Sense* drops into a far more serious tone in order to justify the practice of going to the theatre prepared to disapprove where there is every reason to expect an attempt to force approval from the audience.

At some risk of being considered far gone in antiquarianism I should like to reproduce briefly here some of the evidence from which a history not of the catcall itself but of its use in this period might be reconstructed. Of most importance is the understanding that far too often the audience—or an irrepressible segment of it—came prepared to damn, were often better pleased to damn than to approve. Note that though the instruments laid out before young Townly were available in a variety of materials and a range of pitches, they had only one mode: disapprobation.

It is perhaps fitting that the earliest evidence in this odd footnote to theatrical history should be obscure. It involves a famous Restoration playgoer, Samuel Pepys. Very early in the diary, on Ash Wednesday 7 March 1660, Pepys records a morning of bustle ending with: "Thence I went to the Pope's Head Alley and called on Adam Chard, and bought a catcall there, it cost me two groats. Thence went and gave him a cup of ale." One wishes that since he was circumstantial enough to tell us the cost Pepys had told us the intended use. The puzzle is that it is 18 August before there is any record of play-going.

No unmistakable evidence of a use of the catcall in the theatre[7] appears for a generation after Pepys's comments—at least my own notes reveal nothing until in 1686 two items suggest an established tradition. One is a mock-dedication by Thomas D'Urfey of his *Banditti,* damned at Drury Lane early that spring, "To the extreme witty and judicious gentleman, Sir-Critick-Cat-Call." The other is the appearance, in the same year, of a dedication and a prologue to Thomas Jevon's *Devil of a Wife,* in which catcalls are repeatedly mentioned.

Ten years later an obscure playwright named Henry Higden complained when, to accept his version, a faction of catcallers rejected his *Wary Widdow* (March 1693) while a then equally obscure young man named William Congreve scored a triumph with a bawdy piece called *The Old Bachelor.* Within a little over two years the now better-known Congreve has Scandal, in the brilliant opening scene of *Love for Love,* describe the pictures with which his private chambers are decorated, a set of quite imaginary portraits representing satirical figures in literary fashion. His group portrait of the pit is designed to strike terror into the hearts of the boldest playwrights: "I have another large piece too representing a school, where there are huge proportioned critics, with long wigs, laced coats, Steinkirk cravats, and terrible faces, with cat-calls in their hands, and horn-books about their necks."[8]

A similar instrument was found at this time in France. The *"sifflet"*—natural or instrumental—as a *"marque d'improbation"* as Jules Bonnassies calls it, came into use some time in the sixteen-eighties, was tolerated briefly, and then by 1696 or so sternly forbidden. Pontchartrain, the Chancellor, had a butcher thrown into jail for three months for using a whistle, somewhat impetuously perhaps since he says in his petition for release that he had made use of an *"instrument avec lequel il éveille ses garçons le matin."*[9]

[7] Almost certainly Jerry Blackacre's newly acquired catcall was to be used in the theatre, but Wycherly does not say so specifically (*Plain Dealer* III, i, 400).

[8] William Congreve, *Love for Love*, I, i.

[9] Quoted by John Lough, *Paris Theatre Audiences in the Seventeenth and Eighteenth Centuries*, p. 74.

That anyone would attend an evening's performance prepared for morning reveille strains credulity, but in any case the butcher's fate was enough to show that the authorities meant business. This, so far as I have been able to discover, was the abrupt end of the short history of catcalls in France.[10]

In England no governmental authority intervened, and the cat-callers continued cheerfully to emit their shrill blasts. Fielding and his contemporaries grew at least partially inured to the sound, and Garrick, too, learned an early endurance. *A Letter to Mr. G——k ... with Some Remarks on Lethe* (1749) gives a lively picture of the reception given his first play on its revival.

Before I take my leave, to let you see I am the impartial critic I say I am, I shall make some observations upon your friends and foes in the audience the first night. A gentleman that sat next to me, soon as the play was over, [i.e., before the afterpiece, *Lethe*, began] said to his friend, Now for it; have you got your catcall? Yes, yes, reply'd the other, I never go without my tackle, and immediately try'd the force of his instrument. Others were prepar'd as strenuously to support it; so that I don't think there were three people, besides myself that intended justice.[11]

A month later Garrick presented for the first time another play with which he must have been long acquainted since it had come up to London with him from Lichfield in 1737 with its author, Samuel Johnson. *Mahomet and Irene* was presented for the first time on 6 February 1749 with a remarkable cast, including Garrick himself, Spranger Barry, Mrs. Cibber, and Mrs. Pritchard. The fact that so splendid a company had difficulty keeping the play going for nine nights, so that its author could reap maximum benefits, is less to the point here than is the mood of the audience before a word of the play was spoken. Forty years later James Boswell was to take

[10] Henry Carrington Lancaster, *A History of French Dramatic Literature in the Seventeenth Century*, IV, 47–48. Pierre Mélèse (*Le théâtre et le public à Paris sous Louis XIV, 1659–1715*, pp. 218–220) seems incredulous a spectator would go armed with such an instrument, but he adds a few details that serve to confirm Lancaster.

[11] *A Letter to Mr. G——k, Relative to His Treble Capacity of Manager, Actor, and Author; with Some Remarks on Lethe*, p. 16.

down Dr. Adams's recollections as a member of that first-night audience, recollections made far more vivid by his concern for his friend the author: "Before the curtain drew up, there were catcalls whistling, which alarmed Johnson's friends.[12] The prologue, which was written by himself in a manly strain, soothed the audience, and the play went off tolerably."[13]

Finding the statement about the soothing qualities of the prologue irresistible, Boswell added an elaborate footnote quoting some lines of this manly production, lines which show that the author would not be surprised by the odd chorus that greeted his play.

The expression used by Dr. Adams was "soothed." I should rather think the audience was *awed* by the extraordinary spirit and dignity of the following lines:

> Be this at least his praise, be this his pride,
> To force applause no modern arts are tried:
> Should partial catcalls all his hopes confound,
> He bids no trumpet quell the fatal sound.[14]

It may be contended that this prologue—necessarily written *before* the fact—only pretends acceptance of "partial catcalls," that a more accurate view of the author's feelings appears in a piece written afterwards. At any rate, *Rambler* No. 195 (28 January 1752) takes a much harsher view. This particular number, one in the series describing the education of a young gentleman in the way of the world, recounts his early adventures at the playhouse.

---

[12] The record does not disclose whether the author of a new novel that was to create a sensation on its appearance in the same month was at Drury Lane for this premiere, but if he were we may assume he found this anticipatory whistling old stuff. In his prefatory chapter to the sixteenth book of *Tom Jones*, Henry Fielding offers an ironic justification of prologues, which serve "the critic for an opportunity to try his faculty of hissing, and to tune his catcall to the best advantage; by which means, I have known those musical instruments so well prepared that they have been able to play in full concert at the first rising of the curtain" (XVI, 3). Earlier, in Book XIII, Chapter XI, Sophia had been so frightened by two contending factions at the premiere of a play that she had gone home before the first act was over.

[13] James Boswell, *Boswell's Life of Johnson*, edited by George Birkbeck Hill and Lawrence Fitzroy Powell, I, 196.

[14] *Ibid.*

He was, however, desirous of withdrawing from the subjection which he could not venture to break, and make a secret appointment to assist his companions in the persecution of a play. His footman privately procured him a catcall, on which he practised in a back garret for two hours in the afternoon. At the proper time a chair was called. He pretended an engagement at Lady Flutter's and hastened to the place where his critical associates had assembled. They hurried away to the theatre, full of malignity and denunciations against a man whose name they had never heard and a performance which they could not understand; for they were resolved to judge for themselves, and would not suffer the town to be imposed upon by scribblers.

If there is a note of personal resentment to be detected in the *Rambler*'s remarks, there is quite possibly a note of prophecy also, for the midcentury does mark a turning-point in the public attitude towards catcallers, just as it did in the attitude toward young men crowding on to the stage. Johnson had already been anticipated by his friend Kit Smart in *The Midwife* in "An Oration Spoken to the Clappers, Hissers, and Damners, Attending Both Theatres," which appeared sometime late in 1750 or early in 1751. A brief excerpt will reveal the heavily sarcastic tone.

Riot! Riot! Tear up the benches, break down the king's arms, demolish the orchestre and the fiddles, pelt the players and hiss the author! Clamour, clamour, I say! and display your bravery as usual in a storm of nut-shels, apples, and oranges.

It has been a maxim, time out of mind, *that the most noisy are the most knowing*; and this you have sufficiently verified, who are, and I hope will ever remain, enemies to *taciturnity*, and that other dull thing call'd thinking.

Those wonderful witty gentlemen, who snow down white paper on the ladies in the pit, have my thanks for that elegant and ingenious conceit; and I think myself obliged to all the little boys in both houses, who entertain us with their rattles and their whistle-pipes.[15]

An echo of the last remark appears in a considerably more sophisticated publication, *A Guide to the Stage: or, Select Instructions and Precedents from the Best Authorities towards Forming a Polite*

---

[15] Kit Smart, *The Midwife*, I, 79–80. The collected edition does not give specific dates.

Audience (1751). The title of this pamphlet is in itself of interest since it reveals an ambition Addison and Steele might heartily have approved. The milder tone should not obscure the intention of the author in his attempt "to discover the principal excellencies of a polite audience and point out obstacles to the arriving of such excellencies." His method is chiefly ironic instruction; he advises the playgoer to conduct himself in a certain way, proceeding to describe in some detail the various kinds of offensive behavior—loud talking, inattention, restlessness in general—the audience of the day was too prone to indulge in. Two passages command attention. The first gives a piece of advice to "Mr. Afterday . . . to relinquish his catcal to his nephew, who is a youth of a very promising aspect, and will employ it with greater propriety," and the second serves to show that the reference to the nephew is likewise ironic: "I cannot help thinking it a little out of character, for a polite audience to distort their features by a hiss: however for the sake of some ambitious youths, who thus love to signalize themselves, I shall leave a new play to their mercy. They then are at a liberty to exercise their several talents whether they hiss or groan most successfully or have a greater genius for the cat-call."[16]

It would be hasty to assume that the catcall was abandoned because of a few sarcastic remarks in fugitive pamphlets, but there does appear to be evidence of a gradual disappearance of the annoying little instrument in the latter half of the century as shown by a falling off of allusions to it. My own notes reveal only a dozen or so references to it, almost always in the form of a set phrase in prologues, up to 1792, where I find my own last record, perhaps fittingly in an occasional epilogue. The difficulty in arriving at certainty can be illustrated by two conflicting items just halfway through this span. George Colman's introduction of a character named Catcall in his prelude *New Brooms* in September 1776 would suggest the persistence of the custom, but the failure of Joseph Palmer to men-

---

[16] *A Guide to the Stage: or, Select Instructions and Precedents from the Best Authorities towards Forming a Polite Audience*, 2nd ed., p. 6. I have never seen a copy of the first edition.

tion catcalls as a full measure of English barbarousness at the theatre may actually be more significant. In Letter IX (24 May 1775) of his *Four Months Tour through France,* Palmer comments on the contrasting behavior in Paris:

During the representations here, the attention of the house is remarkable; there is no whistling between the fingers, no bawling for *roast beef,* nor pelting the parterre with oranges, but the public behaviour is such, as becomes those who lay claim to the title of a polished people. Upon the whole, our theatre, when compared to that of Paris, is little better than a bear-garden; and I have no expectation (whatever account our own vanity may make of it) that it will ever bear any reputation among foreigners, before its regulation be totally altered, and no such glaring vestiges of barbarism remain.[17]

There is whistling still, but it would appear to be less offensive since it is more spontaneous and unaugmented by mechanical aids.

2

Another item in Palmer's account discourages any hope that there was appreciable improvement in the conduct of the noisy and irrepressible segment of playgoers. Though the custom of "pelting the parterre with oranges"—"pelting" would hardly be appropriate for an isolated incident or two—was not quite as offensive a sign of premeditation as using a catcall, or would not have been if only oranges were involved, it was more barbarous and vastly more dangerous to the victims on the stage, in the orchestra, or even in the audience. In some ways even more distressing, the incidence of orange-throwing seems to rise as catcalling declines, suggesting a mere change in fashions of disapprobation. Moreover, pelting continues on a fairly high level throughout the century, dispelling any facile assurance of markedly increasing civility.

The first report I have of this particular form of hoodlumism comes at the end of the Restoration period. At this time of occasionally violent warfare between Drury Lane and Lincoln's Inn Fields, who were competing for the attention of a still relatively small

---

[17] Joseph Palmer, *A Four Months Tour Through France,* pp. 76, 77.

theatre-going public, it had become the practice to import exotic entertainment to fill out the more traditional bill. On the evening of 13 December 1700 Colley Cibber's new *Love Makes a Man* was acted for the third time. According to the *London Post* for 13/16 December,

Yesterday a new Play called, *Love Makes a Man: or, The Fop's Good Luck,* was acted at the Theatre Royal in Drury Lane, and there being a French Scaramouch Dance betwixt the second and third Acts, a certain person went in a frolick, incognito, up into the upper gallery, and so pelted the dancers with oranges, that they were forced to quit the stage, and the playhouse was all in an uproar; but some of the auditory perceiving who threw them, cryed out, fling him down into the pit, which so startled him, that he was forced to make the best of his way down stairs; however, a constable having been sent for in the meantime, he was secured; and I am told, sent to the Gatehouse.[18]

One can hardly avoid observing how one form of violence breeds another. "Fling him into the pit!" does indeed sound like summary justice. Yet equally notable is the quickness and apparent uniformity of disapproval, in striking contrast to the placid acceptance of even more violent acts later in the century. For if this incident marked the beginning of a new fashion, it was slow to catch hold. Except for what seems another instance four years later involving what may well have been personal rivalry between operatic singers, there is nothing of this mark of violence for some years.[19]

In the preceding chapter I cited the case of the three young gentlemen who created a prolonged disturbance at Lincoln's Inn Fields on 3 October 1718. It will be recalled that among other demonstrations of their annoyance over being barred from going backstage, "they went into the pit, and with apples, &c. pelted the players in

---

[18] Reproduced by Alfred Jackson, "Play Notices in the Burney Newspapers," *PMLA*, 48 (1933), 815–849.

[19] The Winston Dramatic Register in the Folger Shakespeare Library, Washington, D.C., records an incident, misdating it 5 February 1804: Catherine Tofts' servant threw oranges at Mme. Tofts' rival, Mme. L'Epine, while the latter was singing. Avery reproduces the essentials (*The London Stage*, edited by William van Lennep, et al., pt. 2, p. 56).

a shameful manner," a passage I repeat here for the sake of the last phrase. While there seems to have been no more adequate means of "bringing them to a civil behaviour" than persuasion, since these were "gentlemen," it was possible to describe their conduct as shameful.

Twenty years later, and in far different circumstances, all feelings of shame would seem to have disappeared and the custom of pelting to have been well established. In 1738, shortly after the passage of the provocative Licensing Act, there arose an incident involving a French troupe to whom Sir Robert Walpole's government had given a temporary permit to act, in what appears a brazen flaunting of power. Under such circumstances a considerable amount of premeditation on the part of troublemakers was to be expected. Benjamin Victor later recalled how the dancers who first appeared, "were directly saluted with a bushel or two of peas, which made their capering very unsafe."[20] Oranges might be bought in the theatre itself but hardly dried peas. *Read's Weekly Journal* for 14 October 1738 leaves no doubt of the malice aforethought: "Potatoes and pippins were sold for 18d. a dozen, to pelt the actors." During the same season a French dancer in one of the patent houses was similarly greeted, and similarly, the incident was reported without protest. The *Craftsman* for Saturday 20 January 1739 records blandly, "Tuesday night Mademoiselle Roland was knocked down with an apple as she was dancing upon the stage at Drury Lane Theatre."

John Bull's casual acceptance of violence toward French dancers and actors spread in time to his own countrymen, whether paid performers or paying spectators. The change in attitude came gradually. The next reliable record, for 1 November 1746, shows some remnant of concern, and the *General Advertiser* of Monday 3 November reports that someone in the upper gallery at Drury Lane

. . . threw an apple from thence, with an intent, as is suppos'd to hit some person who was looking through the curtain, but struck a lady of

[20] Benjamin Victor, *The History of the Theatres of London and Dublin*, I, 53.

quality in the face, who sat in the stage box. . . . As it was a publick affront some gentleman would have had him brought on the stage to make a publick acknowledgment of his folly;— and tis hop'd that will be the punishment hereafter, for those who offend in the like manner.[21]

Unfortunately the notion of branding such conduct as "publick affront" requiring public apology did not catch on. In a few short years the practice of pelting was being deplored but tolerated. Only when the damage was too great or the act too flagrant to be ignored was anything more than a simple record made, sometimes accompanied with a note of pained resignation. Richard Cross, who as Garrick's prompter for almost a generation may well have become inured to this violence, records several unpleasant incidents. On 9 February 1751 Edward Moore's *Gil Blas* was performed for the seventh time, after having drawn some strong opposition at the start. Cross reports "a great deal of hissing by some gentlemen in the pit—at the beginning of the 4th act an apple thrown at Mrs. Pritchard."[22] Early in the following season on 18 October 1751 he notes that a blunder in the handling of scenery in a pantomime drew missiles. The mishandling had occurred two nights earlier with only "*great noise* as no more, off, off, &c.," but the repetition called for a stronger show of disapproval, and Cross notes, "A blunder in the same place (the Giants) a great noise—horse beans thrown."[23] A few months later in the same season on 17 February 1752 the audience, having first shown their displeasure over a play, a playwright, or a performer, and then over the scenemen, decided to disapprove the musicians. Cross reports, "A great noise before the play began, occasion'd by the music not playing what they lik'd, they being pelted wou'd not come into the orchestra a branch [chandelier] knock'd down, candles thrown &c.—Mr. Garrick went on, order'd the music in, & all was quiet."[24]

Perhaps Mr. Cross became so used to the pelting that he no longer

[21] *The London Stage*, pt. 3, p. 1259.
[22] Richard Cross, MS diary, 9 February 1751, Folger Shakespeare Library.
[23] *Ibid.*, 18 October 1751.
[24] *Ibid.*, 7 February 1752.

listed details, for his next entry concerning missiles comes as a mere postscript. His neglect is particularly odd because the incident was for a while a *cause célèbre*. In sketchiest form, Garrick and his company chose to violate an unwritten rule of theatrical competition, quite analogous to the rule governing the rival houses of parliament, never to deride the other house. In November 1752 John Rich had revived a pantomime called *The Fair,* adding to it "a wire-dancer and some strange animals . . . from Sadlers Wells," according to the account given by the *Gentleman's Magazine.*[25] Garrick thought it would be amusing to parody these additions by some of his own introduced into Henry Woodward's pantomime *Harlequin Ranger.* He only succeeded in splitting the town into two factions, one of which came nightly for the week beginning 6 November 1752 and showed their displeasure by prolonged hissing until by the following Monday 13 November the Drury Lane managers conceded. Meanwhile, as if to demonstrate once more what mighty contests rise from trivial things, even more violent skirmishes developed within the general framework of theatrical war. "Inspector" Hill ran a series of articles against Garrick and Drury Lane while the *Gentleman's Magazine* supported him and Fielding's *Covent-Garden Journal* poked mild fun at both houses, treating the whole episode in mock-heroic terms.

In this fracas two individuals, a Thaddeus Fitzpatrick in the audience (a decade later the leader of the war against advanced prices) and Henry Woodward on the stage came very close to a duel. It seems that on Friday 10 November Fitzpatrick threw an apple at Woodward, whose only response was a doubtlessly sarcastic "I thank you." The assailant chose, however, to take offense, going about town insisting that Woodward's rejoinder had been "I have noticed you in particular, and I shall meet with you again,"[26] quite clearly a challenge. As was the English custom when differences of this

---

[25] *Gentleman's Magazine,* 22 (1752), 535.

[26] Cross, diary, 10 November 1752. Cross's version quite understandably differs from that of other reporters, notably "Inspector" Hill's in the *London Daily Advertiser,* 16 November 1752.

sort were aired in public, there was a succession of affidavits as to what so-and-so said or so-and-so heard. Inevitably the ever-present Mr. Cross was obliged to make his affidavit. On Sunday 19 November the outraged Mr. Fitzpatrick took his complaint to the Lord Chamberlain, who evidently listened, decided he needed Garrick's version, and then delivered himself in these terms, if we may depend upon the accuracy of Cross: ". . . upon Mr. Fitz. owing he threw an apple at him, my Lord said, that act put [him] upon a footing with the lowest, & judg'd him the agressor—upon which Fitz. desir'd all affidavits &c. shou'd cease & he wou'd drop his resentment. Which was done."[27]

What is most interesting is that Cross had not even bothered to record the apple-throwing when it occurred. It was not until Tuesday 14 November, when he was writing up his notes on the events of the preceding night that his reading of Hill's latest *Inspector*, No. 524 in the *London Daily Advertiser* for Tuesday, prompted him to note the incident: "The *Inspector* very impudent to-day (14th) about Woodward for saying I thank you to Fitzpatrick who threw an apple at him from the stage box on Fryday last."[28] In failing to record such events, Cross seems to be reflecting the general resignation of theatrical managers. My notes from the Drury Lane prompter indicate only widely scattered entries of pelting from 1738 to the end of Cross's career in 1760. An entry for 25 February 1754 is distressingly casual considering the event: "Mr. Carey had his fiddle broke by an apple playing the first music."[29] Almost as revealing is the tone of a note for Saturday 15 November 1755: at the height of the contest over *The Chinese Festival*, there was "amazing noise—no palting [*sic*], except one apple."[30]

If the Drury Lane prompter were the only source of evidence we might take heart, accepting the scarcity of reports as a sign of improvement. But there are, unfortunately, too many other wit-

---

[27] Cross, diary, 18 November 1752.
[28] *Ibid.*, 14 November 1752.
[29] *Ibid.*, 25 February 1754.
[30] *Ibid.*, 15 November 1755.

nesses. Besides, the management felt obliged at least to bluster and
threaten when spectators were exposed to injury; the poor actors
and musicians received no similar protection. In *The London Stage*
Professor Stone reproduces a notice from the *Public Advertiser* of
16 February 1755 in which the Drury Lane managers threaten
prosecution of people throwing "apples, potatoes, and other things
into the pit."[31] Sometimes the management, or the civil authorities,
did act with dispatch, as in a case reported four years later in the
London Chronicle:

On Friday night last [26 October 1759], as the comedy of the Pro-
vok'd Wife was performing at Drury-Lane Playhouse, a lighted serpent
was thrown from the upper gallery into the pit; which terribly frighted
several persons and occasioned so great a confusion, that two or three
ladies were thrown into fits. The person who threw it, being detected,
was immediately committed to the Gatehouse.

Covent Garden may have seemed to lag behind Drury Lane in its
not very exemplary vigilance in protecting patrons from one another. At least the severe critic who in 1768 published his detailed
castigation of *The Conduct of the Four Managers* adopts a tone of
defeatism on that point: "I shall say nothing of the barbarity exercised by the *upper gentry* on the defenceless mortals in the pit, with
oranges and apples." By implication he indicates the reason for
despair so long as the Covent Garden managers collect concession
fees from "the eight *bawling women* who constantly attend at each
of your houses [he here indicates a willingness to include Drury
Lane in his charge] . . . asking about ten times more for *trash*
within doors, than is paid for good fruit without.[32] Perhaps such
criticism did awaken the Covent Garden managers, an item dated
25 October 1769, states:

Last night two men were taken out of the gallery at Covent Garden
Theatre, and carried before Justice Kynaston, who was then sitting at
the Public Office in Bow Street, and by him committed to prison, being
charged with pelting the audience in the pit, and other parts of the

[31] G. W. Stone in *London Stage*, pt. 4, p. 468.
[32] *The Conduct of the Four Managers of Covent-Garden Theatre*, pp. 17–18.

theatre. Several oystershells and other offensive materials provided for
that purpose, were found in their pockets. The offenders will be prose-
cuted, and proper persons are constantly placed in the gallery to prevent such practices.[33]

Threats of arrest and prosecution may have had some effect, for
the frequency of such incidents—at least the frequency of reports—
does diminish somewhat after 1769. However, at the end of the century three cases indicate that the violence of these occasional attacks
offset the decrease in their frequency.

On Saturday evening, a person of the name of Andrew Fleming was
brought up to Bow-Street, for riotous behaviour at Drury-lane Theatre,
previous to the drawing up of the curtain, by throwing an apple from
the Two Shilling Gallery, whereby a gentleman in the orchestra was
nearly deprived of one eye. Mr. Floud, the Sitting Magistrate, after
hearing the charge, which was fully and satisfactorily proved, observed,
it was a practice which he had often seen with indignation and regret.[34]

Public Office, Bow Street, Saturday, November 10, 1798. A caution.
Whereas I, Thomas Ham, did this evening throw from the two shilling gallery of the Theatre-Royal, Drury-Lane, an earthern-ware mug,
which unfortunately struck Mr. Slatter, of the Ordnance Office, in the
Tower of London, who was sitting in the pit . . .[35]

Yesterday [17 October 1799] was brought in custody before Richard
Ford, Esq. at Bow-Street, on a charge of assaulting and wounding Mr.
Thomas Anderson, by throwing a quart glass bottle from the upper
Gallery of Drury-Lane Theatre.—Mr. Anderson said, that on Tuesday
evening he and his wife were in the two shilling gallery of Drury-lane
Theatre, when a quart glass bottle was thrown from the upper gallery,
which falling on his head, broke, and cut him very much; that some of
the pieces struck his wife on the shoulders, and cut the arm of a woman,
who with her child were sitting near them.[36]

Not to prolong this unedifying account I shall stop with a lively
double view afforded by two visitors in 1775. One, the German
Georg Christoph Lichtenberg, quickly became fond of English

---

[33] Newsclipping in Theatre Collection, No. 38, British Museum, London.
[34] *Courier and Evening Gazette,* 25 September 1798.
[35] Winston Collection, British Museum.
[36] *Ibid.*

actors. Garrick he idolized so much that he made him the central attraction of the letters on England he sent to the *Deutsches Museum.* It is in the long account of the low comedian Thomas Weston, however, where he records the most intimate view of the rowdier sections of the English audience.

In the *Rival Candidates*, that play in which he is coaxed and petted by the girl, this year he [Weston] spoke the epilogue in the company of a big dog. . . . On the second occasion on which I saw the play Weston, for the first time, wearied of speaking this epilogue and refused to appear; the audience took this in very bad part, and "Epilogue! Epilogue!" resounded from all the throats which had done their best to wake Richard the Third from the dead; but still Weston did not appear. Several persons left the boxes, but I had made up my mind to await the outcome of the matter. Suddenly there came a shower, first of pears, then oranges, and next quart-bottles, on to the stage, one of them, containing, I should think, three quarts, striking one of the glass chandeliers; and it looked like turning into a riot, when Weston came on the stage with Dragon (that is the dog's name) as calmly as though he were always called for like this. There was a little hissing here and there, but this soon died down.[37]

An account by still another visitor, a Dr. Thomas Campbell from Ireland, fixes the date for the spirited scene just described as 22 February 1775, for, as the Irish visitor learned if the German did not, no actor would dare omit an epilogue merely from weariness. On the tenth night it was customary to drop the epilogue, though sometimes perilous to do so. A passage from Dr. Campbell's diary clarifying the custom relates what he saw and heard at Drury Lane on Saturday 4 March 1775 when the bill was *Braganza* (tenth night) plus *The Rival Candidates* (thirteenth night, the tenth having been on 22 February).

His account, which is too circumstantial to quote in full, is of a similar altercation, this time involving the main piece, *Braganza.* "It was the tenth night of the play & it seems that custom hath decided that after the nineth night the prologue & epilogue shᵈ be dis-

---

[37] Georg Cristoph Lichtenberg, *Lichtenberg's Visits to England*, edited by Margaret Laura Mare and William Henry Quarrell, pp. 28–29.

continued," reports Dr. Campbell. Not only had the managers omitted all mention of prologue and epilogue from the bills; they seem also to have unwisely allowed Mrs. Yates to go home as soon as she had completed her part in the play, unwisely because it was just ten days earlier with precisely the same bill that the scene described by Lichtenberg had taken place. Even worse, there had been a more recent warning. "However when the players came on [at the beginning of the evening's performance] the prologue was called for, & Mr. Palmer—a very handsome mouthing blockhead—answered the call." But at the end of the play, when the company tried to begin the afterpiece, there was trouble. The epilogue was called for, insisted upon, and a succession of actors—Vernon, "the mighty favourite of the Town," Weston, Vernon again, even Yates with a solemn assurance that his wife had gone home ill—all were greeted with oranges and "John Bull roared on." Campbell was much moved by this "scene . . . which strongly marked the English character. . . . The smallest fraction of such language [as he had heard in an exchange in the pit] w^d have produced a duel in the Dublin Theatres—And the millionth part of the submissions made by these poor players w^d have appeased an Irish audience."[38]

So darkly etched a picture of John Bull at the theatre may distort the whole view. With this danger in mind I promise to return to the "more moderate" playgoers in Dr. Campbell's account. Still it is not unfair to say that something near savagery could at times possess some members of the audience, while submissiveness prevailed among the others. It is not always a pretty picture.

3

Up to this point indications of something less than a complete absence of prejudice on the part of spectators have largely been given by individuals. An even more troublesome problem occurs with what in the language of the day was called a cabal, a group pre-organized to cry up or down a play or player or author, often

---

[38] Thomas Campbell, *Dr. Campbell's Diary of a Visit to England in 1775*, pp. 44–45.

quite without regard to merit. A classic picture of this age-old problem, as applicable to English as to French audiences, is found in Molière's *Précieuses Ridicules* (1659).

> It is the custom for authors to come and read their new plays to people of rank, that they may induce us to approve of them and give them a reputation. I leave you to imagine if, when we say anything, the pit dares contradict us. As for me, I am very punctual in these things, and when I have made a promise to a poet, I always cry out "Bravo" before the candles are lighted.[39]

John Dennis, who was no fool but could occasionally talk like one, makes a typically positive statement about the absence of cabals in England in Molière's time—and then turns right around and contradicts himself: "Theatricall Caballs were then unheard of, and those generous and sensible audiences scorn'd to use their Interest for a Foolish play, because the Blockhead who writt it, was their acquaintance." This statement seems clear and forceful enough to settle the question once and for all—if it were not for what follows directly:

> I must confesse the Town was now and then in the wrong, deluded by the enchanting performance of soe just and soe great an Actour as Mr Hart or Mr Mohun, or by the opinion They might have of a celebrated Authour who had pleased them before. But then there were several extraordinary men at Court who wanted neither Zeal nor Capacity, nor Authority to sett them right again. There was Villers Duke of Buckingham, Wilmot Earl of Rochester, the late Earl of Dorsett, the Earl of Mulgrave who was afterwards Duke of Buckinghamshire, Mr Savil, Mr Buckley, Sir John Denham, Mr Waller &c. When these or the Majority of them Declar'd themselves upon any new Dramatick performance, the Town fell Immediately in with them. . . . And when upon the first representations of the *Plain Dealer*, the Town, as The Authour has often told me, appear'd Doubtfull what Judgment to Form

---

[39] Molière, *Précieuses Ridicules*, in *Plays by Molière*, edited by Francis Ferguson, I, 176, ll. 230–237. If Mascarille seems overly eager, he is more patient than the opponents of Francis Stamper's *Modern Character, Introduc'd in the Scenes of Vanbrugh's Aesop* (1751). The opponents were guilty, if Stamper's word is accurate, of "procuring a party to hiss it, long before a syllable of it was wrote" (preface).

of it; the foremention'd gentlemen by their loud aprobation of it, gave it both a sudden and a lasting reputation.[40]

In other words, it is all a matter of definition. "Cabals" are organized by Dennis's enemies, such as Richard Steele. When a friend is involved, there is not a cabal but a group of "extraordinary men" who can set the town right again.

There are enough allusions to cabals early in the period to prompt a rejection of Dennis's denial of their existence. The first of Dryden's prologues, for *The Wild Gallant* (1663), suggests their use, and Dryden was far closer to the scene than Dennis.

> Is it not strange, to hear a poet say,
> He comes to ask you how you like the play?
> You have not seen it yet! alas 'tis true
> But now your love and hatred judge, not you.
> And cruel factions (brib'd by interest) come,
> Not to weigh merit, but to give their doome.

To this is added in the next decade Dennis's own account of the premiere of *The Plain Dealer*, applicable to the 1676–1677 season. Then four years later comes the most unmistakable evidence: faction against faction with public charge against public charge. The heated partisanship of the Popish Plot boiled over onto the stage, most violently perhaps in Thomas Shadwell's *Lancashire Witches*. In his preface the author tells of having heard of a faction forming against his play a whole month before it was acted, but "I had so numerous an assembly of the best sort of men, who stood so generously in my defense for the first three days that they quash'd all the vain attempts of my enemies, the inconsiderable party of hissers yielded, and the play lived in spite of them." A witness from the opposition, Dryden in his *Vindication of the Duke of Guise*, corroborates this account, or *almost* corroborates it: he is discreetly silent on the formation of a party to oppose the play but thinks "it . . . impossible ever to have gotten off the nonsense of three hours for half-a-crown, but for the providence of so congruous an audience."

[40] John Dennis, *Decay and Defects of Dramatick Poetry* in *The Critical Works of John Dennis*, edited by Edward Niles Hooker, II, 276–277.

If the testimony of the sardonic author of *The Country Gentleman's Vade Mecum* (1699) is accepted, the custom of caballing was firmly established by the time Dennis's own plays had begun to appear. In undertaking to describe, in Letter VIII, a crowded theatre on the third night of a new play, the author comes to the playwright's supporters.

In another part of the house sit the poet's friends, which are resolv'd to carry him off, right or wrong; 'tis no matter to them, whether the play be well or ill done, they're engag'd either for friendship, interest, or else by a natural spirit of contradiction, to oppose the other faction.[41]

In one of the best known of all the *Spectators*, No. 2, Steele closes his account of Will Honeycombe with the wry comment, "To conclude his character, where women are not concern'd, he is an honest, worthy man." A slight paraphrase is irresistibly applicable to John Dennis: where Steele was not concerned—perhaps we should have to add Joseph Addison, Alexander Pope, and a few more—Dennis was an honest, worthy man, and a reliable witness. The difficulty often is to find a critical essay by Dennis in the last two decades of his career in which one of these opponents is not concerned. Certainly the caution applies to his statement about cabals repeated at the beginning of this section. A good part of the blame for the decay and defects of dramatic poetry Dennis lays at the feet of "the doge of Drury," as he sarcastically calls Steele. And among the latter's many, many faults is the one now under discussion: the practice of forming cabals. The plain truth is that, though Dennis may have overstated Steele's part in *inventing* the practice, he was not too far off in fixing responsibility.

The full force of Dennis's charge is felt a dozen years earlier on the notable—or notorious—occasion of the first production of *Cato*, in April 1713. Among the numerous statements called forth by Addison's model of neoclassical tragedy were a few not in harmony with the general chorus of praise, among them Dennis's *Remarks*

---

[41] Reproduced by Leslie Hotson, *The Commonwealth and Restoration Stage*, p. 304.

upon Cato, a Tragedy (1713). Of sole importance here is Dennis's attack upon both Addison and his friend and collaborator, Steele, over the formation of a cabal.

> . . . when a poet writes a tragedy, who knows he has judgment and who feels he has genius, that poet presumes upon his own merit and scorns to make a cabal. . . . But when an author writes a tragedy, who knows he has neither genius nor judgment, he has recourse to making a party, and endeavours to make up in industry what he wanted in talent.[42]

In his attack on Steele, "Squire Ironside, that grave offspring of ludicrous ancestors," Dennis may not have known how "industrious" Steele had been in organizing the Whig cabal, but he does attack him for leading a paper cabal of encomiastic essayists. Yet Steele later more than justified Dennis's sarcasm by boasting of his own part in organizing support for *Cato*.

> All the town knows how officious I was in bringing it on; and you that know the town, the theatre, and mankind very well, can judge how necessary it was to take measures for making a performance of that sort, excellent as it is, run into popular applause. I promis'd before it was acted, and performed my duty accordingly to the author, that I would bring together so just an audience on the first days of it, that it should be impossible for the vulgar to put its success or due applause to any hazard.[43]

Pope, himself a compound of Machiavelli and Tom Sawyer in chicane, was maneuvered into writing a prologue for Addison's play and then "clapped into a staunch Whig, sore against [my] will, at almost every two lines" as he ruefully tells his friend John Caryll. *Cato* is actually unique in being the only play, so far as my knowledge extends, to be so ingeniously contrived as to elicit the same kind of response from both its supporters and opponents. It was designed to favor the Whigs and loudly applauded by them, but the Tories could not in good grace protest over speeches in praise of liberty. "The numerous and violent claps of the Whig party on one

---

[42] Dennis, *Critical Works*, II, 41–42.

[43] Richard Steele's dedication to Congreve, inserted into the second edition of Joseph Addison's *Drummer*, 1722.

side of the theatre were echoed back by the Tories on the other," as
Pope told Caryll.[44]

I am tempted, with the problem of space in mind, to let the story
of *Cato* stand as a type of political caballing in the theatre seen
throughout the century. But to do so might be misleading because
the history of Addison's play is fairly unique and the decade following 1713 was more heavily marked by political activity in the
theatre than was any other since the sixteen-eighties. It was with
The Non-Juror of 1717 that Colley Cibber's long war with opponents
in the audience began, or so he professed to think twenty-odd years
later.[45] It was in the second decade that Dudley Ryder records the
frequent response to anything remotely political in the plays he attended.[46] It was in this decade that Lewis Theobald pictured the audience as sitting "stupidly listening for accidental expressions struck
out of the story, which speaks [*sic*] the sense of their own principles
and perswasion."[47] Other periods also saw a rise in political tempera-
ture in the theatre: the opposition to Sir Robert Walpole in the early
seventeen-thirties,[48] the strong feelings generated over the passing

[44] Alexander Pope, *Correspondence*, edited by George Sherburn, I, 175. John
Loftis gives a detailed account in *The Politics of Drama in Augustan England*,
pp. 56–61.

[45] Colley Cibber, *An Apology for the Life of Mr. Colley Cibber*, II, 186–189.
Cibber's friend Victor adds support to the laureate's contention that no play after
The Non-Juror (1717) escaped a severe mauling by the town (see especially
Victor, *History*, II, 95–96, 105). Fielding had already made note of the per-
sistent opposition. His Marplay Junior, in the revised *Author's Farce* (1734),
comments ruefully, "Sir, the town have a prejudice to my family" (I, vi, 42).

[46] Dudley Ryder, *The Diary of Dudley Ryder, 1715–1716*, edited by William
Matthews, pp. 181, 195. See especially the entries for 13 February and 13 March
1716.

[47] Lewis Theobald, *Censor*, No. 93 (25 May 1717).

[48] *Prompter*, No. 47 (22 April 1735), gives a detailed picture of a "house
filled with uproar" when party faces party in this decade of strong political
feeling. For a different kind of example I might cite the absurd case of Captain
Boadens (or Bodens) and *The Modish Couple*, a play performed at Drury Lane
in January 1732. Scouten gives a few details, but for a full account one should
consult C. B. Woods, "Captain B——'s Play," *Harvard Studies and Notes*, 15
(1933), 243–255.

of the Licensing Act in 1737,[49] the troubles that accompanied and
followed the second Jacobite Rebellion in the late seventeen-
forties,[50] the dispute over Wilkes and the *North Briton* in the seven-
teen-sixties, the passionate support of and opposition to the French
Revolution in the last decade of the century[51]—all represent peaks
in a graph by no means even, but none really exceeds the second
decade of the century in its visible or audible effects in the theatre.

4

The organized, premeditated opposition to or support of a play
has until now, had some discernible, though often far from admirable, motivation.[52] A playwright who uses the stage as a soapbox
begs for trouble and a manager who is willing to hazard the safety

[49] Hildebrand Jacob considered himself an innocent victim of the reaction
to Walpole's restrictive bill (see his preface to the unfortunate *Nest of Plays*
[1738]). I suspect that James Miller might with justice have made the same
excuse for the misfortunes of his *Coffee House*, but he chose to think the
Templars opposed his piece on more personal grounds. The Abbé LeBlanc was
persuaded that "the best play in the world would not have succeeded the first
night" of this first season under the act (Jean Bernard LeBlanc, *Letters on the
English and French Nations*, II, 313).

[50] Persistent opposition to invasions by French troupes is a phase of this complex of political feeling. The newspapers of October 1738 or of November 1749
reveal the almost rabid opposition on the part of what the *Daily Post* of 11 October 1738 calls "the Protestant mob." Most curious of all is the affair of *The
Chinese Festival* in November 1755. Garrick had tried to disarm the opposition
by pointing out that Noverre was Swiss and Protestant, Mme. Noverre German.
But John Bull was in no mood for such subtleties. The fact that the troupe of
dancers was from Paris, the posting of French titles for the dances, and perhaps
most critically the insistent support by what in the 1749 episode had been termed
"the Anglo-Gallic Smarts"—these acts sufficed to set the mob in an uproar and
drive the "father of modern ballet" from England.

[51] The newspapers collected by Charles Burney (British Museum) for the
early seventeen-nineties are filled with accounts of displays of political feeling,
accounts, to give just one type, of the insistence on everyone's singing "God Save
the King" over and over.

[52] Though one might insist on allowing a play to stand on its discernible merits,
he can sympathize with a less idealistic stance taken by some persons in the period.
Samuel Johnson might well be their spokesman. When Goldsmith reported an
invitation he had received to go hiss a play, Johnson's rejoinder was, "And did
not you tell him he was a rascal?" (Boswell, *Life of Johnson*, IV, 10). From other

of his company or his property by giving partisan plays should not be surprised if he precipitates a riot. When he fails in his appraisal of the strength of the feeling against foreigners he is possibly more deserving of pity than censure. The motives for caballing are more readily understandable than a form of often disorganized but persistent opposition that is much harder to categorize and explain.

Mr. Spectator in his first number spoke of the wide range of human conduct over which he proposed to rove with well-trained and discerning eye, and indeed the variety and acuteness of his observations helped to set a new style in discourse. Among the hundreds of traits worth public attention that he was eventually to treat, he came in No. 224 to what is now called exhibitionism, a trait especially discernible among young men of the leisure class. True, he called it by a different name, but what he had in mind is unmistakable—and still with us.

> The desire of distinction is not, I think, in any instance more observable than in the variety of outsides and new appearances which the modish part of the world are obliged to provide, in order to make themselves remarkable; for anything glaring and particular, either in behaviour or apparel, is known to have this good effect, that it catches the eye, and will not suffer you to pass over the person so adorned without due notice and observation. . . . To this passionate fondness for distinction are owing various frolicsome and irregular practices, as sallying out into nocturnal exploits, breaking of windows, singing of catches, beating the watch, getting drunk twice a day, killing a great number of horses; with many other enterprises of the like fiery nature: for certainly many a man is more rakish and extravagant than he would willingly be, were there not others to look on and give their approbation.

Since Mr. Spectator was giving only a sample of the more common and annoying manifestations of exhibitionism rather than an exhaustive list he did not include the nuisance in the audience here. The principal motive of the annoying spectator I spoke of in the last chapter, the young man "behind the scenes," was unquestionably

---

accounts, however, we know that Johnson had no such low opinion of *supporting* a play; in fact, he heartily joined in the efforts to support Goldsmith's.

the desire to exhibit himself. As a kind of postscript to the sample above, *Spectator* No. 240 adds a detailed account of this particular show-off, a "sort of beau" who struts about, shows off his clothes, gets in the way of the actors, obstructs the view of the audience, and in general makes a nuisance of himself. Enough was said in the preceding chapter to indicate that neither official disapproval nor public scorn could curb the nuisance. Eventually the special combination of unusual resoluteness on the part of the managers and the accurate aim of the galleries served to rid the audience and players of this considerable annoyance—compelling evidence of the strength of the motive.

To suggest that driving him from the stage was to rid the audience of him is to overstate the case. He only popped up elsewhere, never to be actually repressed. In *Dunciad IV* Pope has fixed and labeled him for all time, like a butterfly impaled in midflight:

> Thro' school and college, thy kind cloud o'ercast,
> Safe and unseen the young Æneas past:
> Thence bursting glorious, all at once let down,
> Stunn'd with his giddy Larum half the town.
> Intrepid then, o'er sea and lands he flew:
> Europe he saw, and Europe saw him too.[53]

With all the Foplings, Novels, Sparkishes, Dappers, Dangles, and what-not thronging the plays and novels of the day, it would seem a work of supererogation to give any more than the sample of specimens already presented. The most notable change perhaps was the change in the principal scene of the show-off's activities. Driven from the stage, he invaded the boxes, where by his loud laughter and distracting conversation he was able to annoy others more interested in the play and thus draw attention to himself. The author of *D–ry-L–ne P–yh–se broke open* reported a suggested remedy for the nuisance of beaux crowding the stage: put mirrors in all the boxes; then they would flock there to admire themselves. This obviously would be no remedy since it was not the desire to

---

[53] Alexander Pope, *The Poems of Alexander Pope*, edited by John Butt, V, 372–373, ll. 289–294.

see themselves but to be seen—and heard—which prompted their actions. With the very considerable increase in the size of the audience and of the theatre, it was possible to get at least intermittent relief by providing more spacious lobbies, especially for the occupants of the boxes, where the young exhibitionist could be seen and heard without disturbing the audience. The popularity of these new provisions for exhibitionism is attested by the numerous uses of such terms as "box-lobby loungers," "box-lobby bucks," "box-lobby swaggerers," "box-lobby beaus," and by the occasional complaints of the disturbance they created, described on at least one occasion as a "box-lobby blast."[54]

The desire of distinction was not the exclusive property of young males though most common among them and most likely to interfere with the chances for peaceful play-going among others. I should not wish to suggest that aging philosophers, of all persons, were guilty of showing off but I do find a note in the memoirs of Joseph Cradock intriguing.

When Rousseau was in England, Mr. Garrick paid him the compliment of playing two characters, on purpose to oblige him; they were Lusignan and Lord Chalkstone [23 January 1766]; and as it was known that Rousseau was to be present, the theatre was of course crowded to excess. Rousseau was highly gratified, but Mrs. Garrick told me, that 'she had never passed a more uncomfortable evening in her life, for the recluse philosopher was so very anxious to display himself, and hung so forward over the front of the box, that she was obliged to hold him by the skirt of his coat, that he might not fall over into the pit.'[55]

Equally distressing are the occasional suggestions that the ladies were not absolved from the same charge. Henry Fielding has Tawdry, in *Miss Lucy in Town* (1742), describe the conduct of "fine ladies" at plays: "Why, if they can, they take a stage-box, where they let the footman sit the first two acts, to show his livery; then they come in to show themselves, spread their fans upon the

---

[54] An unidentified newspaper clipping of 2 December 1789, in the Winston Collection, British Museum.

[55] Joseph Cradock, *Literary and Miscellaneous Memoirs*, I, 206.

spikes, make curtsies to their acquaintance, and then talk and laugh as loud as they are able."[56] A closely similar account appeared in the *Prater*, No. 2, 20 March 1756. Our reporter tells of an evening spent at the theatre, where he seems to have spent more time watching a party of fashionable young ladies than the play. They flounced in a full hour late, in the midst of a highly dramatic scene on the stage. They "fidgetted up and down near a quarter of an hour, before they could place themselves to advantage, that is, make themselves conspicuous." They paid no attention to the play but began their own loud dialogue, punctuated with louder laughter, until the audience finally hissed them to silence.

And finally, Mr. Town in Thomas Holcroft's *Rival Queens* (1794) sneers at his wife's pretensions to high taste and the love of Shakespeare, Otway, and Congreve by suggesting her true motives for going to the theatre, especially her being ". . . stark mad after side-boxes when you find they are all taken for a month to come. . . . You do not go to see but to be seen, Mrs. Town, and, as to Shakespeare, unless fashion and a full house keep you in countenance, you are asham'd of his company."[57]

The pretensions of beaux and their ladies were harmless enough since they had no great effect on the other spectators and their right to enjoy the play in peace. The conduct of some of the young men could be a quite different matter, especially on first nights. A deplorable custom had grown up of attacking a new play on no other grounds than malicious mischief, prompted almost certainly by the exhibitionist motives alluded to in *Spectator* No. 224. Since attacking new plays is not listed among the common "nocturnal exploits" designed to call attention to the perpetrators, perhaps caution should be taken in adding it so early. A few decades later, however, it would appear to belong in the list. At midcentury *Rambler* No. 195 (28 January 1752) provides a picture of young roisterers engaging in precisely the activities listed in the earlier account. They

[56] Henry Fielding, *Miss Lucy in Town*, I, i, 151–157.
[57] Thomas Holcroft, *Rival Queens*, pp. 2–3; MS in Larpent MS play collection, No. 1039, Henry E. Huntington Library, San Marino, California.

drink themselves into a state of "obstreperous jollity," beat the watch, break windows, and do battle with an assembly of chairmen. All this is preceded, however, by another activity—the "persecution of a play."

Though Johnson does not specifically describe the play as a new one, the chances are that it was, for by this time new plays and new authors were considered fair game. Look at the account of what could happen to a new play, this one Anthony Brown's *Fatal Retirement*, which made one disastrous appearance 12 November 1739, its failure evidently being assured by James Quin's refusal to take any part in it on the grounds that it "was the very worst play he had read in his life."

But we ought not entirely to form our Judgment of its being the very worst Play, from what this Gentleman was pleased to say of it, in the Heat of his Resentment for being ill-treated; nor wonder that an Audience should applaud a Sentence which condemned an Author, at a Time when it was the Fashion to condemn them all, right or wrong, without being heard; and when Parties were made to go to new Plays to make Uproars, which they called by the odious Name of The Funn of the first Night.[58]

There is unfortunately a good bit of support for this account, especially in the period following passage of the Licensing Act. In the long discourse on catcalls in *Common Sense* No. 69 (27 May 1738), there is a similar account of a premiere attended by young Townly and his friends, among them the narrator. It is not made clear at the start that this party was intent on damning the play, but after two acts "Townly, at length finding nothing in it to hold his attention, began to tune his flagellet" and was soon joined by "a number of others, in various keys, that it became a *concerto grosso*." Another party having come to support the play, a mighty contest followed in which the poor play failed actually to be heard. At this point the narrator, who favored the opposition party he had originally joined, does a strange about-face. His first impulse is to ap-

---

[58] *A Compleat List of All the Dramatic Authors*, appended to Thomas Whincop, *Scanderbeg* . . . (1747), p. 183.

plaud the young men who consider themselves defenders of liberty
in not accepting a play simply because a party forces it upon them
—much in the manner of the "enemies to English liberty" who
forced the Licensing Act on a free citizenry. Then he suddenly
awakens to the plight of the author.

That a spirit of Opposition should rise up against the licensing of
Dramatick Poetry, is no Wonder:—A true *Briton* would no more have
our Wit excised, than our Wine;—it will render both spiritless and
adulterate. But my objection to the present Practice is, that where the
Resentment is only intended against the Licenser, the Poet may suffer;—like the Frogs in the Fable when pelted by Boys, he may say to
the Audience, that, tho' it be Sport to them, it is Death to him.

The idea that what began as a protest over the invasion of liberty
soon degenerated into a cruel game finds support in other contemporary comments.[59]

5

Throughout this sketch of a "candid" but exigent audience, an
audience sometimes violently responsive to activities on the stage,
I have been aware of the danger of stressing this more dramatic
quality, of leaving the impression that all theatregoers were so partisan or so violent that an actor's only concern was not to arouse
them too much. Such a picture would be distorted since violent reactions are in the long run intermittent and, often enough, the response of something less than the whole audience. My good friend
and sometime collaborator A. H. Scouten fifteen years ago took another student of the theatre to task—and rightly so—for leaving just
such an impression of continuous violence in the eighteenth-century
theatre.[60] In the brief space of a review, however, his altogether too

[59] For other examples see Walpole's letter to Horace Mann, 11 March 1748,
in *Horace Walpole's Correspondence*, edited by Wilmarth Sheldon Lewis, XIX,
469; *A Guide to the Stage*, p. 15; the advertisement ending *Midwife*, I, no. 4
(1751); *Theatrical Disquisitions* (1763), pp. 23–24; David Garrick's letter to
William Woodfall, 13 [February 1776], No. 983, in *Letters*, edited by David
Mason Little and George Morrow Kahrl, III, 1070–1072.

[60] Arthur H. Scouten, Review of *All Right on the Night* by V. C. Clinton-
Baddeley, *Philological Quarterly*, 34 (1955), 256.

stark corrective cancels the real significance of the disposition to violence that did exist—a significance that transcends the theatre itself. Two tendencies were developing simultaneously. First, there was the growing consciousness of the individual's right to express himself, not always accompanied, as Tocqueville had warned, by a sense of responsibility but more often by a love of mischief and self-display. Simultaneously, there was a quieter but actually far more important growth of tolerance for what appeared intolerable to foreigners.

Alistair Cooke, that discerning observer of both British and American attitudes, offers a striking analysis of this general theme of tolerance of the other man's obstreperousness.

In Britain, one of the minor duties of good citizenship is not to disturb the private life of other citizens. In this country, it's the other way around—not to disturb other citizens who are enjoying their private life in public. That, as you see, is a heavily loaded interpretation of an attitude that is universal among Americans. And there are limits. Just the same, the decision of a Washington court of appeal not to let advertisers broadcast in public buses only shows how far you can go in America without being stopped.[61]

The English have changed greatly since 1775, when Joseph Palmer, looking with envy on his French neighbors, reflects the impatience of at least a minority of would-be reformers. His general picture of *pueri robusti* is even more provocative than his view of the English audience.

Some method, I should think, might be invented, for restraining the licentiousness of the populace in London, which is grown to such a pitch, as cannot be paralleled in the most savage country of the globe. The brutality one meets in walking the streets, calls aloud for restraint. If a man is not very nimble, he has his neck broken by a hackney-coachman, or at least his shins by some lamp-lighter, who is permitted to run with his ladder, though in the mist [*sic*] of a crowd. . . . But such is the off-spring of glorious liberty, and these *wild dogs* must not be muzzled, lest in curbing licence, we should touch their sacred birthright, English freedom. I have been often asked, whether any one ever

[61] Alistair Cooke, *One Man's America*, p. 255.

wears a sword in London; for the French seem to conclude, from the opinion every one has of our barbarism, that they should find it necessary to kill a man, every time they walked the streets. In short, the frightful stories every traveller tells of our common people in London, has confirmed an universal opinion of their being below savages, and I doubt whether it is not just.[62]

As in any period, in the eighteenth century most theatergoers were content to watch a play in peace while many were merely bored sophisticates who looked upon the theatre as a convenience for assembly. Perhaps it would be well to examine briefly this last-mentioned minority, thus saving for the last the people whose influence on drama is permanent.

Prompter No. 128 (30 January 1736) says some very harsh things about the people who flock to the theatre just because everyone else does.

. . . what would become of the numbers of people, that constantly spend the hour between six and ten, at a playhouse, if *Pantomime* were abolished? Would they stay at home? No: Believe me, besides the pleasure of the representation, there will always be reasons enough to make the *Fashionable* and *Gay*, frequent play-houses.[63]

A decade earlier John Dennis had noted similar characteristics, especially among the *nouveaux riches* crowding into London.

The Revolution, The union and the protestant succession, has brought to this Town a vast number of strangers who formerly were not seen here. And a new and numerous gentry has risen among us by the Return of our fleets from sea, of our Armies from the Continent, and from the wreck of the South Sea. All these will have their Diversions and their easie partiality leads them against their own palpable interest to the Hundreds of Drury. They goe not thither because tis Just and Reasonable, but because tis become a Fashion.[64]

---

[62] Palmer, *Four Months Tour*, pp. 66–68.

[63] Number 80 is devoted to an analysis of the audience. Much too long and diffuse to quote, it gives a picture that supports the one I have been attempting to outline.

[64] Dennis, *Critical Works*, II, 278. Even earlier, Lady Townley in *Man of Mode* (1676) speaks of her house as "next to the playhouse . . . the common refuge of all the young, idle people" (III, ii, 127–128).

Illustrations of this basic trait of following the fashion—if illustration be required—can be found from one end of this long period to the other. Samuel Pepys, who was often breathless in his pursuit of fashion, reveals the attitude prevalent early in the period.

My wife being gone before, I to the Duke of York's playhouse; where a new play of Etheridge's, called "She Would if she Could"; and though I was there by two o'clock, there was 1000 people put back that could not have room in the pit; and I at last, because my wife was there, made shift to get into the 18d. box, and there saw; but, Lord! how full was the house, and how silly the play, there being nothing in the world good in it, and few people pleased in it. The King was there; but I sat mightily behind, and could see but little, and hear not all.

6 February 1668

So I out, and met my wife in a coach, and stopped her going thither to meet me; and took her, and Mercer, and Deb., to Bartholomew-Fair, and there did see a ridiculous, obscene little stage-play, called "Merry Andrey"; a foolish thing, but seen by every body: and so to Jacob Hall's dancing of the ropes; a thing worth seeing, and mightily followed.

29 August 1668

A midcentury comment in a letter from William Shenstone to his friend Richard Jago (6 February 1741) suggests that fashionable display was still an important reason for attending the theatre.

Comus I have once been at, for the sake of the songs, though I detest it in any light: but as a dramatic piece, that taking of it seems a prodigy; yet indeed such-a-one, as was pretty tolerably accounted for by a gentleman who sate by me in the boxes. This learned sage, being asked how he liked the play, made answer, "He could not tell—pretty well, he thought—or indeed as well as any other play—he always took it, that people only came there to see and to be seen—for as for what was said, he owned, he never understood anything of the matter." I told him, I thought a great many of its admirers were in his case, if they would but own it.[65]

At the close of the century the playwright Frederick Reynolds

---

[65] William Shenstone to Richard Jago, February 6, 1741, in William Shenstone, *The Letters of William Shenstone*, edited by Marjorie Williams, p. 17.

supplies testimony rather than evidence, but it is credible testimony. Commenting on the *Vortigern* fiasco when crowds flocked to the theatre to see this newly recovered play by Shakespeare only to grow disillusioned in midcareer and hiss it off the stage, Reynolds wonders why the management played their cards so clumsily. With more skillful manipulation they could have had the kind of success which, enabling

the box book-keeper to stand up in his place and boldly say, "not a box to be had for a month," regularly secures the letting every box for *a week.* This has often happened, not altogether from the town's desire to see the "new wonder," but partly from the conviction that no fashionable people dare *shew their faces* until they have seen it.[66]

From the point of view of the box-office, theatre-goers impelled by a desire to be fashionable are just as welcome as people more esthetically motivated, and from the point of view of the whole company they are far less annoying than the violent and noisy. Still they hardly represent an ideal. With little or no interest in performers or performance they pass their time in distracting conversation, in visiting from box to box, even on at least a few occasions in sleep. Once more the evidence—in plays, in novels, in essays, in graphic illustrations—is so plentiful that selection becomes difficult. Perhaps the best demonstration of their behavior is provided by an actual playgoer, William Byrd of Virginia, in the careful record he kept during his two-year stay in London.[67] Byrd was hardly an exemplary or even a typical playgoer, but he could possibly qualify as one of the most exasperating persons ever to set foot in a playhouse, for he can be charged with almost every kind of offensive behavior a spectator could be guilty of—except rioting. Byrd seems never to have been interested enough in a play to have so much as raised his voice. Once he quarreled with some footmen, but only for keeping their hats on, a bit of class warfare.

[66] Frederick Reynolds, *The Life and Times of Frederick Reynolds*, II, 241–242.
[67] William Byrd, *The London Diary, 1717–1721, and Other Writings*, edited by Louis Booker Wright and Marion Tinling.

Byrd appears to have had almost no interest in drama. Within certain rather narrow limits he liked people—fashionable people and especially fashionable women or, the latter failing, women of any kind—and these were to be found between six and ten every weekday evening at the theatres. Though he records over a hundred visits to the theatre Byrd rarely gives the title of a play. When he does he makes no comment on either play or performance. On 14 February 1719 his entry sounds almost as if it had been copied verbatim from his more famous predecessor Pepys: ". . . and then went to the play of Tom Killegrew's and was well liked." The syntax is awkward but revealing. The important thing to register—so important he hurries it too much—is how *the public* reacted, not what *he* thought. It would be more economical, however, to deal wholesale in Mr. Byrd's entries. A sample dozen will reveal the American's exasperating habits as a playgoer.

1718

16 January   . . . and then to the play, where was nobody I cared for.

1 February   From hence I went to Will's Coffee-house and from thence to the play, where I slept.

8 February   . . . and then went to the play in Covent Garden and led out Mrs. W–n–m . . .

18 March   About six I went to the new playhouse where there was but indifferent company and I slept.

1 November   . . . and then went to Will's Coffee-house and from thence to the play, where I found indifferent women.

3 November   Then we went to the play where we met two women in B–r–t–n box but could not persuade them to go with us. . . .

4 November   . . . and then went to the play with Mr. Page and was well diverted. Mrs. Lindsay was there and talked all the while with Jack H–r–v–y.

25 November   About 5 o'clock I went to Will's and read the news and then Sir Wilfred Lawson and I went to the play at B–r–t–n box to meet our milliners and they came to us. After the play we went to the Three Tuns and had a fricassee of chicken.

1719

12 September   . . . and then I called at the playhouse which was very

full because it was the first time of acting. However, I did not stay but went to the coffee-house.[68]

13 October . . . and then went to the play where I sat next to Mrs. [Cambridge] and talked abundance to her.

20 October . . . and thence to the play where I saw nobody I liked so went to Will's and stayed about an hour.

5 November . . . and then went to both plays but there was no company at either.

With a comment or two merely emphasizing a few items that may require special attention, I shall allow this amazing cluster of entries to speak for itself. Sad to note, Byrd's behavior was most laudable on the evenings he slept at the playhouse—hardly an exemplary record. The casual report of "abundant" conversation shows him at his worst, though the entry, which is only one of several, telling of his visiting both playhouses in one evening should not be overlooked. Obviously he must have disturbed his neighbors in leaving one house and in entering the other. Playhouse "peepers"[69] were a persistent threat to more regular and considerate playgoers.

6

Turning finally to the really "candid" section of the audience— candid in the then accepted meaning—I face immediate difficulty. For the story, while not precisely like Viola's, a blank, is not an easy one to tell, especially under the heading of behavior. Good behavior always makes poor news and therefore is commonly not reported. And to make matters worse, the considerate, well-behaved spectator is the one who is victimized by his noisier, less considerate neighbor. There were numerous occasions during the eighteenth century when the two were matched, with predictable results, when the meeker spectators did temporarily put aside their meekness to

[68] Avery's entry (*London Stage*, pt. 2, p. 549) shows that this was the Drury Lane offering of *Hamlet* with the full strength of one of the best companies of English actors in the century.

[69] This expressive epithet I take from one of the several newspaper accounts in September 1788 when they were at long last curbed by a new regulation: no money was to be returned once the play started.

assert their right to hear in peace. *Prompter* No. 139 recounts, through an alleged correspondent, the behavior of a group who came to Drury Lane prepared to damn Connolly's *Connoisseur*, 20 February 1736.

That the fact is thus, will be acknowledged by all who frequent the play-houses, except the very men who make the uproar, and by a good many of them too: and tho' *clapping* might be sometimes a match for *hissing alone* at a new play; and the candid part of the audience, might support a justifiable scene upon a fair contest; yet when the auxiliary shouts, cat-calls, and horse-laughs, enter the field, one hundred of these terrible heroes, shall easily prevail against four or five hundred modest persons, who wou'd willingly enjoy a rational entertainment in quiet.

William Popple's account of what happened on the fourth night of his *Lady's Revenge*, 12 January 1734, provides an example of a much rarer outcome, the triumph of the majority who were willing to let a play be heard to the end. Having, according to him, withdrawn the play rather than hurt the manager, John Rich, Popple published it with a detailed account of its fortunes. After surviving a stormy first night the play had been performed without opposition on two more occasions, the third a royal command and the usual author's benefit. Then came the fourth night:

The fourth night a set of about eight or ten young fellows went to the Bedford Coffee-House in the Piazza, and declared publickly that they came purposely to damn the play, and would not leave the play-house till they had encompassed their ends. The same declaration they repeated when in the house to some gentlemen that were there, friends (but unknown to them) of the author. Mr. Ryan coming on to speak the prologue, they began their uproar, but were soon silenced. . . . The play beginning, they began again. . . . Mr. Quin then came on, and told them he found the house was divided, and as the majority was for having the play, he hop'd those who were not, would go out. The house on that were unanimous, and cry'd, Turn them out, Turn them out, but they saved the audience the trouble of doing it, and retired under the general hiss of every person then present.

There are other cases in which a very small group of trouble-makers—Popple's tally may under the circumstances be suspect—

were silenced or evicted by an overwhelming majority. In still others the majority intervened when some outside authority tried to silence a noisy group. The *Morning Post* for 27 April 1791 carried a story of a disturbance brought on by a last-minute substitution in the bill. The protest was evidently confined to the galleries, but when soldiers were sent in to silence the complainers, the whole house rose and protested, or, as the news reporter editorializes, "the audience properly insisted on their removal." More commonly the quiet majority sat in meek resignation, solacing themselves with the hope that their private discomfort was somehow contributing to public welfare.

Usually no disturbance was recorded, and the peaceful majority were allowed to enjoy the play without interruption. In its very full record *The London Stage* provides a day-by-day account demonstrating that it was possible for a theatregoer to attend night after night with no important disruption of his peace and privacy. Given the sometimes turbulent conditions of the times, the general course of the theatre would resemble that of a stream. Where any new departures from a straight course appear, in bends or falls, where obstacles appear in the stream, turbulence develops. More generally the flow is untroubled, even though the placidity may be deceptive.

The remaining phase of audience behavior is seen in the demonstrations of more than passive "candor," the occasional show of generosity or sympathy of which a London audience was capable. Sudden illness, personal misfortune, accidents—if they did not reveal too gross negligence—could call forth the best in an audience. During a performance of *All's Well* at Drury Lane on 16 February 1742 Peg Woffington fainted just before making her entrance in the part of Helena. When it became clear that she was incapable of continuing, "a proper apology being made, the audience with great humanity and patience waited till another person dress'd to read the part."[70]

Demonstrating another kind of candor is Joseph Cradock's report of his misadventures with his first play, *Zobeide*, at Covent

---

[70] Scouten reproduces this newspaper account in *The London Stage*, pt. 3, p. 968.

Garden on 11 December 1771. According to his account, Cradock was the innocent victim of theatrical politics, and his play was given the worst possible treatment by George Colman. Among other indignities

. . . old Mrs. Vincent was forced upon me, dressed in crimson satin, ornamented with fur, as a *Scythian rural Nymph*, attendant on Zobeide. That the audience suffered this, and many other incongruities, particularly meant to offend Mrs. Yates, I can only attribute to that tenderness and partiality which an English audience is always ready to bestow on an *unfledged* author.[71]

A final example of generosity carries special meaning since it involves an actor who knew from bitter experience how unkind an audience could be. Charles Macklin, who was an old man when his right to resume his career was decreed by Lord Mansfield in 1775, showed every indication for more than a decade that he had been exempted from the usual fate of mortals. William Worthen Appleton repeats the veteran's response to George III in May 1787 that he "had been born in the last century, served His Majesty in this one, and hoped to do so in the next."[72] And for another year he seemed equal to the self-imposed assignment. On 9 January 1788, however, his memory failed him early in the play still associated with him, *The Merchant of Venice*. According to the *Gentleman's Magazine* he managed to get through the first act but felt obliged to make an apology before starting the second.

. . . conscious of some few defects, and with much solemnity, he addressed the audience nearly in the following words:
"Ladies and Gentlemen,
Within these very few hours I have been seized with a terror of mind I never in my life felt before;—it has totally destroyed my corporeal, as well as mental faculties. I must, therefore, request your patience this night—a request, which an old man of eighty-nine years of age may hope is not unreasonable. Should it be granted, you may depend this will be the last night, unless my health shall be entirely re-established, of my ever appearing before you in so ridiculous a situation."
This affecting address from an old favourite of the town, of at least

---

[71] Cradock, *Memoirs*, IV, 215.
[72] William Worthen Appleton, *Charles Macklin*, p. 225.

89 years of age, met with enthusiastic reception; which seemed to give a new life to his drooping spirits. He soon recovered, and the play went on with applause to the end.[73]

Though this incident is in all its circumstances unique, it may indicate a trend toward some amelioration in the conduct of the audience. My diffidence and heavy qualification are occasioned by the persistence of quite contrary indications, a good many of which I have already noted. A commentator on theatrical affairs in a contemporary London newspaper of 17 September 1786 comments on the more hopeful sign.

A correspondent remarks, that the people of this country begin to lose that barbarism in the theatre, which formerly characterized them on the representation of new pieces, instead of driving all the players off the stage, and putting an end to the performance before it is half gone through, we seem now to feel for the situation of the performers, to consider them as doing their utmost to please, and if the piece is disapproved of, it dies a natural death by not being attended to by the town.[74]

7

Perhaps the safest judgment would be that an audience often whimsical in its reactions became more and more so as the century progressed. Neander's severe remarks on the *plebs* in Dryden's *Essay of Dramatic Poesy* is provisionally applicable here. "If by the people you understand the multitude, the οἱ πολλοί, 'tis no matter what they think; . . . their judgment is a mere lottery."[75] It is not necessary to restrict the charge of being temperamental to the *plebs*. Just at the time when Dryden was accusing the lower classes of whimsicality Pepys was observing an audience of more elegant persons demonstrate the same trait. The first time he ever sat in a

---

[73] *Gentleman's Magazine* (January 1788), pp. 79–80.

[74] Unidentified newsclipping, Theatre Collection, No. 60, British Museum. Aaron Hill's self-appointed successor, who issued a *Prompter* from October through December 1789, talks a great deal too much about tumult, uproar, and the like to inspire confidence in such assurances. Contemporary newspapers throughout the century report a great many incidents to suggest that nothing remotely like the modern German audience Tynan describes ever appeared.

[75] John Dryden, *Essays of John Dryden*, edited by William Paton Ker, I, 100.

box in his life, at the premiere of *The Black Prince* by Roger Boyle, first Earl of Orrery, on 19 October 1667, with "the house infinite full, the King and the Duke of York there," he saw the mood of the audience change from favorable to unfavorable, all over the reading of a letter which was too long. "After the play done, and nothing pleasing them from the time of the letter to the end of the play, people being put into a bad humour of disliking, which is another thing worth noting."

This remark at the beginning of the long span can be neatly matched by another at the end. A newspaper comment on the varied fortunes of Robert Merry's *Magician*, 2 February 1792, echoes Pepys as it reflects on the importance of "the temporary mood of the audience." Merry had written a couple of tragedies previously and by doing so, according to the informant, had prepared the audience to expect the serious and not the facetious. On a retrial their mood had changed and all went well.[76]

Between these two commentaries on the significance of mood lie numerous accounts of the often mercurial shifts of the audience; the records of the prompters, especially of Richard Cross, are particularly revealing. The many violent reactions to what the actors of that day called "baulks"—last-minute changes in the evening's bill because of alleged illness or the like—were often the result of an audience's mood. Repeatedly the prompters or the newspapers tell of strong reactions to what may have seemed inadequately motivated changes in the bill. Feelings ran so high on occasion that after prolonged opposition to the substitution of an unannounced piece the audience went home without having seen either the originally announced item or the substitute. I trust I am not reading envy into an item in Garrick's diary of his visit to France in 1751 when, on Tuesday 11 June he makes the following note: "In the evening we went to the Italian Comedy to see the XXX [*sic*] as it

---

[76] Enthoven Theatre Collection, Victoria and Albert Museum, London. Tate Wilkinson reports Garrick's concern over having to play tragedy to a house made up in good part of people who could not get in to see one of Rich's pantomimes (*Memoirs of His Own Life*, II, 158).

was so mark'd in the bill, but it was chang'd for Arlequin Sauvage, why I can't tell, for they change their pieces at both theatres as they please without giving their reasons or making any excuse."[77]

If William Byrd provides a striking case history of the more objectionable habits of playgoers, perhaps I ought in fairness to close this account of audience behavior by citing a playgoer more adequately representative, one who, like the audience in general, ranged widely in mood. No better candidate for the post could be found than James Boswell.[78]

Besides revealing a variety of moods, Boswell's accounts are especially useful because they provide full details not only of his actions but also of his emotional state. For he was above all a role-player. As Christopher Morley puts it so well in the preface to the *London Journal*, "Boswell was always a theatre-lover; but his best theatricals were himself. He sat in the pit for a life-long performance of that tragicomedy, James Boswell.[79] Indeed, Steele, anticipating a common theme of modern psychology in *Spectator* 270, thought all men role-players, and a case could doubtless be made for the significance of role-playing in accounting for much of the conduct of an audience. However, I am interested in James Boswell not as a conscious role-player but as a representative playgoer in a variety of moods.

Boswell could on occasion be charged with conduct not greatly superior to that of Byrd. He was even on a few occasions a part-

---

[77] David Garrick, *The Diary of David Garrick, Being a Record of His Memorable Trip to Paris in 1751*, edited by Ryllis Clair Alexander, p. 28.

[78] Of several persons besides Pepys, Byrd, and Boswell who have left detailed accounts of their play-going, only two whom I have encountered would at all match these three. Sylas Neville has left an interesting account of the years between 1767 and 1788, fortunately available in a modern edition, although it is not quite the full record, as Stone's numerous notes from Neville show (see Sylas Neville, *Diary, 1767–1788*, edited by Basil Cozens-Hardy). John Yeoman on the other hand was far less sophisticated and had only a brief acquaintance with London theatres, but his account makes up in its refreshing ingenuousness and wealth of detail what it lacks of Neville's qualities.

[79] James Boswell, *Boswell's London Journal*, edited by Frederick Albert Pottle, p. 27.

time playgoer, visiting both London theatres on the same evening. On the evening of 9 April during his 1762–1763 stay he saw an opera at Covent Garden and an afterpiece at Drury Lane—and made a visit with Erskine's mistress and had a brief encounter with a streetwalker in between. More commonly, however, he went to the theatre to stay for at least the play and did not simply flit in and out. The range of his conduct at the theatre is best expressed in his own language.

Exhibitionist

At Mr. Tytler's, I happened to tell that one evening, a great many years ago, when Dr. Hugh Blair and I were sitting in the pit at Drury Lane playhouse, in a wild freak of youthful extravagance I entertained the audience prodigiously by imitating the lowing of a cow. . . . I was so successful in this boyish frolic, that the universal cry of the galleries was, "*Encore* the cow! *Encore* the cow!" In the pride of my heart, I attempted imitations of some other animals.[80]

Playhouse buck

I went to Foote's theatre in the Haymarket, and saw Sheridan play Brutus. One of the players, I forget his name, I shall call him Carey, was always laughing. Many people around me grumbled, but did no more. "Come," said I, "I'll stop him!" So, as he was going off, I called quite out, "Carey, you rascal, what do you laugh for?" This made him as grave and serious as a bishop. The people around me thought me a great man. "I'll tell you," said I, "if he had continued to laugh, I would have catched hold of the spikes, jump'd upon the stage, and beat him with my stick before the audience." This made me appear as great as Brutus himself. So easily is a momentary admiration to be gained, and so wonderfully inclined am I to be a London playhouse buck.[81]

Patriotic Scot

At night I went to Covent Garden and saw *Love in a Village*, a new comic opera, for the first night. I liked it very much. I saw it from the gallery, but I was first in the pit. Just before the overture began to be played, two Highland officers came in. The mob in the upper gallery

[80] James Boswell, *Boswell's Journal of a Tour to the Hebrides*, edited by Frederick Albert Pottle and Charles Hodges Bennet, p. 387.

[81] James Boswell, *Boswell in Search of a Wife, 1766–1769*, edited by Frank Brady and Frederick Albert Pottle, p. 305.

roared out, "No Scots! No Scots! Out with them!," hissed and pelted them with apples. My heart warmed to my countrymen, my Scotch blood boiled with indignation. I jumped up on the benches, roared out, "Damn you, you rascals!" hissed and was in the greatest rage. I am very sure at that time I should have been the most distinguished of heroes. I hated the English; I wished from my soul that the Union was broke and that we might give them another battle of Bannockburn.[82]

Man of feeling

I went to Drury Lane and saw Mr. Garrick play *King Lear*. So very high is his reputation, even after playing so long, that the pit was full in ten minutes after four, although the play did not begin till half an hour after six. I kept myself at a distance from all acquaintances, and got into a proper frame. Mr. Garrick gave the most satisfaction. I was fully moved, and I shed abundance of tears.[83] The farce was *Polly Honeycomb*, at which I laughed a good deal.[84]

Squire of melting ladies

Next evening I was at the play with them ["Princess" Catherine Blair and her cousin the Duchess of Gordon, in Edinburgh]. It was *Othello*. I sat close behind the Princess, and at the most affecting scenes I pressed my hand upon her waist. She was in tears, and rather leaned on me. The jealous Moor described my very soul.[85]

Wit among wits

At night I went to the opening of Mr. Foote's Little Theatre in the Haymarket for this season, with *The Minor*, in which I saw Wilkinson for the first time, a most admirable-mimic. *The Mayor of Garratt*, a new piece, was also played. I laughed much at it. I sat by Churchill just at the spikes. I was vain to be seen talking with that great bard.[86]

---

[82] Boswell, *London Journal*, p. 83.

[83] To the very end of his life Boswell was able to adopt the proper frame at will. *Mr. Ireland's Vindication of His Conduct* (1796) shows him at his worst, fortunately not in so public a place as the theatre. When asked to add his signature to those of persons willing to state their belief in the authenticity of *Vortigern*, "Mr. Boswell, previous to signing his name, fell upon his knees, and in a tone of enthusiasm, and exultation, thanked God, that he had lived to witness this discovery, and exclaimed that he could now die in peace" (p. 22).

[84] Boswell, *London Journal*, p. 229.

[85] Boswell, *Boswell in Search of a Wife*, p. 117.

[86] Boswell, *London Journal*, p. 250.

Went to the play, having taken a ticket from Sir Joshua in the morning. He had forty places which he was to fill mostly with *wits*, Mrs. Abington being vain of their attendance. Sir Joshua himself dined with so many sea-officers, Mediterranean friends as he called them; and I suppose they had drank like fishes, for he did not appear at the play, when he should have been at our head. However, we had General Johnson, who sat on the seat behind me; but as he could neither see nor hear at such a distance from the stage as a front box, he was quite a cloud amidst all the sunshine of glittering and gaiety.[87]

A final view of Boswell in the significant role of caballer is unfortunately too long and diffuse to give in a quotation. In order to present the full portrait it would be necessary to repeat much of the account in the *London Journal* surrounding 19 January 1763, the day on which Boswell and two of his gay companions were completely routed in their inglorious attack on David Mallet's *Elvira*.[88] The story in Boswell becomes doubly intriguing when compared to corresponding entries in Gibbon's account, because Gibbon and Boswell, soon to be members with Dr. Johnson of the famous Club but as yet unacquainted, found themselves on opposing sides.[89]

[87] Boswell, *The Ominous Years*, p. 102.
[88] Boswell, *London Journal*, pp. 147–150, passim.
[89] Edward Gibbon, *Gibbon's Journal to January 28th, 1763*, edited by David Morrice Low, pp. 202–204.

3. Changing Tastes

THE READINESS OF Polonius to see a camel, a weasel, even a whale in the same cloud was assured by his long years of service at court. Yet it is only just to observe that without such conditioning in obsequiousness he might well have seen a variety of shapes in an object legendary for its shapelessness. Infinitely more amorphous is that abstraction called taste. The wisdom distilled in proverbs indicates that most nations have been baffled in their attempts to describe it, or prescribe for it: *de gustibus non disputandum, chacun a son goût, der Geschmack ist verschieden.* Yet, with the endless varieties, even idiosyncrasies, fashions in taste are discernible, in dress, in cookery, in the arts. There are national dishes, even national cuisines, all of which can be reduced to some rough order if not a rigid taxonomy. And now my process has brought me to a point where some attempt to assess the taste, and the changes in taste, of English audiences is called for.

First, however, let me point out some items that induce caution. On few other topics is greater care in examining evidence required.

The proportion of subjectivity in any given pronouncement makes it essential to examine the credentials of the witness—if available. Like the Erewhonians the people of the eighteenth century felt compelled to be the more positive in their statements the less secure they actually felt in their judgments. The speaker's bias—if discernible—must also be considered. Take the case of a witness already called upon several times, John Dennis. Dennis was not a complete fool or curmudgeon though he was often pictured as one. He could make acute observations about the literature of his day. Yet he had his biases, his blind spots. When noting his comments on Steele or Cibber redoubled caution is needed.

In addition to personal bias there is a professional, and partly factitious, one. It is tempting, for example, to accept the charge made by the author of *An Epistle to Sir Richard Steele on . . . The Conscious Lovers* (1722) that "the greater part of the audience . . . are only pleas'd with the distorted gestures of a comedian, with farce and show,"[1] until it is made clear that the author was trying to substitute something at least as suspect in comedy, "a joy too exquisite for laughter,"[2] to use Steele's own label.

Or again some sophistication in examining rhetoric is called for in studying Nicholas Rowe's complaint:

> O cou'd this age's writers hope to find
> An audience to compassion thus inclin'd,
> The stage would need no farce, no song and dance,
> Nor capering Monsieur brought from active France.[3]

This plea might be more persuasive if it were not for the realization that these lines are designed to win a sympathetic hearing for the tearful *Ambitious Step-Mother* (1700).

Prologues and epilogues in general are both indispensable and invariably suspect.[4] Far too often they are, if rightly taken, the merest

---

[1] Benjamin Victor, *An Epistle to Sir Richard Steele, on His Play, Call'd, The Conscious Lovers*, p. 18.

[2] Preface to Richard Steele, *The Conscious Lovers*.

[3] Prologue to Nicholas Rowe, *Ambitious Step-Mother*, ll. 18–21.

[4] Dane Farnsworth Smith suggests a parallel with the parabasis of Greek

whirrings of the grindstone and should no more be accepted ingenuously than present-day television commercials. Like the latter
they fall into certain patterns: bluster, cajolery, elaborate cuteness,
playing off one group against another, or, even more common,
pitting the past against the present or the present against the past.
A more unusual approach was the attempt to startle an audience
into favor by a presumably novel display of frankness:

> Therefore this Poet to secure his own,
> Seeing the various Humours of the Town,
> Has got some Fancy to please every one.
> To gain the Court, he calls the City, Fools,
> To please the Citts, the Court he ridicules;
> To win the Beaux, that nice i'th'Box appear,
> He laughs at Gall'ry Things that ape an air.
>
> (Prologue to Thomas Baker, *The Humour of the Age*, 1701)

By far the most common theme, and the most suspect, is the
playing off of past against present: "Time was" became almost a
stylized opening.

> True wit has seen its best days long ago,
> It ne're look'd up, since we were dipt in show.
>
> > (Prologue to John Dryden, *Kind Keeper*, 1673)
>
> The time has been, when sence has so prevail'd,
> That of full houses we have never fail'd.
>
> > (Prologue to Thomas Wright, *Female Vertuoso's*, 1693)
>
> Ah, sad, sad times, for since these things must be
> What is become, good sirs, of comedy?
>
> (Prologue to Thomas D'Urfey, *Old Mode and the New*, 1703)
>
> In former days, e're party rag'd so high
> The theatres claim'd the monopoly
> Of wit, to trace the British comedy.
>
> (Prologue to Charles Shadwell, *Humours of the Army*, 1713)

---

comedy, but this parallel accords to these statements a higher place than any but
the very occasional prologue or epilogue deserves (*The Critics in the Audience
of the London Theatres from Buckingham to Sheridan*, p. 144).

The counter-theme of present against past, almost as common, was at least as suspect since it flattered the age—and the audience.

> But, were they now to write, when critics weigh
> Each line, and every word, throughout a play,
> None of them, no, not Jonson in his height,
> Could pass without allowing grains for weight.
> (Epilogue to John Dryden, *Conquest of Granada, Pt. II*, 1670)

> There was a Time, indeed, when factious Rage
> Cou'd damn, with Noise, the Children of the Stage;
> But now our British Audiences appear
> What once the learned Sons of Athens were.
>
> (Prologue to Macnamara Morgan, *Philoclea*, 1754)

Any attempt at exhaustive illustration of the use of prologues and epilogues seems hardly called for here. Examples range from those which form an almost independent part of the entertainment— perhaps best illustrated by the numerous prologues delivered from donkey-back by Jo Haines, William Penkethman, and others or by John Quick's appearance on an elephant at Covent Garden on 13 April 1784—to those which are immediately applicable to the play or occasion—the best, or worst, illustration being Richard Cumberland's unrestrained flattery of Garrick in his prologue to *The Brothers*, 2 December 1769, at the rival theatre.[5] In fact the use of prologue and epilogue would appear to have lived on far beyond any reasonable expectation, in spite of occasional complaints by persons of taste. Two factors helped keep it alive: the gods in the upper gallery, who more than once held up proceedings for an hour or more until a favorite prologue or epilogue was produced, and that natural law of human inertia commonly termed tradition. Aaron Hill put the matter very neatly in a letter to Pope, 23 September 1738: "What you say, against prologues and epilogues, is a truth, which I heartily feel, and come into; but he ought to be very well *mounted*, who is for leaping the hedges of custom."[6]

---

[5] Richard Cumberland, *Memoirs of Richard Cumberland*, I, 266.
[6] Aaron Hill to Alexander Pope, September 23, 1738, in Alexander Pope, *Correspondence*, edited by George Sherburn, IV, 128–129.

More reliable witnesses, unhampered by rhetorical demands or by tradition, would serve the argument better, but these witnesses are not easily found. Educated foreign visitors would be of inestimable value since they would be both sophisticated and comparatively objective, but the number who are capable of making useful observations and who have left a record is quite small. Their lack of familiarity with English customs can be both advantage and handicap. They tend to note, for example, items we find useful but which were so familiar to English commentators they are not recorded. On the other hand their ignorance of custom can cause them to misinterpret what they see. And in the present age of the traveler who becomes an expert overnight one should be cautious of the incautious reporter.

Foreign visitors prove disappointing in still another way: they are not generally given to direct comment on English taste, as opposed to behavior. Pierre Jean Grosley, Georg Christoph Lichtenberg, Gebhard Friedrich August Wendeborn—all have something to say about the English love of liberty which so often found expression in violence. But generalizations on taste are less common, or turn out to be comments on the writer's own taste. The Abbé LeBlanc thought English taste coarse, especially in comedy. Henri Misson makes a brief observation of the flaunting of decorum as expressed in dramatic rules—"*toutes les lois du théatre d'Aristote & des notres.*"

Grosley, whose observation on London theatre roused Garrick's wrath,[7] comments on the bloodiness of English tragedy, which, in a nation given to melancholy, seemed overdone. Although his com-

---

[7] As the most recent editors of Garrick's letters explain, Grosley produced a three-volume account of the English capital—in spite of his knowing no English and of his confining his visit to six weeks. Garrick's letter of 24 September 1770 is a masterpiece of epistolary flaying: "I hope you will excuse my answering you in my own language, as the subject requires great precision, and as I imagine you must be a master of English, from your publication of the three volumes in question." The irony of this is enriched by our knowledge that Garrick himself was but a generation removed from France and completely familiar with Grosley's language (David Garrick, *Letters*, edited by David Mason Little and George Morrow Kahrl, Nos. 602, 610, 611).

ments are perhaps suspect, he does report that both he and his English neighbors were moved to tears.[8] Elie de Beaumont on the other hand tells more about his own tears over *Romeo and Juliet* than about English reactions.[9] And Voltaire is usually too ambivalent in his attitude toward English dramatic violence, as well as often too engaged in other problems and pursuits, to give a clear view of English taste. Visitors from the colonies or the provinces provide nothing that would make them in any way superior to established residents as judges of taste, and their records vary widely in usefulness.

Attention must also be paid to contemporary attacks on the stage, so long as rhetorical flourishes are discounted. Neither the sweeping condemnations of the Colliers and Bedfords nor the more subtle satire of the Swifts and Churchills should be confused with calm, moderate exposition. Yet both condemnation and satire can prove useful.

Best remembered of these satirical pictures of the stage is Alexander Pope's delightfully mocking *First Epistle of the Second Book of Horace* (1737). The poet sketches the English audience in the grotesque but revealing lines of caricature:

> With laughter sure Democritus had dy'd,
> Had he beheld an Audience gape so wide.
> Let Bear or Elephant be e'er so white,
> The people, sure, the people are the sight!
> (ll. 320–323)

Or, with that genius for concision in which he has no equal, he sums up a few lines earlier two generations of theatrical history in one couplet:

---

[8] Pierre Jean Grosley, *A Tour to London*, I, 196. When Grosley told Lord Chesterfield of his reaction, that sophisticated student and teacher of manners assured Grosley that if he (Grosley) had only understood properly he would have laughed (*ibid.*).

[9] Elie de Beaumont, "Un voyageur français en Angleterre en 1764," *Revue Britannique*, 5 (September–October 1895), 140–142.

Taste, that eternal wanderer, which flies
From heads to ears, and now from ears to eyes.
(ll. 312–313)

The passage that immediately precedes is less concise, and less accurate, but it will serve to illustrate the need for caution.

There still remains to mortify a Wit,
The many-headed Monster of the Pit:
A sense-less, worth-less, and unhonour'd crowd;
Who to disturb their betters mighty proud,
Clatt'ring their sticks, before ten lines are spoke,
Call for the Farce, the Bear, or the Black-joke.
What dear delight to Britons Farce affords!
Ever the taste of Mobs, but now of Lords.
(ll. 304–311)

Aside from the exaggeration of *sense-less, worth-less,* and *unhonour'd,* there is a gross inaccuracy in ascription and a self-con-
tradiction. The first couplet is both devastating and inaccurate. *Pit*
makes an obvious rime for *wit,* but *pit* ought not be used generically
for the whole audience. That Pope does so use it is made unmistakable in the next couplet but one. From numerous contemporary
allusions, most famous and frequent being to Addison's Trunkmaker in *Spectator* No. 235, we infer that the practice of beating on
the wainscot or the railings was largely confined to the gods in the
upper gallery as was the shouting for various songs or prologues or
favorite comedians. The contradiction occurs in the reference to
"their betters," presumably in the boxes, in line 307 and the flat
statement four lines later that the taste of the quality is no better
than that of the mob. A brilliant passage in a brilliant poem, but it
can mislead if the poet's intention is ignored. He was ostensibly
hoping to reform his own generation, not to inform succeeding ones.
He was also maintaining the delicate balance between the Augus-
tans and the Neo-Augustans which characterizes these "imitations." The *bear* of line 309 has no place in the London theatre; it
comes directly from Horace, whose coarse audience clamored for
"bears and boxers (*aut ursum aut pugiles*)."

In addition to the problem of adequacy of sources there is the difficulty of dimensions, compounded by the difficulty of change. When Voltaire or Dennis or Beattie speaks of the "audience" it is necessary to ask *which* audience—that is, to require more specific identification of the particular segment of the audience, whether pit or box or gallery, whether attracted by *Rinaldo* or *Hamlet* or *Hurlothrumbo* or *Harlequin Doctor Faustus*, or whether from the beginning or middle or end of the long century and more involved.

A final difficulty, in some ways most troublesome of all, is the one of fixing responsibility. If taste improves, who is to receive the credit? If it declines, who is to blame? No long debate will be required to decide which direction the curve of taste goes in the eighteenth-century theatre, for few would argue that taste improved. The real question is, who is to blame for the decline? The actor, who has become so addicted to applause he will stoop to any posturing to receive it? The dramatist, who is perhaps too impatient to await the bright reversion of posterity and cheapens his wares to gain immediate approval? The producer, who professes a love for high art but finds the lower pays better? The audience, which calls for pageantry or demands edification at the expense of verisimilitude? It would be hard to settle the proportion of iniquity among them. All have had their attackers and defenders. Few would argue seriously, however, that either players or playwrights could in the long run influence the course of taste profoundly. Any serious decision must aim at either of the remaining parties and here, with some notable exceptions, the preponderance of the charges, if not of the evidence, falls upon the audience.

Samuel Johnson's prologue for the opening of Drury Lane offers a sample of charges.

> Hard is his lot, that here by Fortune plac'd,
> Must watch the wild Vicissitudes of Taste;
> With ev'ry Meteor of Caprice must play,
> And chase the new-blown Bubbles of the Day.
> Ah! let not Censure term our Fate our Choice,
> The Stage but echoes back the publick Voice,

> The Drama's laws the Drama's Patrons give,
> For we that live to please, must please to live.[10]

It would be easy but quite unnecessary to bring dozens of similar charges to the support of Johnson's contention. A number of the statements concerning the power of an audience reproduced in Chapter 1 apply here. Perhaps a few additional examples from persons who were in an even better position to observe than was Johnson would be useful.

In 1750 David Garrick, in whose cause Johnson had produced his prologue, opened the season with an even more explicit statement.

> Sacred to Shakespeare, was this spot design'd
> To pierce the heart, and humanize the mind.
> But if an empty house, the actor's curse,
> Shews us our Lears, and Hamlets, lose their force;
> Unwilling, we must change the nobler scene,
> And, in our turn, present you Harlequin;
> Quit poets, and set carpenters to work,
> Shew gaudy scenes, or mount the vaulting Turk,
> For, tho' we actors, one and all, agree
> Boldly to struggle for our—vanity;
> If want comes on, importance must retreat;
> Our first, great, ruling passion, is—to eat.[11]

Twenty years later George Colman, then managing Covent Garden, could speak with authority in an epilogue he wrote for Hugh Kelly's *Clementina* (23 February 1771):

> Thrice happy Britain, where with equal hand,
> Three well-pois'd states unite to rule the land!
> Thus in the theatre, as well as state,
> Three ranks must join to make us bless'd and great.
> Kings, Lords, and Commons, o'er the nation sit;
> Pit, box, and gallery, rule the realms of wit.

Since all three illustrations come under some suspicion as being

---

[10] Samuel Johnson, *The Works of Samuel Johnson*, VI, 89, ll. 47–54.
[11] David Garrick, *Poetical Works of David Garrick, Esq.*, edited by George Kearsley, I, 102–103, ll. 25–36.

items of public rhetoric, I add one more, also from a man long experienced in theatrical management but speaking privately. In his *Original Letters, Dramatic Pieces, and Poems* (1776) Benjamin Victor reproduced a letter he had written Theophilus Cibber in 1751 cautioning him against trying to get his wife barred from the stage because of the public scandal of the notorious Sloper case. To support a generalization he cited an earlier instance in which Cibber had been defeated by opposing the will of the public, the case of the "two Pollies." His comments constitute a warning: "It is at all times dangerous to oppose the public voice."[12]

Although these samples represent but a few from a considerable body of testimony, it is apparent that the audience did in fact carry a large share of the burden of responsibility for theatrical taste and for the changes in taste leading to a general decline in the quality of theatrical presentation. To repeat, Pope's capsule history is too compressed to accept without fuller examination of its basis,

> Taste, that eternal wanderer, which flies
> From heads to ears, and now from ears to eyes.
>
> (ll. 312–313)

Quite aside from its echoing an equally simplified sketch of Roman theatrical history,

> Verum Equitis quoque jam migravit ab aure voluptas
> Omnis, ad incertos oculos, & gaudia vana.
> (Nay, even all the pleasure of our knight is
> now transferred from the ear to the uncertain eye),

---

[12] Benjamin Victor, *Original Letters, Dramatic Pieces, and Poems*, I, 263. One would be hard put to defend Theophilus Cibber from charges of both folly and knavery. The Sloper case concerned an unsavory episode in which Cibber pretty clearly was guilty of trying to profit from an affair between his wife and a man named Sloper. Details may be found in court records of the period. The *DNB* account of Cibber gives a possibly unkind but doubtless accurate review of the case. The "two Pollies" incident came about when Cibber persuaded Fleetwood to produce *The Beggar's Opera* at Drury Lane in 1736–1737 with his wife, Susanna Arne Cibber, in the role of Polly and with Mrs. Clive, who had made a sensation as Polly in earlier seasons, reduced to the lesser role of Lucy. The press and the public leaped into the fray with characteristic zeal, Mrs. Clive made a tearful speech to the audience (reported in the *London Evening Post* of 1 January 1737), and Fleetwood gave up the project forthwith.

and from its inclusion of only two decades of the period, it attempts in a few bold strokes what is far too complex a story to bear such treatment. However, although it does not give an adequate account, it does stress a trend.

2

Another passage from *The First Epistle of the Second Book of Horace* shows Pope in his more accurate state. Speaking of writers in general, in the generation following 1660, Pope declares,

> But for the Wits of either Charles's days,
> The Mob of Gentlemen who wrote with Ease;
> Sprat, Carew, Sedley, and a hundred more,
> (Like twinkling Stars the Miscellanies o'er)
> One Simile, that solitary shines
> In the dry Desert of a thousand lines,
> Or lengthen'd Thought that gleams thro' many a page,
> Has sanctify'd whole Poems for an age.
>
> (ll. 107–114)

John Dryden lends considerable support to this stress on the primacy of the "head" at this stage of literary and theatrical history, though he too tends to cast an eye backward:

As for Comedy, repartee is one of its chiefest graces; the greatest pleasure of the audience is a chace of wit, kept up on both sides, and swiftly managed. And this our forefathers, if not we, have had in Fletcher's plays, to a much higher degree of perfection than the French poets can arrive at.[13]

Dryden was, for his own age, stressing the genteel fashion of taking cues from the king, for Charles II's love of repartee was a common topic. That George Savile, Marquess of Halifax, in his *Character of King Charles the Second* spends somewhat more space on the King's fondness for wit than on his amours is not without significance. Moreover, various sketches of the audience in action in the early decades of this period often support this idea of striving for wit. Wil-

---

[13] John Dryden, *Essays of John Dryden*, edited by William Paton Ker, I, 72.

liam Wycherley's Sparkish, a fop and fool but slavish copier of convention, describes the young men of fashion at the theatre:

Gad, I go to a play as to a country treat; I carry my own wine to one, and my own wit to t'other, or else I'm sure I should not be merry at either. And the reason why we are so often louder than the players is because we think we speak more wit, and so become the poet's rivals in his audience. For to tell you the truth, we hate the silly rogues; nay, so much that we find fault even with their bawdy upon the stage, whilst we talk nothing else in the pit as loud.[14]

And in his diary Pepys paints a picture of Sir Charles Sedley, wit and model of witwoulds, at the theatre:

After dinner, to a play, to see "The Generall"; which is so dull and so ill acted, that I think it is the worst I ever saw or heard in all my days. I happened to sit near to Sir Charles Sedley; who I find a very witty man, and he did at every line take notice of the dullness of the poet and badness of the action, and that most pertinently; which I was mighty taken with.

4 October 1664

To the King's house, to "The Mayd's Tragedy"; but vexed all the while with two talking ladies and Sir Charles Sedley; yet pleased to hear their discourse, he being a stranger.

18 February 1667

Again, Dryden's comments are helpful when appraising the taste of the day, but his numerous quotable opinions—especially when removed from context—often seem contradictory. In every case care must be taken to ascertain the point of view, the role of the moment. His aristocratic scorn of the hoi polloi is stated by Neander, who echoes Horace, "'Tis no matter what they think."[15] This expression of the attitude was not unique.

The liking or disliking of the people gives the play the denomination of good or bad, but does not really make or constitute it such. To please the people ought to be the poet's aim, because plays are made for their de-

---

[14] William Wycherley, *The Country Wife*, III, ii.
[15] Dryden, *Essays*, I, 100.

light; but it does not follow that they are always pleased with good plays, or that the plays which please them are always good.

(*Defence of an Essay of Dramatic Poesy*, 1668)

. . . when I succeed in it [low comedy] (I mean so far as to please the audience), yet I am nothing satisfied with what I have done; but am often vexed to hear the people laugh, and clap, as they perpetually do, where I intended 'em no jest; while they let pass the better things, without taking notice of them. Yet even this confirms me in my opinion of slighting popular applause, and of contemning that approbation which those very people give, equally with me, to the zany of a mounte-bank.

(Preface to *An Evening's Love*, 1671)

While I say this, I accuse myself as well as others; and this very play would rise up in judgment against me, if I would defend all things I have written to be natural: but I confess I have given too much to the people in it, and am ashamed for them as well as for myself, that I have pleased them at so cheap a rate.

(Preface to *An Evenings's Love*, 1671)

I am much deceived if this be not abominable fustian, that is, thoughts and words ill-sorted, and without the least relation to each other; yet I dare not answer for an audience, that they would not clap it on the stage: so little value there is to be given to the common cry, that nothing but madness can please madmen, and a poet must be of a piece with the spectators, to gain a reputation with them.

(Dedication of *The Spanish Friar*, 1681)

So far Dryden the courtier and aristocrat. At other times he is equally conscious of his role as a professional writer. The first of the four quotations just given suggests his awareness of his relationship to the audience, of the proper "poet's aim." Nor was it an easy as-signment.

For my own part, I have both so just a diffidence of myself, and so great a reverence for my audience, that I dare venture nothing without a strict examination; and am as much ashamed to put a loose indigested play upon the public, as I should be to offer brass money in a payment.

(Dedication of *The Spanish Friar*, 1681)

. . . there are many things in plays to be accommodated to the country in which we live; I spoke to the understanding of an English audience.

(Vindication of The Duke of Guise, 1683)

I dare establish it for a rule of practice on the stage, that we are bound to please those whom we pretend to entertain; and that at any price, religion and good manners only excepted.

(Examen Poeticum, 1693)

What do all these contradictions imply? More relevant, what is Dryden's firm estimate of the taste of his day? Without suggesting that it would be a simple matter to reconcile the contradictions, I would assert that a point of view is discernible. With two concessions to reality, Dryden advocates an elite. The professional writer shows through in the concession that applause is appealing, even when wrongly motivated. And the aristocrat can at times be forced to admit that the taste of the few can be as superficial and fickle as that of the many. Yet Dryden commonly rests his case on the cultivated taste of the few. In the passage dismissing the judgment of the hoi polloi as a lottery, Neander speaks of "the mixed audience of the populace and the noblesse," in terms quite favorable to the latter. After the troubled years of the Popish Plot, when the audience had shrunk even more and was possibly even less representative of the whole populace, Dryden could speak in more approving terms of an audience composed "generally [of] persons of honour, noblemen, and ladies, or, at the worst, as one of your authors calls his gallants, men of wit and pleasure about the town."[16]

By 1683 Dryden was approaching the end of his career as dramatist and court poet. If he did entertain hopes of improvement in the taste of the audience, he was forced to abandon them before the decade was out. And by 1694 he had left the theatre though he reserved his valedictory for the preface he supplied to his son's comedy *The Husband His Own Cuckold* (1696).

This I dare venture to maintain, that the tast of the age is wretchedly deprav'd, in all sorts of poetry, nothing almost but what is abominably

---

[16] John Dryden, *The Vindication of the Duke of Guise*, p. 14.

bad can please. . . . yet they raise an unnatural sort of laughter, the common effect of buffoonery; and the rabble which takes this for wit, will endure no better, because 'tis above their understanding.

Though inconsistent in his expressed attitudes, Dryden could at times show pride in the critical and creative attainments of his own age. John Dennis on the other hand persisted in a surly refusal to praise the day. In such early pronouncements as his *Large Account* (1702) he not only demonstrated the changes in taste, to his own satisfaction at any rate, but assessed their causes. Dennis attributed the decline in taste solely to the composition of the audience. In Charles II's day, he claimed, the audience consisted of aristocrats and other persons with the cultivated taste required for high comedy. In his day, it was composed of untutored younger sons of the gentry, great numbers of *nouveaux riches*, and shoals of foreigners. These, especially "the men of business," of whom there were ten times more than during the Restoration, "come to unbend, and are utterly incapable of duly attending to the just and harmonious symetry of a beautiful design." Though Dennis is given to long-windedness, he does from time to time in this essay state in fairly succinct and unmistakable terms his notion of the state of taste.

But, sir, whether the general taste of England ever was good or no, this I think cannot be controverted, that the taste of England for comedy . . . was certainly much better in the reign of King Charles the Second, than it is at present. For it was then extreamly good, and is now excessively bad.[17]

As Dennis grew older and became more involved in controversy —with Pope, with Steele, with Booth, Cibber, and Wilks at Drury Lane—his gloom over the state of taste deepened: "But as the general taste of England could never be said to be good, it was never so bad as it is at present."[18]

Dennis's most elaborate and sustained charge, significantly en-

---

[17] John Dennis, *The Critical Works of John Dennis*, edited by Edward Niles Hooker, II, 289.
[18] *Ibid.*, II, 171.

titled *The Causes of the Decay and Defects of Dramatick Poetry, and of the Degeneracy of the Publick Tast,* was written in 1725.[19] By this time the principal villains had come to be Steele and Cibber or, to use Dennis's more colorful language, the Doge of Drury and the Aegyptian.

Steele found a defender in the anonymous author of a pamphlet of this same year, *A Letter to My Lord . . . on the Present Diversion of the Town* (1725), who contended that the three actor-managers, and especially Cibber, had subverted Steele's every attempt in the cause of good taste. This writer is even more obviously a snob and supporter of the gentry than Dennis at times appeared to be. He joins the quality in its scorn of "the low entertainments of narrow minds, who are delighted with anything that glitters."[20] The difficulty, he says, is that with the increase in the number of persons attending the theatres the range of taste has widened to include the patrons of glitter at one end of town and the people of taste—pretty clearly the nobility and gentry only—at the other. Since there are *two* patent houses, an easy solution would be for each to specialize.

> If we have many such debauch'd sickly minds, that have lost their true relish for wit and sense, and cannot be pleas'd but with these *absurdities,* they may be indulg'd, but not at the expence of those of a better taste. Those of the New House may content themselves with these follies; they have always (it must be said to their praise,) done their utmost to divert by their acting, but they find it impossible: In them therefore it is obliging, in the others it is impudent; in them it is prudence, in the others it is madness.[21]

And the essay trails off into a rumor that the Lord Chamberlain is being urged to exercise his authority, presumably to dictate repertory to the two patent houses. This kind of talk, among English commentators, has an odd sound indeed.

Still another pamphlet of 1725 on theatrical taste, Gabriel Rennel's *Tragi-Comical Reflections,* echoes the theme that Drury Lane

---

[19] *Ibid.,* II, 275–299.
[20] *A Letter to My Lord . . . on the Present Diversions of the Town,* p. 11.
[21] *Ibid.,* p. 20.

was forced to sit impotently by and watch crowds flock to John Rich's pantomime whereas a few years back Drury Lane had been prospering while "the theatre in Lincolns-Inn-Fields, commonly called the New House, was ready to expire under the severest frowns of fortune and the town."[22] Though Rennel falls a good deal short of the author of *A Letter to My Lord* in deploring the taste of the day, he does agree in placing much of the blame on the Drury Lane management. They had grown too self-satisfied and had lost their deference to the public. His account of the sequel also tallies with that of his fellow critic. When Lincoln's Inn Fields began to draw crowds with "Puppet-Shows and Monstrous Tricks," Drury Lane tried to beat them with their own weapons—and failed utterly.

Obviously there are two ways of interpreting these events, supposing they are accurately reported. The triumvirate may well have been guilty of complacency followed by panic. Yet their reaction was prompted by a shift in popularity, crowds now deserting the old house for the new. A writer in the *British Journal* for 18 March 1727, anticipating the theme of "the drama's patrons," places the blame on the public and absolves the managers, of both theatres presumably. He supports his argument with a persuasive bit of reasoning: if the public remained content with conventional drama, which requires little expense, no sane manager would go to the extra expense and effort of mounting elaborate pantomimes.

And, as if to refute the snobbish claims of *A Letter to My Lord*, James Thomson writes to Aaron Hill on 20 October 1726:

A new Torrent of Italian Farces is lately pour'd in upon us. The Advertisement, which just now lies before me, and begins thus—"By his Majesty's Command, at the King's Theatre in the Haymarket, To-morrow, being Friday the 21st of October, will be acted, by the Company of Italian Comedians newly arriv'd, a Comedy call'd *The Inchanted Island of Arcadia, or Arlequin King of the Forests, &c.*" is such a Maze of incredible Impertinence, and promises so much Folly,

---

[22] Gabriel Rennel, *Tragi-Comical Reflections*, p. 7.

that it is to be presum'd the House will be very full, and that, too, with Persons of the first Quality.[23]

3

This chorus of criticism, discordant though it may be, suggests that some change had actually been going on in the repertory, a change for the worse. The chorus persists, with somewhat diminishing vigor, until the end of the century, proving that at least some followers of the drama were not content to have eyes and ears titillated at the expense of the head. With this sample, however, I shall desist from scanning the critics of spectacle and turn more directly to the repertory itself. Since no adequate history of such spectacular features as pantomime in the eighteenth-century English theatre exists, it might be well to devote a few pages to sketching some of that history, particularly as it affects public taste and is affected by it.

Even a casual glance at the theatrical calendar, now fortunately being made accessible through *The London Stage*, will reveal that the mid-seventeen-twenties do in fact represent a kind of watershed in taste. Two changes were rapidly taking place: first, a further flight from head to ears to eyes, the shift to eyes requiring only a season or two; second, a sharp increase in the numbers of theatre-goers. During an interval of less than two decades, while the provisions granting theatrical monopoly were not being strictly enforced, the number of playhouses increased from one (in 1714 and earlier) to five (1732–1737).

The picture by Rennel is not inaccurate or overdrawn so far as John Rich was concerned. Even as late as 1723 he was struggling against almost certain failure, the Lincoln's Inn Fields house, still less than ten years old, clearly doomed to bankruptcy. Then on 22 February 1723 he produced a tragedy by Pope's collaborator Elijah

[23] James Thomson, *Letters and Documents*, edited by Alan Dugald McKillop, p. 55.

Fenton, a piece called *Mariamne*, which the triumvirate at Drury
Lane had rejected. Immediate popular enthusiasm made his fortunes take a sharp turn. Receipts, which had been ranging from a
mere £12 up to the hardly stellar heights of £50, jumped to £124 the
first night and to better than £200 on the author's third-night benefit, a sum which, the *British Journal* of 3 March 1723 states, represents "the greatest audience ever known at either theatre."

The success of *Mariamne* has little to do with the history of taste
since it was only temporary, affecting receipts for half season. But
this half season in the long run proved important, for, as the author
of *The Compleat List* for 1747 was later to recall, "the full houses
for a great number of nights together . . . seemed to show the town
the way to the Theatre, to which they were averse before,"[24] and
by the time the effects of Fenton's play had worn off, Rich was
ready with a new sensation, one far more important in the history
of theatrical taste, a pantomime called *The Necromancer: or, Harlequin Doctor Faustus*. Since this piece was anticipated by a similar
one, called *Harlequin Doctor Faustus*, there would seem to be some
question as to which play started the craze for pantomime. Fortunately it is not necessary to settle that matter here.[25] The important thing is that pantomime as a form of spectacular entertainment
caught on rapidly, especially at Rich's theatre. Partly because it
was elaborate and expensive as well as spectacular, partly because
its effects were more diffuse than in more conventional dramatic
pieces, the single pantomime soon usurped the place formerly occupied by a great variety of "entertainments" at the height of the
season. In 1723–1724 *Harlequin Doctor Faustus* appeared, with
various main pieces, in thirty-six of the ninety-two bills at Drury
Lane between 23 November and 28 March. At Lincoln's Inn Fields

---

[24] Thomas Whincop, *Scanderbeg, . . . To which are added, A Compleat List of
All the Dramatick Authors*, pp. 231–232.

[25] I made some effort to do so in an earlier work, *A Century of English Farce*,
pp. 102–112.

The Necromancer appeared in forty-six of sixty-six bills by the end of March.[26]

The same pattern of a single pantomime for a single season persisted with some variation throughout the century—with obvious effects on the repertory in general and the afterpiece in particular. One form of variation was the occasional failure. Drury Lane attempted a topical pantomime in late November of the 1724–1725 season, a *Harlequin Shephard* based on the career of the notorious Jack Shephard, who had, less than two weeks before the premiere, been cut down from the gibbet at Tyburn. In spite of the topicality and the elaborate sets, "being all painted from the real place of action," as the title page claims, *Harlequin Shephard* failed to attract, and Drury Lane fell back on *Harlequin Doctor Faustus*. In contrast, Rich's luck refused to desert him. Rather than follow his Drury Lane rivals into failure with an imitation he bided his time while his chief pantomime writer, Lewis Theobald, carefully prepared a more conventional piece. *Harlequin a Sorcerer* appeared at Lincoln's Inn Fields in late January, ran for twenty-four nights, and was interrupted only by a fire next door and, following that, the initial run of a new play.

So the story continues. The season of 1725–1726 ran well beyond the Christmas holidays with no new pantomimic venture. Rich used his two stock pieces, *The Necromancer* and *Harlequin a Sorcerer*, until 14 January when he began a long run of Theobald's latest confection, *Apollo and Daphne: or, The Burgomaster Trick'd*, "the contrivance of the whole being very ingenious, and the scenery and decorations as splendid as anything that has yet appeared of that kind," according to the *Daily Post* of 22 January. Now the triumvirate at Drury Lane found themselves cast in a new role, one that pained them and some of their critics, the role of sedulous but inadequate ape to John Rich, who a few short years earlier had seemed beneath contempt. John Thurmond was put

---

[26] This information is drawn from *The London Stage*, edited by William Van Lennep, et al., pt. 2.

hastily to work so as not to lose all the advantages of the height of the season, and by 11 February his *Apollo and Daphne: or, Harlequin's Metamorphoses* was ready. For the next two months both versions of the Faustus story appeared at their respective theatres, much of the time simultaneously, until after Easter and the seasonal slackening of attendance.

Next season Drury Lane tried valiantly to restore its fortunes by reliance on a formula that had succeeded earlier. In what seems a combination of haste and caution, Thurmond prepared a new pantomime for 30 December 1726, but a pantomime drawing further on the Faustus account, for it was entitled *The Miser: or, Wagner and Abericock*; to make its lineage immediately clear, its opening scene was laid in the study of Doctor Faustus. From the scenario, which indicates elaborate sets and the machinery for sudden transformations, and from the fact that "the scenes [were] painted by Messieurs Tillemans, Eberlin, Devoto, and Dominic," it is probable that no expense was spared. The new pantomime started off bravely enough, running nightly from 30 December through 19 January. On the following night Drury Lane dispensed with "entertainments." On 21 January the managers ran *The Miser* once more. On Monday 23 January they returned to the ever reliable *Harlequin Doctor Faustus. The Miser* was quietly dropped.

The rival company at Lincoln's Inn Fields meanwhile played tortoise, making do with their stock pantomimes through January. Then on 7 February Theobald's newest offering, to be called *The Rape of Proserpine: with the Birth and Adventures of Harlequin,* had to be postponed because of the sudden indisposition of Harlequin John Rich, who, under the stage name of Lun, had established himself as king of English harlequins. By Monday 13 February Rich had recovered enough to help launch the new pantomime on a fabulously successful career: it was still a stock piece nearly half a century later. Again the scenario indicates an elaborate set and in the serious part—as usual, the "grotesque" section is scantily outlined—a great many magic transformations with much flying about the stage. During the first week, *Mist's Weekly Journal* commented,

"It is of the nature of pantomimes, partly grotesque, and partly vocal, but far exceeds all ever yet shewn, in the magnificence and beauty of the scenes, the number and richness of the habits, as well as the fable, which is purely poetical, as the Italian operas ought to be."[27]

The reference to Italian operas, though doubtless only coincidental, explains the dedication of the published pantomime, a dedication signed not by Theobald but by Rich. A brief examination of this document reveals that its subject concerned public taste and the effects of pantomime on that taste. Obviously smarting from recent attacks on pantomime and on his own share in developing the form, Rich here undertakes an ingenious defence. His own preference would be, like that of the people of most exquisite taste, for grand opera, in which drama, music, and spectacle all combine to raise the art of the theatre to its highest level.[28] But look at recent attempts to establish grand opera. The subscription system is at best a temporary expedient and has proved ineffective since, with all available funds going to imported singers, it does not provide support for the requisite scenic display. At this critical juncture pantomime comes forward with the missing ingredients, to offer a more nearly balanced diet of drama, music, and scenery and, incidentally, to solve the financial problem left by the failure of the device of subscription. True, Rich loses heart, and persuasiveness, by winding up his dedication on a less confident note: "I will engage, for my own part, that whenever the publick taste shall be disposed to return to the works of drama, no one shall rejoice more sincerely than my self."[29]

If by "return to the works of drama" Rich meant drama unattended by her sister arts, the plain fact is that public taste did not return to simple, unadorned drama within the century. Differently

---

[27] *Ibid.*, p. 908.

[28] Just before the Faustus pantomimes began their spectacular run Rich produced an entertainment called *The Union of the Three Sister Arts* (22 November 1723).

[29] Lewis Theobald, *Rape of Proserpine*, preface.

put, since 1723 English taste had undergone a real change, and the audience had developed an insatiable appetite for the kind of mixed offering Rich's dedication describes.

The 1727–1728 season, to follow the theatrical calendar no further, will illustrate and support this contention. For Rich and Lincoln's Inn Fields it was still another season of surprises and good fortune. No new pantomimes were called for. With the *Rape of Proserpine* and the three earlier successes Rich had formed an extensive enough repertory to last until January 1730, when Theobald came forward with still another sensation, *Perseus and Andromeda*. It was not, however, the continued success of pantomimic display that illustrated Rich's luck but the appearance in this season of the most successful play produced in the century, *The Beggar's Opera*.

The story of triumph involving the happy conjunction of John Rich and John Gay has been told so often that I need not repeat it here. Two observations are, however, relevant to the present topic. First a speculation of the second-guessing variety: Would it be altogether absurd to suggest that the history of Gay's ballad opera— and therefore of ballad and comic opera in general—might have been quite different if Cibber and his partners at Drury Lane had accepted the play? The mood, the frame of mind of an audience is quite important, especially where great novelty is concerned. Rich not only had won over a majority of the audience but also had prepared them for novelty. Their mood was right for Gay's bold venture. This conclusion is borne out by the famous passage, quoted by Dr. Johnson, among others, from the account by Pope recorded in Joseph Spence's *Anecdotes*:

When it was done, neither of us [Pope and Swift] thought that it would succeed. We showed it to Congreve, who, after reading it over, said: "It would either take greatly or be damned confoundedly." We were all at the first night of it in great uncertainty of the event; till we heard the Duke of Argyle, who sat in the next box to us, say: "It will do, it must do! I see it in the eyes of them." This was a good while before the first act was over, and gave us ease soon; for the Duke (besides his own good taste) has a particular knack, as any one now living, in discovering the taste of the public. He was quite right in this, as usual; the good nature of the audience appeared stronger and stronger every act, and ended in a clamor of applause.[30]

My second observation concerns a far from novel kind of irony that was the result of Rich's success. Before 1728 he had been ignored, then contemned, then chastised for his assault on taste. Yet, as he himself had pointed out in the dedication to *The Rape of Proserpine*, it was not the playwrights and producers but the town who had turned to pantomime—and not just the "bear-garden" element but the quality as well. How can this apparent inconsistency be reconciled? An item in a letter dated 7 April 1728 provides an explanation of sorts:

I heartily condole with you upon the very low taste the people of fashion have fallen into to desert the Opera and Old House, where a man of sense might be so well entertained, for the Beggar's Opera which all seem to agree to be hardly fit for the delight of children. But it seems to me to be still more odd that what everybody condemns, everybody should countenance.[31]

If we abandon our survey of the theatrical calendar and return to the accompanying criticism, we are impressed indeed by the notion that "everybody condemns." In addition to the essays of 1725 already quoted there are numerous others ranging considerably in quality and tone but agreeing in attitude. The first two successful pantomimes brought a volley of attacks of which two appearing in 1724 are representative. On his title page the author of *The Dancing Devils* puzzles over the old question of fixing responsibility.

> Pray tell me whether, in a vicious age,
> The stage corrupts the town, or town the stage?

---

[30] Samuel Johnson, *Lives of the English Poets*, edited by George Birkbeck Hill, II, 276–277.

[31] Edward Hughes, *North Country Life in the Eighteenth Century*, I, 385. It may not be irrelevant here to note a kind of popular reaction which is the direct opposite. Joseph Wood Krutch observes the sheeplike following of the critics *against* the natural bent of popular taste in the strange case of *Cato* (*Comedy and Conscience after the Restoration*, pp. 230–231).

> For both concur, when folly makes its way;
> But where the fault begins, 'tis hard to say.

Without precisely answering the question, the author, commonly thought to be Ned Ward, falls upon manager John Rich, who appears in his judgment to have taken the lead in producing such follies.

> In representing to their view
> The tricks old Faustus us'd to shew,
> Hoping e're long he shall obtain
> The with'ring bays from Drury-Lane
> Therefore poor Harlequin's so civil,
> To sign a contract with the Devil,
> That the New-House may damn its rival.
>
> (ll. 245–250)

The British Stage: or, The Exploits of Harlequin (1724) avoids partisanship. As might be expected from the title, this essay is a satire on the present state of the theatre cast in the form of a burlesque pantomime, "as it is performed by a company of wonderful comedians at both theatres, with universal applause." The author, according to his preface, has gone to both theatres during the run of the Faustus pantomimes and, observing the sad decline in taste, declares,

I could not sometimes forbear grinning, and extorting my muscles, at a sight which indeed excited my surprize; a representation of puppets I did not expect, nor a windmill, or a dragon, on our polite stages: But such I found there, and to the immortal honour of this age be it recorded, that they were represented a month together, and met with far greater applause than the politest and most elegant play that ever appear'd upon the British Theatre.[32]

To drive his lesson home he contrives his own "farce," taken from both pantomimes. The resulting scenes have little intrinsic interest, representing a minor—and foredoomed—skirmish in a hopeless war. The list of performers deserves a modest notation. Opposite the names of the characters are the names of leading members of the

---

[32] *The British Stage: or, The Exploits of Harlequin*, preface.

two companies—disemvoweled, to anticipate Fielding's term, but still recognizable. Cibber doubles as Owl and Theatre, Rich of Lincoln's Inn Fields and Thurmond of Drury Lane share honors as Conjurers and Harlequins. Robert Wilks is a ghost. The principal low comedians, William Penkethman and "Dicky" Norris of Drury Lane and John Hippisley of Lincoln's Inn Fields, are puppets. Most ironically cast of all is Drury Lane's principal tragedian Barton Booth, who is down for Punch. The irony is partially of the delayed variety, for Booth was in time to lend his name to the by now familiar form of defense of show, the defense later to be offered in the prologues by Johnson in 1747 and Garrick in 1750. At one point in the proceedings Punch is heard to say ruefully,

What pity 'tis I must quit my acting Station, and that the glorious hero should be the droll of a Puppet-Shew?—But so it is, and I've been a whole half year in learning to dance and cut capers, I can jig it with a Shaw or Thurmond, dance upon my hands, and play a violin standing on my head: For I find there's nothing to be done without a dance and a posture; and if we don't excel the immortal Fawks, we are ruin'd and undone.[33]

Because the Booth speaking here is the butt of satire, the reader is not required to accept him as authentic. The Booth offered by Theophilus Cibber in his biography of 1753 is another matter. Not only does Cibber describe the real Booth, but the following conversation is one Cibber claims to have heard.

I remember being with Mr. Booth at a Coffeehouse, when a number of gentlemen politely addressed him, and gave him their thanks for the extraordinary pleasure they had received the night before from his excellent acting in the part of Varanes. They were unanimous in their almost raptured praises,—and as jointly (but genteely) blamed him, for having tacked to so fine a play that senseless stuff, as they were pleased to call it, of *Perseus and Andromeda*, &c. adding they were much beneath the dignity of the Theatre.—Mr. Booth frankly answered, that he thought a thin audience was a much greater indignity to the stage than any they mentioned, and a full one most likely to keep up the spirit of the actor, and consequently heighten the rep-

[33] *Ibid.*, p. 10.

resentation: He begged them to consider there were many more spectators than men of taste and judgment; and if, by the artifice of a Pantomime, they could entice a greater number to partake of the *Utile Dulci* of a good play than could be drawn without it, he could not see any great harm in it.[34]

What effect the various burlesques of pantomimes appearing in the early seventeen-thirties had on the new theatrical craze is impossible to assess. Such pieces as *Bayes's Opera*, which appeared at Drury Lane in March 1730, or James Ralph's *Fashionable Lady*, at Goodman's Fields the month following, were so coolly received that they could hardly have had even a temporary impact. Henry Fielding's *Author's Farce*, both on its first appearance at the Little Haymarket in April 1730 and at its revival at Drury Lane four years later, was considerably more successful. Again it would be hazardous to assume that even this limited acceptance touched the lovers of pantomime and show. Doubtless these burlesques gave some solace to the opponents of the new entertainments. Obviously Fielding was encouraged to keep up his attack in the highly successful pieces that followed. It must, however, be acknowledged that it was not the success of his attacks on the pleasures of the town but on the politics of the court which led to the act that drove him from the stage in 1737.

Whatever the motivation of the Licensing Act of 1737, it gave the managers the privilege to exercise their monopoly as they chose, and they did not choose to tolerate stage burlesques of pantomimes, their best drawing-cards. But blunting the attack from one direc-

---

[34] Theophilus Cibber, *The Lives and Characters of the Most Eminent Actors and Actresses*, p. 68. While Booth's statement hardly deserves the treatment one would accord a Delphic oracle, these few additional items may be of interest. Aaron Hill's letter to Benjamin Victor dated 5 January 1733 shows that Booth is concerned over the possibility that Hill will attack pantomimes; Hill's *Prompter*, No. 128 (Friday 30 January 1736), an out-and-out attack on pantomimes, begins, "The saying attributed to the late Mr. Booth, *viz.* That empty boxes were the greatest disgrace the stage could suffer, has—done more disservice to the stage than any one thing I know." In the light of Hill's attitude I am unable to suggest where Cibber got the idea, expressed just after the passage quoted above, that Hill thought it not "the business of the directors to be wise to empty boxes."

tion only led to an increase from another. Again Fielding provides an especially apt example. Silenced in attacks employing the stage itself as a platform, he turned to other occupations and to other means of expression. His first efforts in periodical literature, in 1739 in *The Champion*, show his disposition to carry on the war against pantomime and spectacle. In addition to mere occasional sniping, there are at least a few more concerted and elaborate attacks. An opportunity was provided, for example, by the autobiography of his old enemy Colley Cibber, who had appeared in *The Author's Farce* and subsequent burlesques. Fielding developed an elaborate ana- logue in which he compared the pantomimes of Rich, "that truly ingenious and learned *entertainmatic* author," with the elaborate but equally spurious shows making up the history of certain mock heroes as Caligula and, as he warms to his subject, Colley Cibber. In time, however, Fielding became engaged in matters increasingly remote from the theatre and his attitude towards both Rich and Cibber changed gradually to one of amused tolerance.

Also significant is the attitude—far from an uncommon one— revealed about this time by Fielding's latest and greatest rival, Sam- uel Richardson. If close resemblance between the view of the author and an opinion expressed by a fair correspondent can be assumed then a remark in *Familiar Letters* (1741), Letter CLIX, becomes especially interesting. Having been greatly moved by a performance of Hamlet, the writer is distressed to find her feelings dissipated by "the low scenes of Harlequinery" that followed. "My heart was full of Ophelia's distress, and the prince's fate had shaken my soul. In this state of mind to sit two hours to see people run after one another as if they were bewitched, only to cuckold a poor simple-looking husband, put me so much out of patience, that I shall not bear the sight of the stage for some time."[35]

[35] Samuel Richardson's *Familiar Letters on Important Occasions*, edited by Brian W. Downs, p. 217, Letter CLIX. What Richardson's fair correspondent complains of was far worse than the Restoration practice of tacking an absurd epilogue on to a tragedy, the practice that distressed Alexandre Beljame so much (*Men of Letters and the English Public in the Eighteenth Century, 1660–1744*, pp. 63–66).

If Richardson's young lady could only have been able to look a few short months into the future she would have been encouraged by the appearance of David Garrick, who for a decade or so looked very much the hero destined to put the forces of spectacle and folly to rout. A chorus of hope and praise was sounded in 1743 in the various pamphlets prompted by certain widely disapproved acts of the theatrical managers, Fleetwood and Rich. *The Case of Our Present Theatrical Disputes*, by James Ralph, Fielding's collaborator in *The Champion* venture; *The Case between the Managers of the Two Theatres and Their Principal Actors; The Dramatic Congress*—all agree that a new day seems at hand. Pantomime and show have been routed and legitimate drama has been revived, all by the intervention of one man. Letting one speak for all, I take a concentrated bit of recent theatrical history from the last-named pamphlet, a dialogue of the dead in the manner of Lucian. The visitor to the "Shades" told of his report to the late managers and playwrights, Wilks, Booth, Steele, and Congreve on the recent sad state of affairs, with "tumblers, bears, raree-shews, etc. in the room of wit and humour." After so inauspicious a beginning he was able to change his tune and "was highly pleased I could give them an account of the discouragement of pantomimes and the restoration of the drama in the persons of a young hero, who began to bring Shakespear into use again and make him as familiar to the town as A.B.C."[36]

The hopes of the enemies of pantomime and bad taste in general were raised only to be eventually dashed or at least badly adulterated. The new champion who had arisen to defend the cause of legitimate drama failed to retain his zeal, though it must be said in his defense that he never stooped as low as Fleetwood and Rich. The full story of Garrick's effect on the theatre is far too complex to be given here, and anything less than the full story is likely to be misleading. Knowing this I venture to suggest that Garrick's attitude was curiously—exasperatingly—ambivalent. This ambivalence is revealed repeatedly in his letters. One moment he will never

[36] *The Dramatic Congress*, p. 12.

stoop to the level of offering some extravaganza he hears his rivals are about to produce. The next he is anxiously inquiring what his rivals are up to. Two contrasting illustrations occurring just a year apart actually reverse this order of conflicting attitudes.

Do you intend to prepare anything for your alterations in the stage [he writes to his partner John Lacy in July 1750]? I wish we had a shewy thing that might make a stand to his [Rich's] frippery.

Have you seen the *Great Lacy* lately [he writes to Somerset Draper concerning his partner in August 1751]? I wish, when you have that pleasure, that you would hint your great surprise and dislike to Maddox's rope-dancing upon our stage. I cannot possibly agree to such a prostitution upon any account; and nothing but downright starving would induce me to bring such defilement and abomination into the house of *William Shakespeare*. What a mean, mistaken creature is this partner of mine![37]

The tone of the last two sentences suggests that Garrick may well have been prompted by his alarm over his partner's activities to recall his own words in the notable prologue of September 1750, "Sacred to Shakespeare."

Garrick was instrumental in gaining support for the best theatrical taste, but he also gave aid and comfort to the enemy as the *Queen Mab* affair of the 1750–1751 season or the *Jubilee* of 1769, to name just two, will indicate. Perhaps it is justifiable to accept the summary sketch of Garrick's history offered by Sir John Hawkins, keeping in mind the possibility of bias since Hawkins was a dour and "unclubbable" man.[38] In speaking of the Prologue of 1747, Hawkins suggests that Johnson and others were distinctly hopeful of the dawn of a new day in theatrical taste but were soon disillusioned.

. . . but in a few winters they discovered an impatience for pantomime and ballad-farces, and were indulged with them. From that time on Mr. Garrick gave up the hope of correcting the public taste, and at length

[37] Garrick, *Letters*, I, 152–153, 172, Nos. 93, 108.

[38] Sir John Hawkins was not, as Professor Kahrl seems to believe, a disappointed playwright angry over the rejection of his plays. That Hawkins was William, not John (see *ibid.*, I, lxi).

became so indifferent about it, that he once told me, that if the town required him to exhibit the "Pilgrim's Progress" in a drama, he would do it.[39]

Two otherwise obscure items take on some significance in the light of this comment on Garrick and theatrical taste. It will be recalled that Garrick's prologue for the opening of the 1750–1751 season promised loyalty to higher things, especially to Shakespeare. But it had also sounded an ominous note:

> But if an empty house, the actor's curse,
> Shews us our Lears and Hamlets lose their force;
> Unwilling we must change the nobler scene,
> And in our turn present you Harlequin.[40]

In short, Garrick would match Rich's frippery with some of his own. My reversion to the letter of July 1750 is deliberate, for in an earlier section of his inquiry addressed to his partner, Garrick showed his profound concern over Rich's success in out-manoeuvering the Drury Lane managers. "I have been informed that [Spranger] Barry and [Mrs. Susanna Arne] Cibber are certainly engaged with Rich, which neither amazes nor intimidates me:—Let them do their worst, we must have the best company, and by a well layd regular plan, we shall be able to make them as uneasy with Rich, as Rich will be with them."[41] What clearly rankled was the fact that Barry and Mrs. Cibber were deserters from Drury Lane. It is likely that Garrick would all but have conceded to Rich if he could only make these renegades "uneasy." Obviously Londoners could anticipate an interesting season.[42] During the holidays Garrick at-

---

[39] John Hawkins, *The Life of Samuel Johnson, LL.D.*, p. 198.

[40] *The Gentleman's Magazine*, 20 (1750), 422, ll. 25–36.

[41] Garrick, *Letters*, I, 156, no. 93.

[42] During the 1750–1751 season the absurd competition between the two theatres and between the rival Romeos, Garrick and the deserter Barry, led to a solid two weeks of *Romeo and Juliet* at both houses. Seventeen years later *Theatrical Monitor*, No. 2 (24 October 1767), published a letter from one of Garrick's bitter opponents, a letter that rehearses several anti-Garrick anecdotes. One has to do with the 1750 *Romeo and Juliet* war: "[Garrick] was so unequal to Barry in the

tempted to outrival Rich in spectacle. The plain truth is that he did not wait to see whether Hamlet and Lear would lose their force before setting his carpenters to work on a pantomime by Henry Woodward, *Queen Mab*, which appeared on the day after Christmas. It is this triumphant juncture that Patrick O'Brian celebrates in a scene entitled "The Theatrical Steel-Yards of 1750."[43] The caricaturist evidently meant his symbolic picture as a compliment to Garrick, but the result is a bit of unconscious irony. The scene shows the actor-manager of Drury Lane more than a match for his rivals: his weight has already tipped the scales against the leaders at Covent Garden (Barry, Mrs. Cibber, Quin, Peg Woffington) and thrown the unhappy Harlequin-Rich to the ground. Woodward's dashing to his aid with the figure of Queen Mab is an act of supererogation.[44]

The second item comes at the end of Garrick's career and serves as a commentary of sorts upon it. For the opening of his last season, 1775–1776, he prepared a little dramatic prelude called *The Theatrical Candidates*. The candidates at first appear to be two: Tragedy and Comedy. They little more than announce their opposing claims for full sway, however, than they are interrupted by a third and unannounced claimant, Harlequin, whom both agree to scorn. Harlequin appeals to the house:

> Tho' this maid scorns me, this with passion flies out,
> Tho' you may laugh, and you may cry your eyes out;
> For all your airs, sharp looks, and sharper nails,
> Draggled you were, till I held up your tails.

---

part of Romeo, that one night, Juliet asking him, *wherefore art thou Romeo?* Someone archly proclaimed out of the gallery, *because Barry was gone to the other house.*"

[43] Reproduced by George Paston, *Social Caricature in the Eighteenth Century*, opposite p. 45.

[44] Garrick may well have found solace in Warburton's annotations on lines 69–72 of Pope's *Epistle to Augustus*. The small octavo (*Works* [1751], IV, 122–123) sneers at those who profess to like Shakespeare only "because he is in fashion" but really prefer D'Urfey. The larger octavo (IV, 152–153) adds an even more comforting historical note, "Shakespear having once tried to reform the taste [See *Hamlet*] and, on failing, had complied with it, became the favorite Poet of the People."

Mercury, acting as master of ceremonies, is finally obliged to intervene with a ruling from Apollo:

> You, Tragedy, must weep, and love and rage,
> And keep your turn, but not engross the stage;
> And you, gay madam, *gay* to give delight,
> Must not, turn'd prude, encroach upon her right:
> Each sep'rate charm: *you* grave, *you* light as feather,
> Unless that Shakespear bring you both together;
> On both by nature's grant, that Conq'ror seizes,
> To use you *when*, and *where* and *how* he pleases:
>   For you, Monsieur! (*to Har.*) whenever farce or song,
> Are sick or tir'd—then you, without a tongue,
> Or with one if you please—in Drury-Lane,
> As Locum Tenens, may hold up their train.
>   Thus spoke Apollo—but he added too,
> Vain his decrees until confirm'd by you!
>
> [to the audience.]⁴⁵

The closing couplet and gesture of deference would seem to confirm
Sir John's account of Garrick's surrender, and to underline too the
contention that the ultimate arbiter was indeed the public. And the
public had made its wishes clear: there were to be three theatrical
candidates.⁴⁶

4

In telling the story of *Queen Mab* and its sequel I have passed
over another phase of Garrick's career, his share in "processions,"
culminating in *The Jubilee* (1769) or *The Institution of the Garter*

---

⁴⁵ David Garrick, *The Theatrical Candidates*, sequel to *Mayday: or, The Little
Gypsy*, pp. 37 and 39.

⁴⁶ Until Part 5 of *The London Stage* appears it will not be possible to document
as fully as one might wish the story of the three rivals. Genest's account is less
useful for the more ephemeral kinds of drama. The *Gentleman's Magazine* gives
a helpful though intermittent "theatrical register" in the later decades. At
present I should recommend acceptance of a summary word from a scholar who
has known the theatre long and well, Allardyce Nicoll: "Pantomime continued
[1750–1800] on its triumphal career, receiving fresh impetus from the fact that
the minor London theatres, such as those at Sadler's Wells and the Royal Grove,
were permitted by authority to present only musical and pantomimic shows" (*A
History of English Drama, 1660–1900*, III, 208).

(1771). But it would be quite unfair to suggest that Garrick was any more responsible for the invention of this particular form of spectacle than that he was accountable for the use of pantomimes. In the poem that has provided a leitmotiv for this chapter Pope turns at one point to a choice bit of spectacle, specifically Drury Lane spectacle:

> The Play stands still; damn action and discourse,
> Back fly the scenes, and enter foot and horse;
> Pageants on pageants, in long order drawn,
> Peers, Heralds, Bishops, Ermin, Gold, and Lawn;
> The Champion too! and, to complete the jest,
> Old Edward's Armour beams on Cibber's breast![47]

Admittedly the English poet is again under some constraint to follow his Roman model. The lines parallel Horace: "The curtains are kept down for four hours or more, while troops of horse and companies of foot flee over the stage." Admittedly also Pope could have had a recent spectacle in mind. Still there is a strong possibility that he refers to the fall of 1727 and to Drury Lane.

Prompted by the coronation of George II the company had begun a long run of *Henry VIII* on Thursday 26 October 1727. If the opening night had provided an elaborate mis-en-scène its effects were very likely lost, for on that particular evening a woman fancied she saw the stage on fire, lost her head, and started a panic that resulted in a pregnant woman's being crushed to death and others "being very much bruised." Quite understandably the modest space the press could give to theatrical events was devoted to this mishap. By Monday, however, attention could be turned to the production itself; the *Daily Post* of 30 October and 13 November gives two items.

The Play of King Henry the Eighth . . . having met with a very favourable Reception from the Town, we hear that the Players propose to add several different Characters of Dignity to the Procession of Queen Anne Bullen, with other proper Decorations.

[47] Alexander Pope, *The First Epistle of the Second Book of Horace*, in *The Poems of Alexander Pope*, edited by John Butt, IV, 203, ll. 314–319.

We hear King Henry the Eighth, with the magnificent Coronation of Queen Anne Bullen, and the Christning of Queen Elizabeth, still continues to draw numerous Audiences, which is owing to the Excellency of the Performance, and the extraordinary Grandeur of the Decorations.[48]

If at first the excellence of the play or the performance seemed to share on equal terms with the spectacle, the balance began quickly to shift; nine days later on Wednesday 22 November Drury Lane dropped *Henry VIII* and substituted *Virtue Betray'd: or, Anna Bullen*, "with the ceremonial of her coronation in the same manner as it was perform'd in the play of Henry the Eighth." On Friday Drury Lane revived *Henry VIII* for one more performance, with an additional "military ceremony in Westminster Hall, with proper decorations never seen before." On Saturday the managers returned to *Virtue Betray'd*, presumably keeping all the new ceremonial. Then on Monday they ranged further afield, though they kept in the same stream of history, by tacking the coronation and the "ceremony of the Champion in Westminster Hall" to *Jane Shore*. And then as if to suggest that a new relationship had grown up between what had customarily been called—and still was called—*main piece* and *entertainment*, there is an interesting comment in the *Daily Post* of Monday 27 November:

The Coronation of Anna Bullen having met with such extraordinary Success . . . the Players have been encouraged to give the Town an additional and different View of that Solemnity, by shewing the whole Magnificence at once, with the Ceremony of the Champion in Westminster Hall, &c. And we hear that several Persons of Quality being unwilling to lose their usual Variety of Plays, have desired the Comedians to add the Coronation, &c. as a separate Entertainment, to any other Play the Town may be inclin'd to see.

The quality had their wish granted. In regular succession Drury Lane presented: *Wit without Money*, with the Coronation Scene;

[48] I am indebted to Professor Avery for these two items. See *The London Stage*, pt. 2, pp. 941, 943.

The Relapse, with the Coronation Scene; *The Albion Queens,* with the Coronation Scene. And so on into the new year—in fact until 10 January, when Cibber came forward with *The Provoked Husband,* which being new and proving highly popular continued more than a month without any spectacular aids. This success does not, however, mark the end of an interest in the spectacular or even of this particular bit of spectacle. As soon as Cibber's new play finished its initial run, on Monday 12 February, Drury Lane again added the Coronation Scene to almost anything and everything for the rest of that month. During the following fall, when *Henry VIII* was revived on 29 November, Drury Lane also revived their spectacular scene. On 11 December 1728 the managers appear to have aimed at an all-time high in theatrical spectacle by producing *Henry VIII,* with the Coronation Scene, plus *Harlequin Doctor Faustus.*

At the same time that Drury Lane was achieving spectacular success Rich suffered a sharp defeat. On 24 November 1727, just as the Drury Lane company was completing its first month of spectacular coronations, its rival at Lincoln's Inn Fields produced a bill of *The Country House* plus *The Rape of Proserpine,* "in which will be introduced a new scene being a burlesque of the Ceremonial Coronation of Anna Bullen."[49] This last scene may well have been a mere stop-gap, for it was succeeded, on 11 December, by a new burlesque pantomime entitled *Harlequin Anna Bullen.* This piece ran only seven performances, a disastrously short time for anything elaborately mounted, and then was quietly dropped. We are forced to conclude from Rich's failure that theatregoers did not take kindly to satire of a favorite amusement.

In his 1747 prologue Samuel Johnson would appear to confirm what Pope had already said about the flight from head to ear to eye.

> Yet still did virtue deign the stage to tread;
> Philosophy remained though nature fled;
> But forced at length her ancient reign to quit,
> She saw great Faustus lay the ghost of wit

[49] *The Daily Post,* 24 November 1727.

Exulting folly hailed the joyous day,
And Pantomime and song confirmed her sway.[50]

Although prologues can show bias or oversimplification—Johnson himself might have said that prologists, like writers of lapidary inscriptions, were not under oath—there is at least some accuracy in the account as it applies to the second quarter of the eighteenth century. What about the future, to which Johnson immediately turns?

But who the coming changes can presage,
And mark the future periods of the stage?
Perhaps if skill could distant times explore,
New Behns, new Durfeys, yet remain in store;
Perhaps where Lear has raved and Hamlet died,
On flying cars new sorcerers may ride;
Perhaps (for who can guess the effects of chance?)
Here Hunt may box, or Mahomet may dance.[51]

Fortunately the history of English theatrical taste is not quite as desperately bad as Johnson seemed to be predicting, though there were times when it seemed so. Forty years later when a pugilist appeared in a new pantomime, *Aladdin: or, The Wonderful Lamp*, at Covent Garden on 26 December 1788, a newspaper commentator recalled Johnson's speculation and announced that the day had arrived: "For last night Humphreys, the celebrated bruiser, made his appearance at this theatre in the pantomime."[52] A few theatregoers disapproved but most applauded, the critic claims. Not to neglect what was really thematic in the earlier prologues, he absolves the managers from all blame since they have to fit the taste of the day. He concludes his commentary with Johnson's couplet concerning "drama's laws."

Though the commentator was perhaps overstating the case, the fact remains that the love of spectacle did not diminish as the

---

[50] Johnson, *Works*, VI, 89, ll. 33–38.

[51] *Ibid.*, ll. 39–46.

[52] Clipping from *Public Advertiser*, 30 December 1788, in Enthoven Collection, Victoria and Albert Museum, London.

years passed. Even greater sensations than prize fighters appeared. According to one account, a real horse was brought on the stage of Covent Garden on 29 September 1769, in a Coronation scene to which was added a "representation of Westminster Hall and the Ceremony of the Champion."[53] This bit of extravaganza revived one pageant, to use an expression of our own day, and anticipated another, Garrick's *Jubilee,* which appeared at Drury Lane two weeks later and which featured a procession "with bells ringing, fifes playing, drums beating, and cannons firing,"[54] among a great, great many other things. In *The London Stage* Stone does not seem to have recorded any horses at Drury Lane during the original run or numerous revivals of *The Jubilee,* but Walley Chamberlain Oulton states, typically without revealing his source, "that this season [1775–1776] Mr. and (the late) Mrs. Astley made their first appearance *on horseback* in the entertainment of the *Jubilee.*" Oulton also describes a tournament and jousting at Drury Lane in a run of *Cymon* around New Year's Day in 1792 in which "three of Hughes' horses were introduced and managed with much dexterity."[55] Just over a year later, 23 January 1793, the *Thespian Magazine* records another revival of *Cymon.* "The procession is certainly the most splendid spectacle we ever witnessed: three beautiful white horses were introduced in the tournament." Playbills in the British Museum leave no doubt about realism. The bill for a royal command at Covent Garden on 4 February 1793 calls for *Notoriety* plus *Harlequin's Museum* plus *The Fox Chase,* "with real horses and hounds." Two years later the Drury Lane managers were paying Hughes, Astley's rival, for attending the theatre with horses.[56] It is with some relief that I report an item from 1798: the appearance on 16 Janu-

[53] Henry Saxe Wyndham, *The Annals of Covent Garden Theatre from 1732 to 1897,* I, 182.

[54] Walley Chamberlain Oulton, *The History of the Theatres of London,* I, 43–44.

[55] *Ibid.,* II, 215. It was this attraction, "by far the greatest spectacle ever seen upon the stage," which three nights later drew a crowd so large and unruly that a man was trampled to death.

[56] Winston Collection, British Museum, London.

ary of *Blue-Beard,* by George Colman the younger, with not only
horses but also an elephant and two camels—"all artificial," we
are mercifully assured.

This brief sketch of what the theatrical calendar reveals of the
history of taste clearly suggests that some at least of Johnson's worst
fears were justified. The love of spectacle by no means diminished.
Perhaps as satisfactory a means as any of showing what the calendar was actually like in the closing years would be to compare the
theatrical calendar at the end of the century with that of midcentury. Since *The London Stage* for the later period is not yet available the list comes from *Gentleman's Magazine.* The "Theatrical
Register" in the February 1798 issue gives the plays for both January and February, the height of the season. Of the forty-seven bills
offered at each of the two theatres by far the majority of main
pieces consist of such now mercifully forgotten plays as *The Castle
Spectre, The Wheel of Fortune, Knave or Not, False Impressions,
Secrets Worth Knowing,* and *He's Much to Blame.* Better than two-
thirds of the afterpieces consist of spectacular and puerile items like
Blue Beard, The Shipwreck, Joan of Arc, The Round Tower, and
Harlequin and Quixote. True enough, the worst of Dr. Johnson's
fears were not realized: the new sorcerers did not actually *replace*
Lear and Hamlet; they only elbowed their way into a status
amounting to at least equality. Less figuratively, *Hamlet* does appear three times in these two months, and there are eight other
Shakespearean performances. Add to these some two dozen earlier
plays or adaptations of some stature, *A Trip to Scarborough* for
example, and two of Handel's oratorios. Though the prospect is not
quite hopeless, it is not encouraging.

The calendar reproduced in *The London Stage* for the corresponding months of the season introduced by Johnson's prologue
(1747–1748) presents an interesting comparison. The Shakespearean offerings almost exactly balance those in the 1798 calendar. It
is in the other main pieces and the entertainments that the vast
difference occurs. Sentimentalism sees an increase over earlier

years, as shown by the attention given plays by Otway, Rowe, and Steele and by the one new play offered, Edward Moore's *Foundling*, but there are plays of substance by Congreve, Vanbrugh, and even earlier writers. Most significant of all, Drury Lane mounted not one pantomime, and the fourteen performances of *The Royal Chase* at Covent Garden account for not quite half the bills at that theatre.

4. Morality and Sensibility

PROFESSOR ERNEST BERNBAUM begins his *Drama of Sensibility* with a chapter on "The New Ethics" of the eighteenth century, stating that, "a new ethics had arisen, and new forms of literature were thereby demanded."[1] The new forms were of course bourgeois tragedy and—to use a long familiar though possibly self-contradictory term—sentimental comedy, forms which by the end of the century had taken over a good share of the theatrical repertory. To understand the development of these forms it is necessary to examine the role of the audience in developing the new ethic. In doing so I shall broaden somewhat Bernbaum's concept and devote attention to the simultaneous development of moral prudishness and sensibility. These two concepts though often closely intermingled are by no means identical: *Tom Jones* has been called sentimental and, indeed, does show at least one important strain of sentimental-

[1] Ernest Bernbaum, *The Drama of Sensibility*, p. 10.

ity, but I have yet to discover anyone who considers it an example of moral squeamishness.

Still the two concepts often do appear side by side during the period, often as if they were two aspects of the same thing. Among the earliest writers cited in conventional accounts of the new ethic on the stage are Colley Cibber and Richard Steele, who speak of prudishness and sentimentality as occupying the same ground. Joseph Wood Krutch sums up the views of both Cibber and Steele in his chapter on "The Theory of Sentimental Comedy"[2] and thereby presents as compact and incisive a statement as can be found anywhere of the problem of what Mr. Alfred Dolittle called middle-class morality. Steele, as Krutch clearly sees, is more than any other figure the pioneer, the exponent, the exemplar of the new ethic. His works, from *The Christian Hero*, through the famed essay periodicals and pamphlets, to *The Conscious Lovers*, set the tone for the rising middle class and provide both inducement and guidance for them to refine their morals and manners.[3] Miss Lois Whitney has traced the origins of benevolence in at least one exemplary though fictitious character, Courtney Melmoth's Benignus (*Liberal Opinions*, 1775–1777), to "the Bible and old numbers of the *Spectator*."[4] That these two sources were the proper, and even sufficient, streams from which to seek such nourishment many of Melmoth's countrymen would have agreed. Professor Frederick A. Pottle similarly accounts for the early education of a quite true-to-life and somewhat less exemplary character, James Boswell, whose biographical sketch drawn up for Rousseau's benefit contained this interesting item:

However, from the age of eight to the age of twelve I enjoyed reasonably good health. I had a governor who was not without sentiment and

[2] Joseph Wood Krutch, *Comedy and Conscience after the Restoration*, pp. 228–258.

[3] Benjamin Victor, in his *Epistle to Sir Richard Steele* (1722), defending the author of *The Conscious Lovers* from Dennis's severe attack, may well have been expressing the public's view in accepting Steele seriously as "Publick Censor of Great Britain" (p. 9).

[4] Lois Whitney, *Primitivism and the Idea of Progress*, p. 62.

sensibility. He began to form my mind in a manner that delighted me. He set me to reading *The Spectator*; and it was then that I acquired my first notions of taste for the fine arts and of the pleasure there is in considering the variety of human nature.[5]

Since much as been said in previous studies about the development of sensibility and a stricter morality in eighteenth-century drama, I shall dispense with retraversing well-trodden ground and confine my attention to audience reaction—insofar as it can be identified or isolated, for it is no simple matter to discover precisely the way in which the "town" made its wishes known. It would be ingenuous to depend upon evidence provided by the box office, even were such evidence available in all key cases. As disapproval of an older play too coarse for refining taste builds up, the parsimonious account would run, the attendance falls off. The testimony of one highly successful playwright, George Farquhar, suggests that such easy logic could prove a trap. In the preface to his *Twin Rivals*, first performed at Drury Lane on 14 December 1702, he tells how, under the pressure of Jeremy Collier and other reformers, he altered the pattern then customary to provide punishment for the wicked, reward for the good. But he was disappointed in the response of the "greater share of the English audience."

I thought indeed to have soothed the splenetic zeal of the city, by making a gentleman a knave, and punishing their great grievance—a whoremaster; but a certain virtuoso of that fraternity has told me since, that the citizens were never more disappointed in any entertainment: "For," said he, "however pious we may appear to be at home, yet we never go to that end of the town but with an intention to be lewd."

More serviceable as illustration is the history of one play, Sir George Etherege's *The Man of Mode*. This Restoration masterpiece is particularly interesting because it was *The Man of Mode* that Steele singled out as the first in a series of "our most applauded plays" to see if it would stand up under searching scrutiny, not of "the generality of opinion" but of "reason, truth, and nature." In *Spectator* No. 65 Steele makes short work of his scrutiny of this

[5] Frederick Albert Pottle, *James Boswell: The Earlier Years, 1740–1769*, p. 2.

"pattern of genteel comedy." The gay young hero turns out to be a black villain, the heroine not much better. It is unnecessary to point out how badly out of focus was his microscope of reason, truth, and nature or to suggest that Steele was pretending a literal-mindedness he did not possess. The best refutation of Steele is not the able rejoinder supplied by Dennis in *The Defence of Sir Fopling Flutter* but Steele's own words in a later *Spectator*, No. 266. Here he shows scorn for what he calls the "outrageously virtuous"—anticipating Burns's "unco guid"—and demonstrates in his high praise of the audacious irony of Wycherley's dedication of *The Plain Dealer* that he is quite capable of reading irony as it should be read. It hardly matters now whether Steele's moral righteousness over *The Man of Mode* was in good part factitious. He was riding the wave of the future, perhaps just a bit ahead of the crest.

At any rate, the effect of his devastating analysis was not strikingly immediate. *The Man of Mode* stayed in the repertory for nearly a half century longer, enjoying the same moderate attention it had claimed before Steele's attack. As the century progressed its three performances a season gradually slackened to one annual revival. Still, when box-office receipts are available, it seems to have done about as well as the usual run of older plays. A house of only £80 for a revival at Drury Lane on 26 November 1753 would seem to spell doom, but a performance of *As You Like It* at the same theatre a week earlier drew the same amount. And a season later, on 25 April 1755, *The Man of Mode* brought £220 for an annual benefit of two minor actors. Perhaps more telling than receipts is the attitude revealed in Richard Cross's somewhat cryptic diary note on the performance the following fall, 31 October 1755: "Much dislik'd & hiss'd, imperfect, &c." If the epithet "imperfect" merely indicated a shabby performance by actors unfamiliar with the play we might ignore the hissing, but the October 31 cast is almost identical with that of the two performances given in the preceding spring.[6] The day of doom for *The Man of Mode*, prematurely

[6] A good share of the facts in this paragraph come from the indispensable *London Stage*.

heralded by Steele in 1711, had finally arrived. Bourgeois morality had overcome the mode of a more cavalier day.

What happened to Etherege's best play is typical of the fate of most Restoration comedies except that its demise, though gradual, was complete. Other plays of the type were dropped as tastes became more squeamish, especially in the seventeen-fifties and sixties, although some were revived after considerable changes had been made. Dryden's *Amphitryon*, to take another kind of play, one marked by the frankness or downright coarseness of the classical theatre, was revived in greatly altered form by John Hawkesworth in 1756. The prologue, reproduced in *Gentleman's Magazine*, gives the proper tone.

> The scenes which Plautus drew, to-night we show,
> Touch'd by Moliere, by Dryden taught to glow.
> Dryden!—in evil days his genius rose,
> When wit and decency were constant foes:
> Wit then defil'd in manners and in mind,
> Whene'er he sought to please, disgrac'd mankind.
> Freed from his faults, we bring him to the fair;
> And urge once more his claim to beauty's care.[7]

Or take even more famous comedies, those of Wycherley and Congreve. Most of their best plays underwent bowdlerizing, the homage virtue pays to vice, because the later eighteenth-century audience was clearly reluctant to give up these brilliant plays altogether in favor of the Lenten fare provided by writers like Richard Cumberland and Hugh Kelly. Wycherley nearly joined Etherege in oblivion at midcentury. *The Plain Dealer*, considered in the last quarter of the seventeenth century a nonpareil of British satirical comedy, was dropped as early as 1743 after a series of lean seasons. *The Country Wife*, a far saltier play, lasted another decade and would doubtless have preceded *The Man of Mode* into the theatrical museum if it had not been for the vogue of revision and revival that struck the theatres in the mid-sixties.[8] Actually it may be moot

---

[7] *Gentleman's Magazine*, 26 (1756), 585, ll. 7–14.
[8] Emmett L. Avery, "The Reputation of Wycherley's Comedies as Stage Plays

to classify *The Country Wife* as still surviving in the two-act after-piece to which it was reduced by John Lee for his benefit performance at Drury Lane 26 April 1765. Meanwhile Isaac Bickerstaffe was preparing a version of *The Plain Dealer* that would pass the more exigent moral test of the time, and in December his recreation, from which most of the quite vigorous language and some of the more unsavory episodes had been pruned, was presented at Drury Lane. Even more drastic surgery was necessary if *The Country Wife* was to be preserved as a main piece, and this delicate task the manager of Drury Lane accepted himself. Garrick's version, which, as Sheridan's Puff would have said, showed the marks of the ax rather than of the pruning-knife, appeared in October 1776, with the title altered to *The Country Girl* and the principal male character, Horner, omitted entirely. Both Wycherley plays survived these operations for a time, but both were dead by the end of the century.

A chance remark made in connection with these revisions reveals one of the less admirable facets of the new attitude: a tendency toward smugness. In the fall of 1766 while Garrick was readying his *Country Girl* for production the *Public Advertiser* provided some advance publicity. A note in the issue of 13 October informs the town of the coming revival of what had been "the indecent and obscene" *Country Wife* with a new actress, Miss Reynolds of Bath, in the title role. But an even more revealing comment was made in the same paper two days earlier in connection with an announcement of plans at the rival theatre. It seems that four seasons earlier when John Beard had recruited Ann Elliot for ingenue roles at Covent Garden, she had expressed a desire to play Margery Pinchwife, but Wycherley's play had been "judged unfit for *the present correct taste of the town* [emphasis supplied]" and someone—it turned out to be Arthur Murphy—had been assigned the task of returning to Wycherley's original French source to supply *The*

School for Guardians, which was to provide humor "without the immorality and indecency of Wycherley."

Congreve received a lighter sentence, or a longer reprieve, than his older colleagues. His four comedies were all being produced years after the original versions of Etherege's and Wycherley's works had been abandoned. A comment in the "Theatrical Article" of the *London Packet* of 18–20 November 1776 on the recent revision of *The Old Bachelor* even anticipates the tone of modern film publicity, which neatly combines moral reassurance and titillation: "The play as it stands is yet sufficiently rich; the most modest may hear it without a blush, and yet those who like relishing dishes will find it savoury enough for their palates." An attack in an unidentified daily of 21 November indicates, however, that approval of the new version was not unanimous.[9] The writer's objection to a revival of *The Old Bachelor* turns out, however, to be hardly less equivocal. The reviewer begins by assuring everyone that he too disapproves of Restoration bawdy but continues by saying that, if these plays are to be kept in the repertory, the audience should not be squeamish and try to clean up the dialogue. To drive home the charge he quotes "Lady Booby's waiting gentlewoman": "Some people's ears are the nicest part about them."

It must have been just about this time, too, that Fanny Burney's Evelina was forced to blush over Congreve. It will be recalled that the fair heroine had no sooner arrived in London than she found herself at Drury Lane, in raptures over Garrick as Ranger, a role the actor had a few years earlier been obliged to defend against a charge of indecency brought by his French friend Marie Jeanne Riccoboni.[10] Evelina gives no hint that Ranger required any defence, but Congreve's characters were another matter. On her next visit to the theatre, not counting a night of opera, she found herself in a side-box at Drury Lane.

[9] Column entitled "Stage Gazette" clipped from an unidentified newspaper and preserved in the Winston Collection of the British Museum, London.

[10] David Garrick, *Letters,* edited by David Mason Little and George Morrow Kahrl, II, 626–627, No. 519.

The Play was Love for Love; and though it is fraught with wit and entertainment, I hope I shall never see it represented again; for it is so extremely indelicate,—to use the softest word I can, that Miss Mirvan and I were perpetually out of countenance, and could neither make any observations our selves, nor venture to listen to those of others.[11]

If Congreve's plays could barely survive, it is easy to imagine what happened to such coarser pieces as *The Rover* or *The London Cuckolds*. As early as 1741 the ladies at any rate were objecting to the vulgarity of Ned Blunt in Mrs. Behn's play, especially to his losing his breeches right on the stage. Lacy Ryan chose the play for his annual benefit on 16 March only to find himself engaged in a brief but spirited debate in the newspapers over this episode. His forthright insistence that such a scene was essential in bringing out the folly of the character quieted opposition briefly, but the play was doomed and did not survive the decade. What prompted John Rich to revive it twenty years later, on 19 February 1757, and not only to revive it but to repeat it several times at the height of the season, is puzzling. He did not do so with impunity. One critic, in the *London Chronicle* of 22–24 February, took the opportunity provided to charge ambivalence or hyprocrisy. He pictures the various parts of the house as they react to Blunt's plight. The ladies would be shocked, but on peeking through the sticks of their fans would be even more disappointed on finding that Blunt was still wearing drawers.[12] The gentlemen would be more interested in observing the ladies' reactions than in following the play. The rabble in the upper gallery—"It is a matter of wonder that the upper gallery don't call for a hornpipe, or, 'Down with the drawers,' according to their usual custom of insisting upon as much as they can get for their money."

When Rich persisted in flaunting this bit of Restoration coarseness before a town rapidly approaching correctness of taste another newspaper critic fell upon him, if the following clippings preserved

[11] Fanny Burney, *Evelina*, 4th ed, I, 130.
[12] James Jeremiah Lynch quotes a similar charge of ambivalence from Lyttleton's *Letters from a Persian in England*, in his *Box, Pit, and Gallery*, p. 268.

in the British Museum are actually by the same commentator, as they seem to be:

[10 March 1757] Covent Garden, same day. For *The Wonder*, which was mentioned by mistake in our last, read *The Rover* again, as it was acted on Tuesday night. On Thursday *The Rover* again! And this present Saturday night, *The Rover* again!—Not excepting *The Fair Quaker of Deal*, *The Rover* is the worst play on the stage; and we hope we shall not have occasion to mention it again for some time, as the playbills inform us that the tragedy of *Douglas* is to be acted on Monday next; the beauty and morality of which, we are informed, will compensate for the dullness and ribaldry of *The Rover*.

[12 March] Covent Garden. Same day. Was performed, instead of *Rover* again! as we mentioned in our last, a comedy written by Mr. Cibber, called *The Refusal*. We are pleased to find that we have prevailed with the manager to interrupt the run of so licentious a performance as the *Rover* and to introduce so good a comedy as the *Refusal*.[13]

Though the newspaper critic may have been no more than Æsop's fly on the coach wheel, he was headed in the right direction. *The Rover* lasted for another dozen performances in the next three seasons and then was allowed to die quietly.

The passing of *The London Cuckolds* made more noise. Edward Ravenscroft's lively old collection of fabliau materials had long enjoyed the sort of popularity remarked earlier in connection with *The Beggar's Opera*. Sneerwell, cynical critic in Fielding's *Pasquin*, had expressed the general view: " 'Tis very true [that pantomimes are in bad taste], and I have heard a hundred say the same thing, who never failed being present at them." Despite the new ethic, *The London Cuckolds*, a high-seasoned play even by Restoration standards, remained in the repertory season after season. The German visitor Zacharias Konrad von Uffenbach remarked, on seeing a performance in June 1710, "when this play is given, there are always prodigious crowds."[14]

John Rich had no aversion to crowds and no particular squeam-

---

[13] Newsclippings in Charles Burney, "Theatrical Register," British Museum.
[14] Zacharias Konrad von Uffenbach, *London in 1710*, edited by William Henry Quarrell and Margaret Mare, p. 38.

ishness about the quality of audience he could attract, especially in the early years at Lincoln's Inn Fields when it looked as if he were destined never to attract any crowds. His Drury Lane rivals evidently decided to drop *The London Cuckolds* after the summer of 1722, but Rich took it up and on 29 October 1722, the eve of Lord Mayor's Day, began what was to grow into a custom encouraged by the apprentices who turned out in large numbers for the annual City festival. With a few gaps in the late seventeen-twenties, Rich ran Lord Mayor's Eve performances of *The London Cuckolds*, especially after his opening of Covent Garden, for a quarter of a century. That the general populace had lost some of its relish for such high seasoning is suggested by the tendency to offer the piece only twice a year: on the eve of Lord Mayor's Day and at least once during the Christmas holidays, because this season, too, brought out the very occasional playgoer from the lower classes. Drury Lane meanwhile struck a kind of compromise by continuing to neglect *The London Cuckolds* while offering plays with special appeal to the City, *The Beggar's Opera* being frequently done.

Garrick, with all his early promise of exalted fare, found copying Rich irresistible. In his very first season he offered *The Committee* followed by another Ravenscroft favorite, *The Anatomist*, for Lord Mayor's Eve. But in 1748 Drury Lane joined in the game of catering to the lower orders by offering *The London Cuckolds* on 29 October. For two seasons Garrick matched Rich, offering both Ravenscroft plays in 1749 and 1750. At this point pressure of another kind began to be exerted. In its list of plays for October 1750 *Gentleman's Magazine* deliberately left 29 October blank in order to provide the emphasis of a subjoined note: "On the 29th both theatres acted (as usual) the *London Cuckolds*—which a remarker observes is affronting and immoral, and that *George Barnwell* would be more proper for youth to see on a holiday."[15]

A few months later *Gentleman's Magazine* returned to the attack. In the February 1751 issue a long and generally unfavorable

[15] *Gentleman's Magazine*, 20 (1750), 439.

review of *Gil Blas*, new at Drury Lane, includes this interesting comment:

There is not one elegant expression, or moral sentiment in the dialogue; nor indeed one character in the drama, from which either could be expected. It is however to be wished that the Town, which opposed this play with so much zeal, would exclude from the theatre every other in which there is not more merit; for partiality and prejudice will always be suspected in the treatment of new plays, while such pieces as the *London Cuckolds*, and the *City Wives Confederacy*, are suffered to waste the time, and debauch the morals of society.[16]

When Lord Mayor's Day came round again and Garrick showed signs of yielding to pressure from the reform group by substituting the revived Jacobean *Eastward Hoe*, "instead of the *London Cuckolds* by way of compliment to the City," as prompter Cross puts it, the *Gentleman's Magazine* neglected to observe the change though Dr. John Hill's *Inspector* No. 206 (29 October 1751) applauded it as providing more wholesome fare for "the morals of the trading youth."

Not until a full year later, when on the eve of Lord Mayor's Day (now become 9 November because of the calendar reform of 1752) the Drury Lane company chose to ignore the apprentices completely, or perhaps to compliment the City in more subtle fashion by offering *The Merchant of Venice*, did *Gentleman's Magazine* see fit to note the occasion.

It appears by this list [of plays acted in November], that Mr. Garrick is solicitous to banish *vice* from the theatre, by his having first omitted to exhibit that scandalous piece the *London Cuckolds*, on the evening of lord mayor's day, contrary to immemorial custom, and the practice of the other house.[17]

Rich was obliged in time to yield to public pressure, though he was slow about it. On 9 November 1759 he gave *The London Cuckolds* to an audience of apprentices—and of streetwalkers if a reporter in the *London Chronicle* is to be believed—for the last time.

[16] *Ibid*, 21 (1751), 77–78.
[17] *Ibid*., 22 (1752), 535.

There was an attempt to revive the play nearly a generation later as an afterpiece. On 10 April 1782 John Quick, leading comedian at Covent Garden, chose for his benefit performance to add *The London Cuckolds* to Charles Johnson's *Wife's Relief*, a coarse play also from an earlier day. Sylas Neville, who saw the performance, approved of the actor but disliked both parts of the bill, largely on moral grounds. "If the 'London Cuckolds' was no better in its original state than when it appeared this evening cut down into an entertainment I never saw a sillier thing. They must be cits indeed, if not cuckolds, who can relish such low and absurd stuff."[18] The fact that Quick drew a large crowd—"I never saw a fuller house," reports Neville—would seem to indicate that he rather than Neville was more nearly attuned to the times. Yet there are quite adequate indications that the coarser taste represented by this benefit bill was rapidly changing. According to those self-appointed spokesmen for the town, the newspapers, London audiences had already developed moral and aesthetic attitudes far different from those of a century earlier. Two items from the 1780–1781 season give the tone. On 8 March 1781 a sharply divided audience gathered at Covent Garden to see the first performance of Frederick Pilon's afterpiece, *Thelyphthora: or, More Wives than One*. The author had prudently raised a noisy band of supporters but found himself overwhelmed by an even larger and noisier band of opponents who had come prepared —aroused perhaps by the subtitle—to be offended. And offended they were, "even before any part of the dialogue was spoken." The commentator was himself offended by the burlesque scenes in a bagnio since these bordered on indelicacy, which, it appears, should never be mixed with humor. The second clipping, reporting events at the same theatre sixteen days later, suggested that even Hannah Cowley was found too indelicate for the times. Her *World as It Goes* having been condemned on its first appearance in February was now revived as *Second Thoughts are Best*, the same play with the offending passages deleted. True, the grounds for

---

[18] Sylas Neville, *Diary, 1767–1788*, edited by Basil Cozens-Hardy, p. 292, 10 April 1782.

rejection seem to have been somewhat more general. As the commentator suggests, "something more is necessary for the support of a comedy than the negative merit of *not being indecent*."[19]

Outcries against indelicacy in new plays and revivals become so frequent in the last quarter of the century that extensive illustration seems unnecessary. It is easy enough in our day to understand how an age preening itself on its moral delicacy could find Restoration comedy or the more robust plays of John Fletcher and his age too shocking for acceptance. More effort is required to understand how plays produced by the age itself, often by persons otherwise noted for their sensibility, could be offensive. Perhaps, in the interest of economy, one fairly striking case can serve as representative of a whole class. Typical of this class was a petite piece by Mrs. Elizabeth Inchbald, who is now somewhat vaguely remembered, if at all, as a leading exponent of sensibility in both plays and novels.

On Saturday 22 October 1785 Mrs. Inchbald's *Appearance is against Them* appeared at Covent Garden as an afterpiece to *Henry IV, Part I*. On Monday the *Public Advertiser* reported a warm reception for the play and praised it highly. A little later the *European Magazine* joined in and predicted continuing success "if the public have not lost their good taste." The *Morning Chronicle,* which under William Woodfall had become the leading advocate of good sense and good taste in theatrical criticism, was even warmer in its praise.[20] "Upon the whole, we have not seen a farce for some years with such merit and less commonplace in it."

Thus far the voice of common sense. The outrageously virtuous had not as yet been heard from, but they were not long silent. The *Morning Herald* was fairly moderate in its moral disapproval, but the *General Advertiser* came fairly close to being outrageous. The first comment, perhaps not by coincidence echoing the *Morning*

[19] Unidentified newspaper clippings, Enthoven Collection, Victoria and Albert Museum, London.

[20] I assume the editor of the *Morning Chronicle* to be the one alluded to in a blustering epilogue delivered by Miss Younge, "brandishing a cane," found in *Gentleman's Magazine*, 51 (1781), 135. There is a reference to "Woodfall Lieutenant-general of the Pit" in line 9.

Chronicle's "upon the whole," was that justice required the play to be labeled "the worst of any farce on the stage, unless a total regard to decency [clearly *disregard* is meant] in language be a recommendation." A little more than a week later, on 8 November, the *General Advertiser* somewhat prematurely pronounced the play dead and preened itself on its share in the execution. The *Monthly Review* joined in the assault or, rather, expanded it to include all female scribblers.

Ladies are observed, by malicious wits, to have a remarkable pruriency in their writings: appearances are against them. As we may fairly say of Mrs. Inchbald, what Pope has said before of Mrs. Behn.

> The stage how loosely does Astrea tread,
> Who fairly puts all characters to bed.[21]

Both Woodfall papers continued to defend Mrs. Inchbald, or really to speak up in opposition to such patent irresponsibilities carried on in the name of morality. As early as 2 November the *Morning Chronicle* showed its awareness that more than the fate of a single afterpiece was involved.

The malignant and dull may continue to abuse Mrs. Inchbald's farce but the candid and liberal will not resign the evidence of their senses. Repeating at this time the hackneyed falsehood that the piece is replete with indecency is sinning in the face of conviction.

Ten days later Henry Sampson Woodfall's *Public Advertiser* ran a little burlesque item entitled "Theatrical Force-Meat Balls, or, Newspaper Stuffing," in which *Appearance is against Them* is referred to in mock consternation as "indecent" and "diabolical." The item further declares that the play was "received with universal horror." On 16 November the *Morning Chronicle* called attention to the fact that the play had been in print for some days now, thus giving everyone an opportunity to see how false the charges of indecency were. On 17 November the same paper triumphantly called attention to the royal command on the preceding evening.

All of which makes the persistence of criticism in the *General*

---

[21] *The Monthly Review*, 74 (1786), 231.

Advertiser more intriguing. On 17 November an item congratulates the public on its steadily improving morality and notes that everyone is flocking to see Thomas Holcroft's chaste opera (*The Cholerick Man*) but that no one goes to see "the last new farce" because it is indecent. The managers of both theatres are meanwhile to be congratulated for having "shelved" *Love for Love* and *The Old Bachelor*. These comments serve as a sample, to which a great deal more evidence could be added, that as the century advanced the numbers of outrageously virtuous greatly increased. Spectators of a sort observed by a commentator in the *Morning Chronicle* at a performance of Thomas Hull's *Henry the Second: or, The Fall of Rosamund* on 12 January 1774 were growing in numbers and influence: ". . . the theatre was last night crowded with those who doat on dramas of a moral or religious tendency, and wish the stage to teem with nothing but dialogue sermons."

2

In light of these developments a book published at midcentury takes on added interest. In 1757 appeared *An Estimate of the Manners and Principles of the Times* by John Brown, parson and author of one highly popular tragedy, *Barbarossa*. "Estimate" Brown, as he is still labeled in histories of the period, was given to the kind of oversimplification that marks such broad sociological surveys, old and new, but he was not lacking in common sense and, at times, acuity. He pretty quickly dismisses the usual notion that his age was marked by "profligacy." A better label, he thought, would be "effeminacy." The ruling class, which was the only class he undertook to survey, had by its self-pampering degenerated into "vain, luxurious, and selfish effeminacy." Like many of the writers surveyed by Miss Whitney in her valuable study, Brown managed somehow to combine the doctrines of both primitivism and progress. The luxury that had "destroyed our force of taste" had been offset by the disappearance of "our grossness of obscenity" though this too was not pure gain, for now double entendres are substituted for plain-spoken ribaldry.[22]

The effeminacy that Brown saw in English manners had in his judgment brought about—or been accompanied by—an interesting leveling effect. As women had become bolder, men had become softer, far more given to the expression of tender emotions. When, a generation later, Edmund Burke refers to "the tears that Garrick formerly, or that Mrs. Siddons not long since, have extorted from me,"[23] we may assume he is not being merely rhetorical, that he considers tears and manhood not antithetic. It had not always been so. Shortly after Brown had delivered his appraisal of English sensibilities, a correspondent styling himself "Humanus" writes to the *Theatrical Review* (May 1763) to complain that London audiences refused to give full vent to their feelings over a tragic scene but instead contrived to spoil the effect for more sensitive souls like himself "by a universal blowing of noses and a fit of coughing, which at that moment seizes the major part of the audience." Even as early as February 1735, according to an exchange in *Gentleman's Magazine*, the ladies had developed a resistance to tears, which in the days of the *Spectator* could be counted on when Otway or Southerne was played. In a letter addressed to Mr. Stonecastle of the *Universal Spectator*, "J. Drama" decries this feminine insensitivity.

But our modern fine ladies will not redden their eyes for any poet that ever wrote: no; tragedy has a quite contrary effect; in those parts where the most moving woes seem real, where pity should possess all the faculties of the soul, instead of the anxious look, the heaving breast, and the silent tear, we see the affected whisper and ridiculous smile at

---

[22] John Brown, *An Estimate of the Manners and Principles of the Times*, I, 29, 44–45. Oliver Goldsmith made the same point in his essay "On Education" in *The Bee*: "I have found by experience, that they, who have spent all their lives in cities, contract not only an effeminacy of habit, but even of thinking" (*Collected Works*, edited by Arthur Friedman, I, 456).

[23] Edmund Burke, *Reflections on the Revolution in France*, edited by Thomas H. D. Mahoney, pp. 91–92.

some ill-bred lady, who may discover the meanness of her taste, by the *tenderness* of her heart.[24]

Despite these protests, a change was beginning, and by the time Humanus voiced his complaint in 1763 some criticism of excessive sentimentality was being heard. On 30 April 1770 Garrick wrote to the Reverend Charles Jenner, who had the preceding January submitted his adaptation of Diderot's sentimental *Père de famille*,

I could wish that you would think of giving a Comedy of Character to yᵉ S[tage]—One calculated more to make an audience laugh, than cry —the Comedie Larmoyante is getting too much ground upon us, & if those who can write the better species of yᵉ comic drama don't make a stand for yᵉ genuine comedy & vis comic[a] the stage in a few years, will be (as Hamlet says) like Niobe all tears.

Jenner's answer expressed agreement: ". . . the stage may be getting too much into the handkerchief strain."[25]

The importance of French influence on English taste is indicated by Jenner's source and by Garrick's use of the term *comédie larmoyante*. Less than a year before, Garrick's French friend Mme Riccoboni, something of an exquisite and emoter herself, had in a letter dated 3 May 1769 deplored the temper of her countrymen and its effect on the drama.

. . . la nature et la plaisanterie sont banies de leurs pièces, et comme il est très *ignoble* de rire, ils cherchent à faire pleurer.
Dans nôtre brillante capitale, où dominent les airs et la mode, s'attendrir, s'emouvoir, s'affliger; c'est le bon ton du moment. La bonté, la sensibilité, la tendre humanité, sont devenues la fantaisie universelle.[26]

A pair of these French *pleureurs* appeared in the English audience about this time. Elie de Beaumont attended a performance of *Romeo and Juliet* at Covent Garden on 21 September 1764 that not only reduced him to tears but also threw him into a state of pro-

[24] *Gentleman's Magazine*, 5 (1735), 87.
[25] Garrick, *Letters*, II, 689–690, No. 583 and n. 1.
[26] David Garrick, *The Private Correspondence of David Garrick*, edited by James Boaden, II, 561.

found depression.[27] Pierre Jean Grosley relates that he also wept over an unidentified tragedy he saw in a London theatre the following season.[28] Since Mr. Grosley seems to have known very little English—the inaccuracies in his later study of the theatre may be said to have thrown Garrick into a state of depression—he would seem to lend support to Mme Riccoboni's contention that the French had all succumbed to the goddess of spleen: "On se croit *bon* quand on est sombre, *excellent* quand on est triste."[29] Grosley came prepared to weep.

The mode had begun to affect many of the English. Boswell, who might have been better advised to avoid tragedy because of his natural tendency to melancholy, seems deliberately to have sought occasion to indulge in tears.[30] In his accounts of his attendance at the theatre Boswell displays the gamut of emotions, from the gayest to the most lachrymose. So Shandean a range of feeling could hardly be expected from Horace Walpole. It is enough to discover him moved to tears by even a bad performance of William Mason's *Elfrida*—if indeed he was not simply trying to flatter his friend the author.[31] If a man, and a supercilious one at that, could be moved by a weak performance of a tragedy marked by frigid caution, what might be expected of a more sensitive and less inhibited lady, exposed as she was to a tender scene movingly enacted by the most accomplished drawer of tears of the period? What effect would

[27] Elie de Beaumont, "Un voyageur français en Angleterre en 1764," *Revue Britannique*, 5 (September–October 1895), 133–154, 349–362.

[28] Pierre Jean Grosley, *A Tour to London*, I, 196.

[29] Garrick, *Private Correspondence*, II, 561.

[30] Richardson's Lovelace may well have reflected the bourgeois views of his creator in taking the opposite attitude: "I loved not tragedies. . . . I had too much feeling. . . . There was enough in the World to make our hearts sad, without carrying grief into our diversions, and making the distresses of others our own." Justification for assigning the sentiments to the author can be found in Richardson's *Postscript*, where he returns to the passage on his very first page (Samuel Richardson, *Clarrissa: Preface, Hints of Prefaces, and Postscripts*, Augustan Reprint Society, No. 103, edited by R. F. Brissenden).

[31] Letter to William Mason, 19 November 1773, in Horace Walpole, *Correspondence*, edited by Wilmarth Sheldon Lewis, XXVIII, 109–111.

Sarah Siddons have, as Isabella or Matilda or Mrs. Beverly, on her feminine hearers as their sensibilities presumably deepened? Typical of the feminine sensibility were the reactions of Lady Ravensworth and Mrs. Piozzi.

Lady R. [avensworth] had ventured to the play . . . attracted by the fame of the superior merit of Mrs. Siddons, who, in her opinion, is intitled to all the praise and admiration she has received. From this testimony you will conceive an high idea of her merit. You can have no adequate notion of her powers till you see her. Mrs. Crespigny, I was told in London, went to the theatre rather prejudiced against her, criticized and found fault at the beginning, but soon began to doubt her judgement and was actually in hysterics before the conclusion of the play.[32]

On 13th April [1789] Mrs. Piozzi writes from Hanover Square after a visit at Drury Lane: "I have scarcely slept since for the strong agitation into which Sothern and Siddons threw me last night in Isabella"; while her husband adds a P.S.: "I assure you I cried oll (*sic*) the Tragedy."[33]

These episodes introduce the last decade of the century and the period referred to by Miss Whitney in her conclusion or "Afterthoughts":

We saw, for instance, the roots of sensibility in the Cambridge Platonists in the seventeenth century; but the climax of the popular vogue came, I should say, in the last quarter of the eighteenth century. In the nineties one gets expressions of it so exaggerated as to border on burlesque, side by side with actual burlesque of the fashion and the pronouncement that it is already dead.[34]

3

The story of official censorship in the eighteenth century, though not very helpful as an indicator of moral attitudes, merits at least brief attention. There was a period, around the time of Jeremy Collier, when there was considerable amount of quasi-legal censor-

[32] Edward Hughes, *North Country Life in the Eighteenth Century*, I, 387.

[33] *The Intimate Letters of Hester Piozzi and Penelope Pennington, 1788–1821*, edited by Oswald Greenways Knapp, pp. 19–20.

[34] Whitney, *Primitivism and Progress*, p. 329.

ship of the watch-and-ward variety. As the pendulum of morality and of politics swung away from the freedom of the Restoration period, the signs of reform became increasingly evident. Of particular interest are the activities of certain self-appointed public censors banded together in such organizations as the Society for the Reformation of Manners. Taking down, from their stations among the audience, the allegedly "profane" speeches uttered by the actors, they contrived to make utter nuisances of themselves by bringing suit against innocent persons engaged in their profession. Since these vigilantes are not to be counted as regular playgoers—they were actually sworn enemies of the theatre—they hardly count in the attempt to appraise the temper and taste of the audience. This is not of course to say that they had no influence on the drama or, in the long run, on the public attitude toward the theatre. The Act of Anne, dated 1704 and listing certain prohibitions involving the drama and the theatre, was assured passage in part because of just such reform activities. Later, when such amateurs of morality as Steele took up the task of reform, they found a public prepared for their message.

A similar judgment would apply to the rulers of the City, under the leadership of Sir John Barnard, who showed their displeasure with the theatre in 1735 by attempting to push a restrictive bill through Parliament. Again, the clarity of their motives, chiefly to have Goodman's Fields in the East End closed because it attracted idle apprentices and harmed trade as well as morality, and the haste with which they abandoned the project when they discovered their powerful ally the Prime Minister had quite different motives suggest caution in accepting their activities as informative about the tastes and attitudes of actual theatregoers. There is after all no period, even at the height of theatrical glory, when some persons cannot be found who would gladly abolish all plays and players. One man, not a member of the rabble or a tradesman but a claimant of sorts to membership in the gentry, can speak for the entire City. Sir John Hawkins writing in 1787 leaves no doubt as to how he would deal with the theatre.

And here let me observe, that although of plays it is said that they teach morality, and of the stage that it is the mirror of human life, these assertions are mere declamation, and have no foundation in truth or experience: on the contrary, a play-house, and the regions about it, are the very hot-beds of vice: how else comes it to pass that no sooner is a playhouse opened in any part of the kingdom, than it becomes surrounded by an halo of brothels? Of this truth, the neighbourhood of the place I am now speaking of has had experience; one parish alone, adjacent thereto, having to my knowledge, expended the sum of £1300. in prosecutions for the purpose of removing those inhabitants, whom, for instruction in the science of human life, the playhouse had drawn thither.[35]

The event that provoked this jeremiad involves another kind of censorship, one of scarcely greater significance than the puritanical attempts to abolish the stage. In one of the numerous and extended digressions in what might in more than one sense be called his *extravagant* biography, Sir John devotes considerable space to the Licensing Act, evidently on the ground that it was passed at the time Johnson and Garrick arrived in London to start their careers. In doing so he touches upon the motive that is far more forceful than puritanism in the story of censorship, namely, politics.

The Stuarts had had enough experience with puritans to insure their taking no chances. The language of the patents granted Davenant and Killegrew is heavily rhetorical—and quite misleading. Charles II's concern, if his proclamation is taken seriously, is with "prophanation and scurrility," with avoiding the mistakes of the past, when the drama, "which, if well managed, might serve as morall instructions in humane life, as the same are now used doe for the most part tende to the debauchinge of the manners of such as are present at them, and are very scandalous and offensive to all pious and well-disposed persons."[36] Stuart tolerance of prophanation and scurrility actually proved so great that playwrights and actors were lulled into the assumption that anything would be acceptable. Pepys gives a brief but eloquent account of their disillu-

---

[35] John Hawkins, *Life of Samuel Johnson, LL.D.*, pp. 75–76.
[36] Quoted by Watson Nicholson, *The Struggle for a Free Stage in London*, p. 2.

sionment in his diary. On 15 April 1667 he caught a cold from having to stand just inside the door of a packed house to see the premiere of Edward Howard's *Change of Crowns*, which was "a great play and serious; only Lacy did act the country-gentleman come up to Court, who do abuse the Court with all the imaginable wit and plainness about selling of places, and doing everything for money. The play took very much." The next night Pepys was back,

. . . in haste to carry my wife to see the new play I saw yesterday, she not knowing it. But there, contrary to expectation, find "The Silent Woman." However, in; and there Knipp come into the pit. I took her by me, and here we met with Mrs. Horsly, the pretty woman—an acquaintance of Mercer's, whose house is burnt. Knipp tells me the King was so angry at the liberty taken by Lacy's part to abuse him to his face, that he commanded they should act no more, till Moone went and got leave for them to act again, but not this play. The King mighty angry; and it was bitter indeed, but very fine and witty.

The period of greatest activity among political censors, however, was in the ministry of Sir Robert Walpole, at the point where Sir John digressed. The story of Walpole's increasing sensitivity to the repeated attacks of Gay and Fielding and others in the decade between 1728 and 1737 has been told and retold. The period begins with *The Beggar's Opera*, which raised an alarm, not so much because of its moral tendencies as because of its political satire. The great success of Gay's piece brought on the first move of the censor in years, the suppression by the Lord Chamberlain of its sequel, *Polly*. And for the next few seasons the government seems to have been unusually sensitive, even to the point of stopping or trying to stop the acting of several plays and in 1733 making an abortive attempt to bring in a bill providing strict controls.

When finally in 1737 Walpole and his followers did succeed in getting their Licensing Act they set about providing for its careful execution. In his chapter on "The Licensing Act in Practice, 1737–1787," Watson Nicholson tells of the noise made by the earliest proscription of plays,[37] one of which gained more lasting notoriety

---

[37] *Ibid.*, pp. 72–73. Courtney's successors in Johnsonian bibliography, Chap-

than its importance warranted simply because Samuel Johnson chose to occupy an exceedingly temporary role as "opposition patriot" by opposing the stopping of *Gustavas Vasa* (published 1739). Only one more item is needed to paint a graphic picture of the sensitivity and consequent vigilance of the Walpole faction. Thomas Cooke, having had some difficulty getting his *Mournful Nuptials* produced, decided to publish his play anyway, in 1739, and take advantage of the occasion by adding a "Preface containing Some Observations on Satire." This discursive essay comments at one point on the sensitivity of the present administration.

I have myself often seen a thin pale man looking over the prompter's book at the stagedoor almost during the performance of the whole play; and upon enquiry I was informed that he was the Deputy Licenser, and that he stood there to see if any words were spoken on the stage which were not in the book. What, in the name of wonder, could the man be apprehensive of!

After a few seasons such zealous policing seems to have proved unnecessary or onerous, and authorities began to look the other way. By 1741, a little more than three years after the act went into effect their vigilance had become so lax that they permitted Henry Giffard to resume operations at Goodman's Fields under a transparent device of offering concerts with free plays. And when an occasional voice was raised for more scrupulous censoring of passages tending to vice in new plays, the licenser soon learned how to manage such self-appointed censors.[38]

A quite adequate illustration of this management is provided by

---

man and Hazen, add even further evidence of Walpole's sensitivity: "Of all Johnson's pamphlets (excluding Proposals) this is certainly the rarest, and there can be little doubt that it was suppressed" (Robert William Chapman and Allen T. Hazen, "Johnsonian Bibliography: A Supplement to Courtney," *Oxford Bibliographical Society Proceedings and Papers*, 5 [1938], 124).

[38] Stone calls attention (*London Stage*, pt. 4, pp. 29–70) to a long passage in *Gentleman's Magazine* (21 [November 1751], 513–514) in which Swift's Plan, appearing in *A Project for the Advancement of Religion and the Reformation of Manners* (1709) and calling for the setting up of an office of public censor of plays, was proposed as if no such office existed at midcentury.

a letter to Garrick published by James Boaden. The central figure in this episode is Samuel Foote, who was at the time playing very much the English Aristophanes and consequently frightening everyone. In 1758 he had introduced a Welsh acquaintance named Apreece into his *Author*, first performed at Drury Lane on 5 February 1757. The suggestion has been made that Apreece prompted Foote to make him the butt of his play,[39] and, though it may strain credulity that any sane man would ask to be so treated, Foote seems to have been unmolested for nearly two full seasons. In December 1758, however, the offended Welshman approached the Lord Chamberlain and obtained an injunction against Foote's performing the play as he had intended on 18 December. With this fact in mind, one is impelled to accept the dedication of Foote's next play, *The Minor* (first performed at the Little Haymarket 28 June 1760, first published in July 1760) as ironic since it compliments the Duke of Devonshire, then Lord Chamberlain, on his commendable restraint in the use of his power to ban plays. A letter from Devonshire to Garrick hints of something like connivance between the Lord Chamberlain and the managers of the theatres. True, it was written after Foote's dedication, but it does suggest the public censor's readiness to cooperate.

I had long conversation with his Grace [The Archbishop of Canterbury], who would have authorized me to have used his name to stop "The Minor," but I got off from it, and concluded with sending a recommendation by Mr. Pelham to the author, to alter those passages that are liable to objection: his Grace would not point them out, so I think very little alteration may do. This to yourself; let me hear what has passed.[40]

As long as Foote and his colleagues focused their attention on Welsh genealogists and Methodist preachers and left the government in peace the minister in charge of censorship was not too exigent in his requirements.

[39] Mary Megie Belden, *The Dramatic Work of Samuel Foote*, pp. 73–80; Lynch, *Box, Pit, and Gallery*, pp. 221–222.

[40] Duke of Devonshire to David Garrick in Garrick, *Private Correspondence*, I, 120.

A problem in censorship, which seems at times almost to monopolize the attention of twentieth-century critics, the problem of dress —more accurately the lack of dress—on the stage did not exist in this period. The histories of costumes show clearly that feminine attire was designed to cover adequately. The severe décolletage to be observed in portraits of Restoration actresses was confined to a relatively small class of women and a relatively brief period—if I may rely on my admittedly casual and largely incidental notation. Aside from some comments, often sharply worded, on the costumes worn by the social elite at masquerades, there are only half a dozen references to the problem, and even these are sometimes cryptic. A caustic comment in a newsclipping suggests that Mrs. Gardner offended at least one sensitive soul by playing a favorite breeches part at her benefit on 20 September 1775: "A correspondent who was present at Mrs. Gardner's appearance the other evening in the Commissary remarks that the impudence of the stage historian was too great to admit a laugh, and that he expects the bills will announce her standing on her head without drawers, for the amusement of the Scavoir Vivre and other Macaroni clubs."[41]

Another rather indirect comment occurs almost at the end of the century in a clipping affixed to the back of a playbill marking the premiere of the younger Colman's *Blue-Beard* on 16 January 1798. The commentator takes pains to compliment Mrs. Crouch on the decency of her dress, chiefly, it would appear, to provide occasion to lecture Miss Decamp, who had recourse to indelicacy "to display the symmetry of her person."[42]

No such delicacy in expressing disapproval of indelicacy occurs, however, in widely scattered charges against female dancers, especially French dancers. At almost the very time Miss Decamp was causing eyebrows to be raised at Drury Lane no less a peer than the Bishop of Durham was fulminating in the House of Lords against scantily clad French dancers. George Paston reports that this dignitary saw these young ladies as part of a conspiracy by the French

[41] Theatre Collection, No. 4, British Museum.
[42] Playbills collection, British Museum.

government, which, unable to prevail over British arms, was insidiously attacking British morals.[43]

Sixty years earlier the *Grub-Street Journal* seems to have appointed itself to the important post of censor of French dancers. Number 269 (20 February 1735) carries a burlesque of an absurd bill to be performed by a troupe of French invaders. Among the various attractions is "Camaigo from Paris, who shews more in dancing than any lady whatever." A season later Number 315 (8 January 1736) reproduces a letter from "Cato" complaining about Mlle Roland's dancing at Drury Lane:

... every one who has seen her dance knows, that at the end of the dance she is lifted by Poitier, that she may cut the higher, and represent to the whole house as immodest a sight as the most abandoned women in Drury-lane can shew. Her whole behaviour is of a stamp with this; for during the whole dance, her only endeavour is to shew above her knees as often as she can.

Easily the most sensational record involves another Poitier, possibly a daughter of Mlle Roland's partner, at a royal command at Covent Garden on 30 December 1762. The *Public Advertiser* states that the new sensation by Isaac Bickerstaffe, *Love in a Village*, was being performed for the fifteenth time and would be followed by dancing, among other specified items "a hornpipe by Miss Poitier." A correspondent styling himself "the Volunteer Manager" reported a few days later in the *Theatrical Review* on the sensation caused by this dance, or rather by Mme Poitier's costume, which seems to have been scanty indeed. If his criticism were intended as an early assault on British morale and morality, it was a striking failure. A disapproving murmur and "the Court turned instantly from the stage"! Precisely how our resolute reporter managed to observe the conduct of the royal party while not missing a

[43] George Paston, *Social Caricature in the Eighteenth Century*, p. 54. The Print Room of the British Museum preserves a number of amusing cartoons by Gillray, Isaac Cruikshank, and others celebrating the occasion (see Mary Dorothy George, *Catalogue of Political and Personal Satire Preserved in the Department of Prints and Drawings in the British Museum*, VII, 507–510).

lurid detail of the dance—or the dancer—I shall leave to the histor-
ians of journalism. The reader who wishes full details of this early
triumph of the English monarch later celebrated by Byron for his
domestic virtues can find them in *The London Stage*.

4

The Beggar's Opera had an important place in the history of censorship. It had an even more important place in the story of moral
attitudes of the audience, for it represented better than any other a
type of play that was considered especially dangerous because of
the immediacy of its effect. In his important preface to *The Conscious Lovers* (1722), that chief proponent of bourgeois attitudes,
Richard Steele, states the doctrine of immediacy in clearest terms:
". . . it must be remembered a play is to be seen, and is made to be
represented with the advantage of action, nor can appear but with
half the spirit without it. For the greatest effect of a play in reading
is to excite the reader to go see it; and when he does so, it is then a
play has the effect of example and precept."[44] Steele is here introducing a model play designed primarily to induce observers to good
conduct by good example and sound precept. A decade earlier, in
Spectator No. 65, he could have spelled out the converse idea in
equally plain language when he undertook to point out the dangers
of bad conduct and bad advice in *The Man of Mode*.

Two pieces of supposedly immediate but quite opposite effects,
The Beggar's Opera and *The London Merchant*, suffice to show the
changing morality and the importance of these changes to audience
reaction. Henry Ellison, North Country visitor to London in the

---

[44] We may assume that Fielding has a somewhat more subtle and complex
idea in mind when, in his dedication of *Tom Jones*, he appears to be saying much
the same thing: "I declare that to recommend goodness and innocence hath been
my sincere endeavour in this history. This honest purpose you have been pleased
to think I have attained: and to say the truth, it is likeliest to be attained in books
of this kind; for an example is a kind of picture, in which virtue becomes as it
were an object of sight, and strikes us with an idea of that loveliness, which
Plato asserts there is in her naked charms" (Henry Fielding, *The History of Tom
Jones, A Foundling*, I, xii).

spring of 1728, demonstrates the ambivalent attitude with which the public had greeted Gay's novel play: ". . . it seems to me to be still more odd that what everybody condemns, everybody should countenance."[45] Many people did condemn *The Beggar's Opera* from the start, though at first ostensibly moral approval and disapproval sometimes turned out on closer examination to be politically motivated. Johnson sums up the varied reaction in his study of Gay in *The Lives of the Poets*:

Of this performance, when it was printed, the reception was different, according to the different opinion of its readers. Swift commended it for the excellence of its morality, as a piece that "placed all kinds of vice in the strongest and most odious light"; but others, and among them Dr. Herring, afterwards archbishop of Canterbury, censured it as giving encouragement not only to vice but to crimes, by making a highwayman the hero, and dismissing him at last unpunished. It has been said, that, after the exhibition of *The Beggar's Opera*, the gangs of robbers were evidently multiplied.

Both these decisions are surely exaggerated. The play, like many others, was plainly written only to divert, without any moral purpose, and is therefore not likely to do good; nor can it be conceived, without more speculation than life requires or admits, to be productive of much evil. Highwaymen and house-breakers seldom frequent the play-house, or mingle in any elegant diversion; nor is it possible for any one to imagine that he may rob with safety, because he sees Macheath reprieved upon the stage.[46]

Not everyone was prompted to speak for or against *The Beggar's Opera*, especially as years passed and the topical allusions in the play, vague and subtle as they were in any case, began to lose their point. Most of the attention given the play by moralists was understandably in the form of opposition, most of it was utterly naïve,

[45] Hughes, *North Country Life*, I, 385.
[46] Samuel Johnson, *The Lives of the Poets*, II, 278. It was on 18 April 1775 in the wide-ranging conversation at "Mr. Cambridge's beautiful villa on the banks of the Thames" that Boswell records Johnson on the same subject and in the same general vein, though perhaps what is equally memorable is the pronouncement in Johnsonese: "There is such a *labefactation* of all principles as may be injurious to morality" (James Boswell, *Boswell's Life of Johnson*).

none of it was very memorable except perhaps for a wry comment by Bernard de Mandeville, who considered himself a fellow sufferer with Gay in the hands of ingenuous moralists.[47]

In spite of the commotion it had created—and to some extent, because of this commotion—*The Beggar's Opera* was triumphantly performed scores of times, decade after decade, until the end of the century. Occasional rumblings of protest from the rigidly righteous also continued, and almost half a century after its premiere the piece met concerted opposition of the type that leaves no doubt as to the persistence of immediate effect. Sir John Fielding, who had carried on the great burden left by his more famous brother at the office in Bow Street, seems to have become convinced that the play did indeed encourage crime and increase the numbers of wretches who daily appeared before his court, so conveniently located between the theatres.[48] He turned to the managers but in vain. *Westminster Magazine* for September 1773 reports, "Drury-Lane Theatre opened, on Saturday the 18th instant, with the *Beggar's Opera*, notwithstanding Mr. Garrick was requested, by the Bench of Justices in Bow-Street, to suppress it, as they were of the opinion it had done a great deal of mischief among the lower class of people."[49] The *London Evening Post* for 26–28 October discloses that the rival theatre gave its first performance of the old play on Wednesday 27 October.

Yesterday the Magistrates of Bow-street sent a card to Mr. Colman,

---

[47] See William Eben Schultz, *Gay's Beggar's Opera*, pp. 239–240. Schultz devotes an entire chapter to "The Morality Question."

[48] *Gentleman's Magazine* in its "Historical Chronicle" for September 1773 gives, under Wednesday 15, an account of Sir John's plea before the Bench of Justices for aid in approaching the managers, his own plea the preceding year having been ineffectual. The Justices readily joined in, "and a polite card was dispatched to Mr. Garrick." In the October list of books, *Gentleman's Magazine* includes a burlesque, *Bow-street Opera*, which proves on examination to be an anti-Fielding pamphlet. The piece is dedicated to Garrick as a commendation for his stand against magisterial interference. The magistrates are led by the most unscrupulous and high-handed of them all, Justice Blindman—Sir John Fielding had always been blind.

[49] *Westminster Magazine*, I (1773), 557.

manager of Covent Garden Theatre, requesting he would not suffer The Beggar's Opera to be played that evening, as they were all assured that every representation of it made some thieves.—Mr. Colman sent them a letter, acquainting the Justices, he was very sorry to differ in sentiments from them, for he was assured that his house was one of the few about Covent-Garden that did *not encourage thievery*.

The same newspaper contains a note addressed to Colman, congratulating him on his stand in opposition to "an over-bearing magistrate." Still another note in the same number of the *London Evening Post* is addressed in mockery to Sir John, jeering at his small success with "cruel, cruel Colman," right after his having "no triumph over little David."

The defeat of authority turned out to be less than complete in the long run. The retirement of Garrick in June 1776 and the transfer of Colman's interest from Covent Garden to the Haymarket in the spring of 1777 would appear to have provided the occasion finally to do something, but something far short of deletion, about *The Beggar's Opera*. An obscure tinker of plays named Edward Thompson was commissioned by James Harris to write a reformation scene in which Macheath is condemned to labor on the hulks at Woolwich and content to be so since he is now repentant and reformed. W. C. Oulton reports that "this alteration was suggested by Mr. Garrick," though he does not divulge the source of his information.[50] Oulton's further suggestion that "the managers" soon realized the absurdity of the alterations and soon laid them aside indicates the possibility that both theatres were involved though Harris alone signed the petition for a license. Again it would be imprudent to miss the point here: the alterations provided by Thompson do approach the absurd both aesthetically and morally,

---

[50] *The Morning Chronicle* of 22 September 1777 indicates that Garrick's part in the revision was commonly assumed: "There is no doubt that the catastrophe of the Beggar's Opera has been altered by Mr. Garrick; the purport of the alteration is, Macheath is supposed to receive the punishment due to his crimes, and the opera, which with the above alterations will in a short time be performed at the Theatre Royal in Drury-lane, will conclude with a lesson of morality, and consequently remove all the objections which have been lately made to its representation."

but the trend toward an ever greater ingenuousness in the moral expectations of the audience—and the continued deference of the managers—is clear.

John Gay would probably have been puzzled by this stir since, as Johnson points out, *The Beggar's Opera* "was plainly written only to divert."[51] In contrast, every circumstance surrounding the writing and production of John Lillo's *London Merchant* testifies to the author's purpose of providing example and precept, particularly for the apprentices who might come to be edified. The dedication, significantly to an alderman and former lord mayor, makes Lillo's intention clear: "If tragick poetry be, as Mr. Dryden has some where said, the most excellent and most useful kind of writing, the more extensively useful the moral of any tragedy is, the more excellent that piece must be of its kind." The moral calculus implied is obviously intended as just that. True, it remained for Lillo's French imitator Fenoullot de Falbaire to spell out the lesson in its most ingenuous form, and Lillo would certainly have accepted the clearer statement in the preface to *Le Fabricant de Londres* (1771):

Quand nous sortons du spectacle, après la représentation d'une belle tragédie, nous rencontrons rarement des princes fugitifs, des rois détrônés, qui puissent profiter de l'attendrissement que nous venons d'éprouver. Mais nous voyons chaque jour enlever et vendre les effets de citoyens malheureux, qui auraient besoin de notre commisération, auxquels nous pourrions accorder d'utiles secours, et dont une pitié généreuse préviendrait la ruine.[52]

When the London merchant-playwright undertakes to quote Shakespeare, in businesslike display of his credentials, he chooses the obvious passage: Hamlet's observations on the effectiveness of plays in catching consciences.

Lillo's play is about as stilted as the sketchy morality that brings

---

[51] Gebhard Friedrich August Wendeborn, among others, agrees that, "Most of those who frequent the theatre, go there for the sake of pleasure and entertainment" (*A View of England toward the Close of the Eighteenth Century*, II, 182).

[52] Quoted by John Lough, *Paris Theatre Audiences in the Seventeenth and Eighteenth Centuries*, p. 255.

Claudius out of his seat shouting for lights and is infinitely more preachy. Charles Lamb's epithet for the play, "nauseous sermon," is scarcely too strong. Yet sermon is precisely what Lillo had in mind and, more significantly, what the public seemed to expect. Almost thirty years earlier, in a far more sophisticated play, *The Lying Lover* (1703), Steele had tried to help wit "recover from its apostacy, [so] that, by being encourag'd in the interests of virtue, 'twill strip vice of the gay habit in which it has too long appear'd, and cloath it in its native dress of shame, contempt, and dishonour,"[53] only to find the public not interested. In his *Apology* of 1713 addressed to the House of Commons, Steele looked back on his difficulties with *The Lying Lover* to comment wryly on his fate as "a martyr and confessor for the church; for this play was damned for its piety."[54]

By the seventeen-thirties, however, public taste, at least that segment of it representative of the City, was so altered that Lillo's sermon was quickly accepted. Sound judgment prompted the introduction of *The London Merchant* to a summer audience—it was first performed by the Drury Lane summer company 22 June 1731 —when the more sophisticated playgoers would have been out of town. By fall it was well entrenched, having gained the support of "certain eminent merchants of the City of London," who began to bespeak the play. Whether the glowing account of the new status of tradesmen given principally in Thorowgood's speeches had any weight in this early popularity with a group commonly opposed to the theatre must remain conjectural.

At the beginning of the 1731–1732 season *The London Merchant* was taken up by the Goodman's Fields company since its subject matter was better suited to the City locale than to the theatres in Westminster, but by 16 October Drury Lane was offering it again and by 28 October offering it, not simply "at the particular desire of several persons of distinction, and eminent merchants of the City of London," but by royal command. The House of Hanover was

[53] Richard Steele, *The Lying Lover*, p. [vii].
[54] Richard Steele, *Mr. Steele's Apology for Himself and His Writings*, p. 48.

quite aware of its debt of gratitude to the City. Though I find no published statement of it, probably many spectators were aware of the symbolic link when the Drury Lane company offered the play again the following evening, 29 October, the eve of Lord Mayor's Day.

The next appropriate date of *The London Merchant* as a City play would be right after Christmas, and on Monday 27 December both Drury Lane and Goodman's Fields offered it for holiday theatregoers. It must be sadly acknowledged that John Rich chose this evening to revive an older play of rather less edifying tone, *The London Cuckolds*, but before the 1731–1732 season was over Rich too fell into line by adding Lillo's play to his repertory at Lincoln's Inns Fields on Monday 22 May. To make acceptance unanimous, the Little Haymarket, which just a year before was playing cat and mouse with the legal authorities, finally joined the ranks of good citizens by adding the play to its repertory on 1 June 1732, some weeks short of its first anniversary.

Though no special effort seems to have been required to keep Lillo's play before the eyes and minds of London audiences, an occasional journalistic exhortation does appear recommending it to London merchants as salutary for their errant apprentices, a theme sounded at the very start by a correspondent to the *Daily Post* and echoed from time to time in other journals. The most concerted effort and most dramatic account of the moral efficacy of *The London Merchant* came much later in its career. In 1787 while trying to win public support for the new theatre he had built in the East End in defiance of authority, John Palmer received an able assist from Isaac Jackman in a long and well-written pamphlet called *Royal and Royalty Theatre*. Quite aware of the kind of argument that would be most persuasive, Jackman solicited and reprinted a letter from veteran actor David Ross, a moving testimonial to the efficacy of stage plays, proper stage plays. During the Christmas holidays of 1751, Ross recalls, he performed George Barnwell to Mrs. Pritchard's Millwood.[55] The direct result of that performance was to

[55] An examination of *The London Stage* reveals that 26 December 1751 was a

throw a real-life George Barnwell into violent fever and so terrible a state of remorse that his life was despaired of. Dr. Barrowby, of the staff of St. Bartholomew's Hospital, was called in to minister to the youngster, and it was from Dr. Barrowby that Ross learned of his own unwitting venture into psychotherapy. Doubts have been cast upon some details of Ross's account,[56] though the annual gift of ten guineas from a mysterious donor with the message "a tribute of ... Barnwell"—if the message were still forthcoming—would serve as authentication. In fact, the authenticity of every detail is not significant in this context; of importance is the knowledge that such a story could be used to justify the erection of a theatre and to support the cause of drama as a moral force.

---

first for Ross in the part of Barnwell and the only time he ever played opposite Mrs. Pritchard in Millwood.

[56] Adolphus William Ward, in his introduction to the Belles Lettres edition of George Lillo's *London Merchant,* calls attention to the DNB account of "the celebrated (or notorious) Dr. Barrowby," which has him dying on 30 December 1751, a fact that does not destroy the story but does suggest very close timing. On the other side of the ledger is a repetition of the story, in somewhat garbled form, in the *Thespian Magazine* for October 1792, an indication that Ross's account was becoming a legend.

5. A Mixed Assembly

Few know that elegance of soul refined
Whose soft sensation feels a quicker joy
From melancholy's scenes.[1]

So INTONED THOMAS WARTON just before the midpoint of the century. The notion that some quality of spirit—be it an exquisite sense of honor, a refined taste, a highly sensitive set of nerves—is confined to a tiny fraction of the populace, of which the speaker is always a member, is not an invention of the eighteenth century. If the claim went no further than to state that by some accident of nature—even more, of nurture—there often does exist a considerable range of taste, no objection could be raised. It is only when the claimant begins to announce terms of exclusion, to insist that mere accident of birth or breeding is enough to assure membership among the exalted and exclusion of those less fortunate that the quarrel begins.

[1] Thomas Warton, *The Pleasures of Melancholy*, ll. 93–95.

In many cases careless usage accounts for what may seem a fraudulent claim. Casual use, and misuse, of the term "nature" will provide an analogue. The Old Man urges Dr. Faustus to repent, if it is not too late already, "if sin by custom grow not into nature." Lady Cockwood's maid, in Sir George Etherege's *She Wou'd If She Cou'd*, indicates that her mistress has passed the point of no return because "custom has made it [hypocrisy] so natural, she cannot help it." Quite possibly a similar carelessness is at the base of a remark more apposite to theatrical taste in the epilogue to Thomas Cooke's *Mournful Nuptials* (1739):

> They who are born to taste with pleasure throng
> To Shakespear's sense, or Farinello's song
> The tasteless vulgar, as experience tells,
> Warmly espouse their Harlequins and Nells.
>
> (ll. 3–6)

Bishop Hurd, less likely to be merely casual, does not quite so clearly assume a genetic basis for taste: "I fear the *tender and pitiable* in comedy, though it must afford the highest pleasure to sensible and elegant minds, is not perfectly suited to the apprehensions of the generality."[2]

What happens when the notion of the refined few is applied to an audience growing increasingly *sensible*, getting more and more, to apply the Reverend Charles Jenner's phrase, into "the handkerchief strain"? If we take seriously the claim that refinement is the mark of the few, we are plunged into an insoluble problem in logic. As the theatrical fare grows increasingly refined and sentimental, to fit the taste of the refined few, then the crowds should decrease. The facts, unfortunately for the logic, are far different: the size of the theatre-going public was steadily increasing throughout the century. How, then, can the apparent antithesis of increasing refinement and growing public be reconciled?

Any attempt to make sweeping generalizations about the compo-

---

[2] "Dissertation Concerning the Provinces of the Several Species of the Drama," in Horace, *Q. Horatii Flacci: Epistolae ad Pisones et Augustum*, edited by Richard Hurd, 2nd ed. (1753), I, [2]72–73.

sition of the audience, if by composition is meant class structure, is likely to end in folly or frustration. Too many tangible and intangible facts must be considered: the nights, the play, the part of the season.

Take the days of the week as an example. Comments are too infrequent over the long span to support confident generalization, but there is enough information to suggest that there were differences in audience composition on different days. Tuesdays and Saturdays were "opera nights" during much of the eighteenth century (earlier it was Wednesdays and Saturdays, as we learn from the nonmusical Swift, seeking consolation from his friends' desertion by writing to Stella). On these nights the upper classes, who did and do provide the bulk of the operatic audience, were poorly represented at the playhouse. The week of warfare over *The Chinese Festival* in November 1755 serves as dramatic illustration of audience composition and comes closest to an example of class warfare. Prompter Cross, who recorded every development in the quarrel, designates the opposing sides as "boxes" and "pit," with strong auxiliaries for the latter in the "galleries." The boxes held the upper hand the first three nights, Wednesday through Friday, but on Saturday the fortunes of war turned sharply in favor of the pit and galleries, to the point of Lacy's giving up the dancers. As Cross perhaps ingenuously puts it, "being Sat. our friends were at the opera & the common people had leisure to do mischief."[3]

Three years later *A Letter to Mr. Garrick on the Opening of the Theatre* adds further evidence of a shift toward a more bourgeois if not a more plebeian audience on opera nights.

If it be true that Saturday adds always a fifth part to the receit of the house, it may become you to consider that you owe to the people some acknowledgement for this advantage. It would be ungenerous to give an inferior entertainment on that day, because you knew more would partake of it; and if the merchants of the city prefer the decency and good sense of a theatrical representation, to the boisterous folly of

[3] Richard Cross, MS diary, 5 November 1755, Folger Shakespeare Library, Washington, D. C.

tavern-meetings, for relaxing the mind after the attention of the week, the publick, not they alone, will interest themselves, to wish you would always preserve that decency, especially the performances of those nights which has occasioned the preference.[4]

One more item, a letter in the *Public Advertiser* for 11 December 1766 from a self-styled milliner who professes to be an ardent admirer of the theatre and especially of Garrick and his company, suggests the composition of the Saturday audience: ". . . whenever my mistress will give me leave and my pocket will allow me that pleasure I post myself to the two shilling gallery at Drury Lane playhouse. I seldom miss on a Saturday night."

This meager evidence is not enough to warrant assurance, particularly when it is offset by other bits pointing to other nights as being popular among tradespeople. When in November 1748 John Rich gave Tom Harbin his choice of nights for a benefit he chose a Wednesday, "as being a night of most leisure amongst people eminent in trade, on whom the City depends."[5] Much later in the century Monday seemed favored by the lower classes, if a casual generalization or two may be relied on. On Monday 17 May 1784 according to a note in the *Public Advertiser*, "Fosbrook and Martin, so far favoured as to have a Monday night which we understand makes a probable addition to the receipts of 50£, got together great pit and galleries." Similarly a reviewer in the *General Advertiser* for 6 December 1785 reports on a performance of *Richard II* at Covent Garden, claiming that "the audience seemed much inclined to merriment, and to their disgrace be it said, laughed in some of the best scenes. But it was Monday, and all is allowable in the galleries."

If the proportion of classes varied for different days of the week, it varied at least as much in different parts of the season. Both ends were poor times to draw the affluent and genteel, the leisure class in the fullest sense of the word, for they simply were not in town. A disappointed playwright, Mary Latter, complains of the readiness

---

[4] *A Letter to Mr. Garrick on the Opening of the Theatre*, p. 7.
[5] *General Advertiser*, 8 November 1748, MS copy in Burney Notebook 939d 10, British Museum, London.

with which managers offer a new author benefits late in the season, for "in April and May, tickets are mere drugs, which the managers are glad to get any to partake of."[6] Joseph Reed, in his *Retort Courteous* (1787) suggests that the theatrical managers will have to resort to extraordinary measures to draw crowds during the fall: "As parliament does not meet till late in January, depend on't, gentlemen, you will have great need of novelty, much novelty, to bring good houses."[7] And finally, to show that seasons did vary somewhat, there is the *Morning Chronicle*'s advice of 17 September 1788 to the Drury Lane management to wake up and emulate their competitors at Covent Garden, who have been drawing crowds and being heartily applauded while Drury Lane is "very thinly attended." Even though it is only 17 September "there were more people in town than at this time of year was generally imagined."

The composition of the audience changed sharply on certain traditional nights of every season. For some decades, especially before and around midcentury, the eve of Lord Mayor's Day called out the City in force, to be entertained by "City" plays, most notoriously *The London Cuckolds*. The event, shifted with the change in calendar in 1752 from 29 October to 9 November, continued to be celebrated but with a rather different bill later in the century. A common attitude toward the audience of the evening is expressed in a review of *The Fair Quaker of Deal* in the *London Evening Post* for 9–11 November 1773. After terming the play "vulgar," "barren," and "contemptible" the reviewer winds up with a generalization: "The Fair Quaker is a good gallery play, and therefore a proper exhibition for the evening of a Lord Mayor's Day."

John Bull had for years been fond of showing his British patriotism and Protestant zeal by attending a performance of Nicholas Rowe's *Tamerlane* on 4 and 5 November, the anniversaries of King William's birthday and the landing at Torbay. In the fall of 1716, spurred by the recent Jacobite uprising, the Drury Lane company

---

[6] Mary Latter, Preface ("Stage-Craft, an Essay") to *Siege of Jerusalem* (1763), which was never produced.

[7] Joseph Reed, *Retort Courteous*, p. 14.

under Steele's leadership revived Rowe's fustian tragedy with a new prologue memorializing the events of 1688. Dudley Ryder, later to become attorney general, was keeping a diary of, among other things, his frequent visits to the theatre. There were doubtless more sensitive playgoers but none more stirred by Whiggish zeal than Ryder, whose earlier comments on politics in the theatre foretell his attendance on 6 November 1716 and his observations: "Went to see the tragedy of *Tamerlane* which was acted with a new prologue in honor of King William and in memory of what he did for us. The play itself is good, but I find myself too much moved and affected with tragedies to take much pleasure in them." From this time on for much of the century both theatres dutifully produced Rowe's play at the appropriate time, but by the seventeen-eighties much of the early zeal had evaporated. A correspondent to the *Sunday Chronicle* for 9 November 1788 laments that even on "this Centennial Anniversary" no one had observed the occasion in the theatres by offering *Tamerlane*.

The lower classes were also attracted to the theatre during the Christmas and Easter holidays. Box-office receipts are not available for many of the seasons and when available account usually for only one of the companies. Even so, these spotty records reveal that during the holidays receipts rose sharply.[8] Since the increase seems largely due to the lower classes, the managers were quick to defer to them. Pantomime and show, boisterous comedy—these were the favorites and were sure to increase, during the Christmas holidays especially. Pantomime serves as a clear illustration of the holiday fare. John Rich's elaborate harlequinades are perhaps only distant cousins of the English Christmas pantomimes, today as much a part of the season as holly and plum pudding, but they are related. The history of the term, if nothing else, would indicate the relationship, for perhaps the most notable feature of the present-day pantomime is the fact that it is no longer actually pantomimic. Today tradition seems to be the rule. In the eighteenth century the tra-

---

[8] Harry William Pedicord gives some samples (*The Theatrical Public in the Time of Garrick*, Appendix B).

dition was just beginning and therefore novelty was considered a necessary ingredient. Hence the practice already noted of producing a new pantomime for each season. The calendar in *The London Stage* or, a more concentrated kind of evidence, the lists provided by Allardyce Nicoll will make this clear. Henry Woodward's offerings, for example, run to fifteen, of which nine are pantomimes. Of these nine, six were offered to London audiences for the first time right after Christmas, one in mid-November, and two in January. Although the marvelously combined appeals of success and show provided by Dick Whittington were not fully exploited until the nineteenth century, audiences of the eighteenth century made the initial discovery of these delights; Nicoll lists a performance of *Whittington and His Cat* at Astley's Amphitheatre for 4 May 1795. The chief attraction of pantomime from the beginning had of course been scenic display, especially as assisted by "magic." It is not surprising, therefore, that John O'Keeffe started Aladdin and his "wonderful lamp" on their long career on the day after Christmas 1788.

The popularity of magic suggests still another component of the audience, young people or even children, for the holiday seasons were beginning to attract families to the theatre and therefore beginning to create some demand for wholesome family fare. It would be misleading to count attendance by younger members of the royal family as evidence. The children of all first families are too often on exhibition themselves to count as mere spectators. Nor were such families as the young Burneys typical. As a musician their father would have had professional connections with the theatre, they had lost their mother, and their friendship with the childless David Garrick, who adored them as much as they did him, made access to his private box quite simple and easy.[9] Ruling out

---

[9] "As soon as the young Burneys were old enough to go to the theatre—and that seemed to be from the age of three or four—[Garrick] frequently offered them his wife's box at Drury Lane" (Joyce Hemlow, *The History of Fanny Burney*, p. 12). Burke's son too had the favor of Garrick's box. In one of his letters Garrick apologizes for the boxkeeper's not looking after the eight-year-

such exceptions, we still find an occasional youngster who had no such ready access and who therefore may be counted. Mrs. Thrale recalled that she was only six when she saw Quin in *Cato*.[10] And even if feminine memory of birthdays is suspect—Mrs. Thrale managed to forget a year or two when Johnson composed his impromptu on her thirty-fifth birthday—there is no need to question another young person who saw Quin the preceding season. Richard Cumberland, grandson of a bishop on one side and of the greatest of English classical scholars on the other, simply compels belief. He saw Quin and Garrick and Susanna Arne Cibber in the *Fair Penitent* during the season of 1746–1747 when John Rich had the splendid trio under contract at Covent Garden. Cumberland was a schoolboy of fourteen at Westminster at the time.[11]

By fourteen another Westminster boy, Frederick Reynolds, must have been a seasoned playgoer. He claims that he saw the Barrys in *Othello* when he was "in my sixth year." He spoils his story, however, by remembering too many details, among others a visit to the greenroom where he was greeted by Mrs. Barry, a friend of his mother, and startled by an actor whom she identified as Edward Shuter. Since the Barrys and Shuter were never in the same company until the former deserted Garrick for Covent Garden in 1774–1775 and since other details lend some support to these more incidental items in Reynolds's memory, it is necessary to double the young enthusiast's remembered age.[12] Two other accounts by Reynolds, equally circumstantial but not so readily checked, emphasize his youthful interest in the theatre.

There is some virtually on-the-spot corroboration of the common attendance of quite young people at holiday plays during the last quarter century and more. An item connected with the *Beggar's Opera* story will provide an example. When the elder Colman

----
old properly (David Garrick, *Letters*, edited by David Mason Little and George Morrow Kahrl, II, 490, No. 385).

[10] James Lowry Clifford, *Hester Lynch Piozzi*, p. 12.

[11] Richard Cumberland, *Memoirs of Richard Cumberland*, I, 80–82.

[12] Frederick Reynolds, *The Life and Times of Frederick Reynolds*, I, 14–16.

seemed especially determined to flaunt the Westminster justices, he was sharply attacked in the *Public Advertiser* of 15 January 1774 for offering the old ballad opera "on execution days, on Christmas holidays, and in the first run of a new pantomime. . . . The boxes at such seasons are crouded with the sweet cherubs from the boarding schools, and the nation's blooming hope from Eaton, Winton, Harrow, &c." In another decade or so the attendance of children during the holidays must have become commonplace. A playbill in the Burney collection for a mid-August 1784 production at the Hammersmith theatre may not establish the emergence of a youthful audience, but there is significance in the legend "Children half price"—for *Bold Stroke for a Wife* plus *Flitch of Bacon!* A newsclipping concerning the highly popular *Harlequin's Chaplet*, introduced at Covent Garden three days before Christmas 1789, does seem to confirm the trend: "*Harlequin's Chaplet* is likely to run more than the holidays; it not only pleases the children, but those who have long since left off going to school."[13]

Clearly the composition of the audience varied with the season, and children accounted for a growing segment during holidays. Though it is difficult to assess the effect of their presence on the fare, except that the kind of scenic display and mock magic associated with the pantomime was obviously increased with children in mind, a few conjectures seem in order. It is fair to assume that the decidedly more "adult" plays of the earliest years of the century would almost guarantee the exclusion of children and adolescents— I say *almost* simply because I lack corroborating evidence and because parents do sometimes act in unaccountable ways with their charges. Certainly Grosley had cause to wonder how the English, by nature given to melancholia, could expose themselves to the shock of ghosts, murders, and so forth on the stage. Even more surprising, he says, "They are very ready to carry their children to the playhouse, alledging the same reasons for this practice that are

---

[13] Undated and unidentified newsclipping in the Enthoven Collection, Victoria and Albert Museum, London. The date was obviously around 6 January 1790.

elsewhere given for sending young persons to public executions."
Grosley enforces his point by citing the case of his landlord's son,
nine or ten years old, who had nightmares in which "he thought he
was haunted by all the ghosts in the tragedy of Richard the Third,
and by all the dead bodies in the churchyards of London."[14] *Harlequin's Chaplet* may not have represented very exalted fare, but it
sounds like an improvement over *Richard III* for children.

The chief supposition is that in an indefinable way these younger
persons had some effect on the theatrical fare generally, increasing
the emphasis on wholesomeness, on the strongly didactic, on the
movement from head to eye and ear. Before assigning them too
much credit or blame we should recall that they were not a significantly large group at all seasons and that they did not write
letters to the newspapers and otherwise badger the managers to
change their offerings. In fact, their presence is far more important
as a symptom than as a cause. Their increasing attendance, even
at restricted seasons, indicates an increasing tolerance, even approval, of the theatre.

The existence of audience variety and the appearance of identi-
fiable groups on certain days is strengthened by the activity of certain organizations—the Masons, the Marine Society, the Robin Hood
Society, even what appears to be a mutual admiration society calling
themselves "Selected Albions"—who on occasion attended the theatre in a body. On some nights national or ethnic groups—Scots,
Jews, Irish, French, West Indians—assembled to applaud or oppose
a particular play or performer. Even trades groups were known to
have occupied at least part of the house on special occasions, as when
the tailors filled the galleries at the Little Haymarket "to see themselves exalted into heroes and demi-gods" as the *Morning Chronicle*
reports concerning a new afterpiece called *The Taylors*, played after
The Beggar's Opera on 16 September 1776. On another night, when
a play about tailors promised satire rather than exaltation they
organized against it,[15] just as in 1765 the barbers objected—it is not

---

[14] Pierre Jean Grosley, *A Tour to London*, I, 198.
[15] *The Thespian Magazine*, III, 225, tells the story of a delegation of tailors

clear that they attended in a body—not to a play about barbers but to the economic threat posed by an actor's temerity in wearing his own hair.[16]

Candor forces recognition of the presence, in season and out, of still another group of what might euphemistically be called tradespeople, that group variously known as "the ladies of Drury," "the flesh market," or, to use a term popular before Queen Anne's edict destroyed its usefulness, "the vizard masks." Sir John Hawkins's assertion of the inevitable kinship between prostitutes and the theatre is overwhelmingly substantiated by the many references to the relationship in newspapers, diaries, and letters.

John Dryden can once more represent his own period, for no one was readier than he to follow the advice offered in the epilogue to *The Second Part of the Conquest of Granada* (1671):

> They, who have best succeeded on the stage,
> Have still conform'd their genius to their age.

Scattered throughout the long list of Dryden's prologues and epilogues are numerous allusions to prostitutes in the theatre. Uniformly these references are both casual, or downright blasé, and cynical. If any sign of disapproval appears, it is commonly a mild protest that these ladies create a disturbance by distracting gallants from the proper business of an audience, attention to the play. Dryden's first allusion to vizard masks occurs in the prologue to *The Second Part of the Conquest of Granada*. Though the tone of sophisticated banter is already there, and the charge of distracting gallants, it is not altogether clear that the term refers exclusively to streetwalkers. The fashion of wearing masks at the theatre was apparently less than ten years old, for it was on 12 June of 1663 that Pepys, who was perhaps no genius but a champion conformer,

---

who paid a visit to the actor Quick, who planned to perform in a new satirical bit called *Now's Your Time, Taylors* at his benefit in March or April 1794. Group pressure was enough to cause Quick to cancel his plans.

[16] A clipping in the British Museum Theatre Collection, 38, 23 February 1765, tells of disturbance by "a knot of barbers" in the upper gallery protesting Maddock's action.

reports seeing Lady Mary Cromwell masked at the play and hints of his own impatience to dash off to the Exchange after the play to buy his wife one, since wearing masks "of late is become a great fashion among the ladies." As Dryden's lines show the gallants in heated debate over the identity of the wearer, it would appear that they suspect another Lady Mary behind the bit of black gauze or velvet rather than Mother Bennet or one of her minions.

Other allusions in following decades show no shift in circumstances, or in Dryden's blasé attitude. The only real change is in the term "vizard mask" itself. By the sixteen-eighties the possibility of equivocation has largely disappeared. The epilogue "To the King and Queen, at the Opening of Their Theatre, 1692" leaves no doubt:

> But stay: methinks some vizard masque I see,
> Cast out her lure from the mid gallery:
> About her all the flutt'ring sparks are rang'd;
> The noise continues though the scene is chang'd.[17]

Any sign of disapproval of these ladies or of the theatre for harboring them must be sought, before the close of the seventeenth century, in more general satire or in attacks upon the stage. Montague Summers, who provides much additional material on this unsavory topic, quotes from such pieces as Robert Gould's *Play-House* (1689) and from *The Fire-Ships* (1691), two bitter attacks on the theatres and on prostitutes.[18] By 1699, however, even the comparatively mild *Historia Histrionica* can be heard to protest, "Whereas of late, the Play-houses are so extreamly pestered with Vizard-masks and their Trade, (occasioning continual Quarrels and Abuses) that many of the more Civilized Part of the Town are uneasy in the Company, and shun the Theatre as they would a House of Scandal."[19]

---

[17] Other allusions by Dryden appear in his prologue to *Marriage A-la-Mode* (c. 1672), his epilogue for the opening of the new Drury Lane (26 March 1674), and his prologue to Mrs. Behn's *Widdow Ranter* (1689).

[18] Montague Summers, *The Restoration Theatre*, pp. 89–90, 297–321.

[19] This well-known document of 1699 has been reprinted by Robert Lowe in the prefatory material to his edition of Colley Cibber, *An Apology for the Life of Mr. Colley Cibber*, I, xix–li.

Reform being in the air at the turn of the century, the theatrical managers were finally impelled to action in their own defence by attempting to ban masks from their houses; at least I assume this to be the object of a note at the foot of a bill in the *Daily Courant* for Wednesday 20 January 1703 announcing a performance at Drury Lane the following Saturday of *The Country House* and "a consort of musick": "And no persons to be admitted in masks." This feeble attempt no doubt proving ineffective, the government was asked to intervene. On 17 January 1704 Queen Anne issued an edict providing among other things that "no woman be allowed or presume to wear a vizard mask in either of the theatres."[20]

Probably a consensus had been reached, very likely not shared by the ladies in question, for hardly any similar edict seems ever to have met with such swift and complete success. By June a new song appeared at Lincoln's Inn Fields during a benefit for Mrs. Boman, a song sung by Mr. Boman and entitled *The Misses' Lamentation for Want of Their Vizard Masks in the Play-house.* And by January 1705 the practice is referred to as a thing of the past:

> Nay, oft, neglecting Beauty, Sense, and Wit,
> With ugly Masks you've stoln out of the Pit.
> Thanks to good Orders, now that Sport is over;
> The Hoods o're nose have charms still for a Rover.[21]

When, five years later, a German visitor comments on seeing masked women, "generally harlots," in London, he refers to women in the park or on the streets.[22]

It is perhaps not necessary to point out that Queen Anne was ruling against vizard masks in the original and literal sense. For masks in the literal sense were all that disappeared from the theatre. True, there was a kind of conspiracy of silence about metonymic

---

[20] *Daily Courant*, 24 January 1704.

[21] Prologue to Peter Anthony Motteux, *Farewel Folly*, 18 January 1705, Drury Lane.

[22] Zacharias Konrad von Uffenbach, *London in 1710*, edited by William Henry Quarrell and Margaret Mare, p. 12.

"masks" in the first half of the eighteenth century. The custom of casual reference to punks and whores in prologue and epilogue was largely abandoned, though there were enough allusions to them in plays and newspaper accounts to dispel any supposition that the ladies had in fact disappeared from the audience.[23]

By midcentury, however, comments about the problem had begun to increase, indicating no tendency on the part of the ladies to desist, and the tone of disapproval had become much more vigorous. The term "flesh market" was invented about this time as a sufficiently descriptive label. The ladies themselves had moved up in the world, no doubt as a result of increasing British affluence, and now occupied, instead of their old haunts in pit or middle gallery, the upper side boxes, often called green boxes. There are charges that "the front rows of the green boxes . . . are kept for them as their stand,"[24] and though these allegations would appear grossly exaggerated they may not have been completely without foundation. The indignant author of *Observations on the Importance and Use of Theatres* (1759) likewise charges that the boxkeepers accept half-crown bribes from these ladies so that they may sit, not in the obscurity of the galleries but in the view of everyone. This author is in fact so indignant over such flaunting of immorality before decent people that he urges audiences to "rise with a universal hiss upon the entrance of one of these infamous women into their places."[25] Then, his voice taking on what must have seemed to many a quite un-English shrillness, he calls for his countrymen to follow the King of France by using the power of the state to banish

[23] There are allusions in Charles Shadwell's *Humours of the Navy* (1713) and in Charles Molloy's *Coquet* (1718); Dennis mentions them along with other drunken and profane members of the audience in his *Stage Defended* (1726); César de Saussure mentions them in his *Lettres et Voyages, en Allemagne, en Hollande et en Angleterre*, Letter XII (June 1728); *Grub-Street Journal*, No. 352, and *A Seasonable Examination of the Pleas and Pretensions of the Proprietors of, and Subscribers to, Play-houses* (both 1735) use the familiar link between theatres and prostitutes to join in the parliamentary attack then in progress.

[24] *Theatrical Monitor*, no. 4 (14 November 1767).

[25] *Observations on the Importance and Use of Theatres*, p. 21.

these creatures from the theatre. Though such sentiments were very likely shared by others, no concerted response was forthcoming, and no movement to license playgoers as well as plays was started.

An item from *Lloyd's Evening Post* of 10–13 November 1758, is perhaps more typical in its complaints because it is unequivocal in its disapproval but not so desperate as to demand intervention by the state. The graphic picture of the audience must be viewed with some caution, both because of the likelihood of exaggeration and because the particular audience is not to be considered as representing the usual pattern. It was the eve of Lord Mayor's Day, the theatre was Covent Garden, the play was *The London Cuckolds*, and the commentator admits being biased from the start.

There were several men of distinction in the boxes at this Play, and I think eight Ladies. What their inward feelings might be, I know not; but if one might judge of their thoughts by the gravity of their looks, they were rather mortified than diverted. But of the women of the town, who, as we may suppose, were unwilling to let slip a fair opportunity of getting a supper and a bed-fellow, there were crouds both in the pit and green boxes, and in fact we should almost be tempted to think, that this play is acted now and then in consideration of the Manager's kind hearted neighbors, not one of whom, as may easily be guessed, went out of the house without a companion. Let me add, that the upper-gallery was crowded with applauding spectators, and once for all, that the *London Cuckolds* is a spectacle fit only to be represented before common w—— and blackguards.

More, many more, examples could be cited, but the foregoing excerpt should be quite enough to emphasize that among the varied ingredients of the eighteenth-century audience one staple was prostitutes, and that among those whose opinions were voiced publicly the attitude toward this staple was increasingly disapproving. The Brothers Woodfall, in their highly influential newspapers, present evidence of the persistence of the problem. William in his *Diary or Woodfall's Register* for 13 September 1792 reports in matter-of-fact tones that "the number of prostitutes, who frequent the theatres, encrease rapidly," whereas on the following day Henry Sampson Woodfall's *Public Advertiser* congratulates—prematurely as it turned out—the managers of Covent Garden for getting rid of the denizens of the upper gallery and then goes on to ask for further reforms:

While the managers of the theatre are to be praised for suppressing that disgraceful nuisance the Upper Gallery, which is in general only visited by rabble who delight in noise and mischief, they should endeavor to protect the frequenters of the Boxes against riotous and inebriated women of the town, who are now become offensive in the extreme. Peace officers should be found who will *do their duty* when those women will not pursue their unhappy calling without disturbing the audience.

2

In attempting to define the composition of the eighteenth-century audience I hope I have established at least the complexity of any adequate answer. There were stable elements, not always the best. There were much less stable or at least seasonally recurrent elements. But I still have not answered or even assaulted the question of class structure. What about the view that the audience was increasingly middle class? An immediate reaction to this question is ready acceptance. Since both the audience in the theatre and the middle class in English society were quite measurably increasing, it would seem logical to assume that the theatre audience was becoming more middle class. Unfortunately such an answer is more logical than useful. It is like the pronouncement that this or that age is transitional. What age is not? To obtain a satisfactory answer, a definition of classes that is both accurate and helpful is necessary.

The period between 1660 and 1800 continued a development started long before but accelerated in the earlier seventeenth century: the rise in numbers and power of persons independent economically and politically—and esthetically—of the ruling minority. What made the development more readily possible is what makes definition harder: the increasing fluidity and amorphousness of classes, permitting a Simon Eyre or a Dick Whittington to travel far across class boundaries, which in the rush were being trampled out.

The temptation to draw what would seem logical conclusions from the considerable range in prices for various parts of the theatre or to assume that the relatively high cost of admission to any part of the house barred all but the affluent can be readily dismissed. John Lough well into that trap in his study of Parisian audiences:

> . . . the very existence of different theatre prices, ranging from those paid for the expensive "premières loges" and seats on the stage down to the more modest "quinze sous" for the right to stand in the *parterre*, presupposes considerable differences in purse and possibly in rank among the spectators.[26]

Let the worthy clerk of the King's Ships take Professor Lough in hand. On 1 January 1668 Pepys went to see his favorite play, *Sir Martin Mar-all*, at the Duke's Theatre. After some comments on the pleasure Dryden's play always gives him, he turns to sober reflection on a theme that had to wait until the twentieth century and Professor Veblen for exhaustive treatment:

> Here a mighty company of citizens, 'prentices, and others; and it makes me observe, that when I began first to be able to bestow a play on myself, I do not remember that I saw so many by half of the ordinary 'prentices and mean people in the pit at 2s. 6d. a-piece as now; I going for several years no higher than the 12d. and then the 18d. places, though I strained hard to go in when I did: so much the vanity and prodigality of the age is to be observed in this particular.

Nor is Pepys's moral indignation over prodigality any stronger than his chagrin seven years earlier in an equally apposite case. On 19 January 1661 he "went to the theatre, where I saw 'The Lost Lady,' which do not please me much. Here I was troubled to be seen by four of our office clerkes, which sat in the half-crowne box, and I in the 1s.od."[27]

---

[26] John Lough, *Paris Theatre Audiences in the Seventeenth and Eighteenth Centuries*, p. 56. Oddly enough, Professor Lough had just quoted a passage from Lancaster, remarking that the great scholar's works should be "carefully weighed," a passage dismissing the very argument Lough is about to advance: "Nor is the question of expense a serious argument."

[27] It might be well to give a few essentials concerning prices here; a full account would require several pages. "Common prices" after the Restoration

It is likewise hazardous to make assumptions about the composition of the audience on the basis of curtain time. The fact that this important event in the day tended to become later and later, moving from around 3:00 P.M. in Pepys's day to around 6:30 P.M. at the end of the eighteenth century,[28] coupled with the fact that late hours were considered to be "quality" hours,[29] would seem by a

---

were: boxes 2/6, pit 1/6, middle gallery 1/0, upper gallery 0/6. Whenever it was possible to plead extra expense for scenery and costumes, Davenant instituted "advanced prices" of 4/0, 2/6, 1/6, 1/0, which by the first quarter of the next century had become "common" so that new "advanced" prices of 5/0, 3/0, 2/0, 1/0 were introduced. By the start of Garrick's management, these "advanced" prices had become common, but instead of requiring a new set of advanced prices the managers had by now settled on the practice of refusing to allow "half-price" after the third act of the main piece. That is, when the bill called for a standard play or plays from the repertory without extra expense for new sets and the like, it had become customary to allow latecomers to enter at the end of Act III for a fixed sum approximating half the regular price. After the riots at both houses in the early months of 1763, an agreement of sorts was reached that in effect prevented the managers from insisting on full prices for insignificant expenditures. These prices (5/0, 3/0, 2/0, 1/0) prevailed until the last decade of the eighteenth century when the Drury Lane company, using the occasion of its expensive move to the opera house in the fall of 1791, succeeded in moving the prices up still another notch to 6/0, 3/6, 2/0, 1/0.

[28] Pepys is not as specific as he might be, though he is detailed. In the interest of brevity I should say that the details he does give would indicate that the time clearly set on the title page of Davenant's *Cruelty of the Spaniards in Peru*, which Leslie Hotson judges to be some time before 25 July 1658 (*The Commonwealth and Restoration Stage*, p. 156), "Represented daily at the Cockpit in Drury Lane, at three after noone punctually," would have held for at least a decade. By the beginning of the eighteenth century curtain time during the winter season had crept up to 5:00 P.M. and seemed already to be advancing still farther to 5:30 P.M. In another fifteen years the curtain rose at 6:00 P.M., the usual hour for the next sixty years. By the beginning of the last quarter of the century it had moved to 6:15 P.M., and there it remained until 1800 and beyond. These figures apply, it must be emphasized, to plays and to the main season from midfall to midspring. Oratorios and operas were commonly half an hour to an hour later. The longer days of summer brought near chaos early in the period, although by the middle of the eighteenth century a settled policy was established by the patent houses of beginning some fifteen minutes later during the first and last months of the season.

[29] In *The London Stage* (pt. 2) Avery quotes some play announcements for

simple equation to signify the overwhelming importance of the
genteel part of the audience in settling theatrical affairs. Again
there are complications. It is true that late hours were quality
hours—and urban hours. In town at least the hour for dinner,
always closely tied to curtain time, became later and later.[30] But
the quality were not the only ones fond of late hours. The members
of the business community joined in the pressure to delay the evening's performance, as seems inevitable since the more affluent were
bound to follow the lead of their more genteel countrymen. Social
climbing was not, however, the only motive. Plain business had
much to do with it. Though Mr. Gradgrind's grim statistical clock
was as yet unknown, time was beginning to be recognized as a
commodity not to be squandered in activities that encroached on
business hours. I find little evidence that the demands of commerce
had any influence in setting the hour of curtain time, but they did
affect the theatrical schedule at the two other points: the time of

---

the first years of the century in which the time is given as having been set for
the "conveniency of the gentry" (6 December 1700) or "conveniency of the
quality" (11 June 1703). At the other end of the century, the *Thespian Magazine* for March 1793 scolds an actress, evidently Mrs. Jordan, who has been so
"partial . . . to *quality hours*" that she has held up the performance for nearly
forty-five minutes.

[30] Again it is hard to be certain about the times, often vaguer than they at
first look, given by Pepys, but it would appear to be between 1:00 P.M. and
2:00 P.M. In support of this conclusion is the schedule of Mrs. Behn's fashionable lady in *Sir Patient Fancy* (1768), who dresses till 12:00 and dines until
2:00 P.M. In 1717–1719 William Byrd routinely records dining at 2:00 P.M. By
midcentury the fashionable hour had become 4:00 P.M. according to a Conti-
nental visitor, Frederick Kielmansegg (*Diary of a Journey to England in the
Years 1761–1762*, p. 28). In 1775 Boswell informs us that the Thrales dine at
5:00 P.M. and omit supper (*The Ominous Years*, p. 106, 28 March 1775). Still
a generation later Joseph Farington dines at 5:00 P.M. and at 5:15 P.M. but finds
an older custom and an earlier hour of 4:00 P.M. prevailing at Windsor in 1797
(*The Farington Diary*, edited by James Greig, I, 3, 21 July 1793). As evidence
that the later hour was both aristocratic and urban is Jane Austen's consciousness
that her family hour of 3:30 P.M. was both rural and old-fashioned (Jane Austen,
Jane Austen's Letters, edited by Robert William Chapman, p. 39).

opening the doors and the time—at least the growing tendency to specify the time—of half-price admittance.[31]

Clearly the one term that best fits the audience is the one used both early and late: mixed. Dryden speaks, through his persona Neander in *An Essay of Dramatic Poesy* (1668), of "the mixed audience of the populace and the noblesse." Tom Davies, defending pantomime in his *Life of David Garrick* (1780), refers to what would appear to be much the same thing in the phrase "a mixed company."[32]

Throughout the period there are indications that all levels of the populace are represented. No neat rows of figures inviting tabulation are available, and all classes are not equally or even adequately represented at all seasons—far from it. To quote Dryden again, this time in his *Vindication of the Duke of Guise* (1683): "Are the audience of a play-house, which are generally persons of honour, noblemen, and ladies, or, at worst, as one of your authors calls his gallants, men of wit and pleasure about the town,—are these the rabble of Mr. Hunt?"[33] Yet only thirteen years later, according to Dryden's own account in the preface to his son's play, *The Husband*

[31] J. Brownsmith's *Dramatic Time-piece* (1767) was designed for both the leisure class and business people. It would enable those with carriages and servants to know quite precisely when the play ended so they could be properly attended, and it would inform those prevented by business from getting to the play on time to estimate the time for "the latter account." *Theatrical Review* for March 1763 publishes a letter from "Barnaby Flog" in which he says, among other things: "A multitude of people are engaged in business till 8 o'clock, as great a number may not possibly choose to go at six. . . . Should they all be made to pay the full price?" (I, 76).

[32] Thomas Davies, *Memoirs of the Life of David Garrick*, I, 76. Richardson's Lovelace, in a discursive letter dated Friday, July 28, comments on a first-night audience and pleads for quiet, since everyone is entitled to see quietly what he paid for in "that mixed multitude" (*Clarissa*, VI, 285). Foote uses precisely the same term in the preface to *Taste* (1752). Late-century accounts of the who-was-there type provide details of the mixture. See especially *London Magazine* for May 1776; the later *Prompter*, No. 5 (31 October 1789); or, more generally, the various gossipy accounts in such newspapers as the *Morning Post* in the last two decades of the century.

[33] John Dryden, *Vindication of the Duke of Guise*, p. 14.

His Own Cuckold (1696), the true rabble were evidently back: "There is scarce a man or woman of God's making in all their farces: yet they raise an unnatural sort of laughter, the common effect of buffoonery; and the rabble which takes this for wit will endure no better, because 'tis above their understanding."

Indeed, a sampling of comment giving any details on the possible make-up of the audience supports the idea of a mixture at all periods. A Frenchman, Henri Misson, who visited London sometime between 1683 and 1696 describes the range:

The pit is an amphitheatre, fill'd with benches without backboards, and adorn'd and cover'd with a green cloth. Men of quality, particularly the younger sort, some ladies of reputation and vertue, and abundance of damsels that hunt for prey, sit all together in this place, higgledy-piggledy, chatter, toy, play, hear, hear not. Farther up, against the wall, under the first gallery, and just opposite to the stage, rises another amphitheater, which is taken up by persons of the best quality, among whom are generally very few men. The galleries, whereof there are only two rows, are fill'd with none but ordinary people, particularly the upper one.[34]

An English observer's description in the last decade of the seventeenth century supports Misson.

In our Playhouses at London, besides an Upper-Gallery for Footmen, Coachmen, Mendicants, &c. we have three other different and distinct classes; the first is called the Boxes, where there is one peculiar to the King and Royal Family, and the rest for persons of Quality, and for the Ladies and Gentlemen of the highest Rank, unless some Fools that have more wit than money, or perhaps more Impudence than both, crowd in among 'em. The Second is call'd the Pit, where sit the Judges, Wits and Censurers, . . . in common with these sit the Squires, Sharpers, Beaus, Bullies, and Whores, and here and there an extravagant Male and Female Cit. The Third is distinguisht by the Title of the Middle Gallery, where the Citizens Wives and Daughters, together with the Abigails, Serving-men, Journeymen and Apprentices commonly take their Places.[35]

---

[34] Henri Misson, *Mr. Misson's Memoirs and Observations*, entry for *Plays*.
[35] *The Country Gentleman's Vade Mecum*, Letter VII.

In the seventeen-thirties two depositions suggest much the same effect. The author of *A Seasonable Examination to the Pleas and Pretenses* (1735) does not support plays in general, feeling that "the diversions of the stage have taken no small hold of the minds of the lower class of people." [36] And Thomas Cooke, in the "Observations on Satire" prefacing his *Mournful Nuptials* (1739), proclaims that "there never was a time in England when our people of high rank, and indeed those of lower condition in London, shewed a greater inclination to encourage public entertainments than now."[37]

Fifteen years later in a passage awkwardly long for full quotation *Connoisseur* No. 43 (21 November 1754) gives a highly detailed picture of the range of playgoers, from "the stage-box to the upper gallery." There are still beaus on the stage—there will be for another decade. The "flesh market" infests the upper boxes and even threatens to invade the lower. "The court of criticism" still occupies the pit. Most interesting, however, are the boxes, which seem to be occupied by the glittering and chattering leisure class, who come "not to see the play but 'because every body is there,' " and at least some "gentlemen, who draw the pen from under [*sic*] their right ears about seven o'clock, clap on a bag-wig and a sword, and drop into the boxes at the end of the third act."

The author of *Reflections upon Theatrical Expression in Tragedy* (1755) is equally long-winded in covering the same ground though not quite as explicit on the range of classes, referring somewhat more vaguely to "men of fortune" and "women of genteel deportment" in the pit. His chief concern is with deportment of the spectators, since he wishes "to intimate to the town, that the *excellence* of theatrical expression has great dependance upon *their* conduct," and he spends most of his energy in chiding the noisy, restless audience and little in reporting who is there.

Garrick's French correspondent Mme Riccoboni claimed the

---

[36] *A Seasonable Examination of the Pleas and Pretensions of the Proprietors of, and Subscribers to, Play-houses, Erected in Defiance of the Royal Licence*, p. 17.

[37] Thomas Cooke, *Mournful Nuptials*, pp. xii–xiii.

English audience in 1769 was composed of the middle and lower classes only, but she was depending on information—or what she thought was information—conveyed by English visitors to France, for she never visited England. She was quickly challenged by Garrick, and the picture she gives—"À Londres, les personnes distinguées vont rarement à la comédie [plays in general]"[38]—is sharply contradicted by an on-the-spot sketch in the *Theatrical Monitor* of 19 March 1768:

During the time of the representation of a play, the quality in the boxes are totally employed in finding out and beckening to their acquaintances, male and female; they criticize on fashions, whisper cross the benches, make significant nods, and give hints of this and that, and t'other body.

This part of the audience is, however, balanced by crowds of

the vulgar [who] gather from all parts and crowd the pitt, slips and galleries. . . . The exhibition of a new piece now-a-days, is to be supported by a legion of clappers, drawn out in front lines over the house, and are, right or wrong suffered to disturb the audience. . . . and this in a country which we boast to be free; indeed it is too much so, with the vulgar part, who by repeated encouragements, think they have a right to abuse without distinction.

Oxford Magazine of three years later provides further evidence of a mixed audience in an open letter to Garrick from Sir Robert Talbot. In the letter Talbot repeats his description of London audiences given to a Parisian acquaintance: "As it was at Athens . . . the playhouse at London is for all the classes of the nation. The peer of the realm, the gentleman, the merchant, the citizen, the clergyman, the tradesman, and their wives, equally resort thither to take places, and the crowd is great."[39]

A foreign observer, writing some twenty years later than Mme Riccoboni, describes what he actually saw about 1789. Gebhard Friedrich August Wendeborn was no observer from afar or week-

---

[38] *Le nouveau théâtre anglois*, edited by Marie Jeanne Riccoboni, I, viii–ix.

[39] Sir Robert Talbot, letter, *Oxford Magazine*, VII (July–December 1771 and Supplement), 272.

end visitor but a resident of London for more than twenty years. His description, which is possibly intended to generalize for much of the last quarter century, shows clearly a range of classes.

Many traits of the national character of a people may be observed in their public entertainments; and it appears to me, as if the English intended to shew that liberty, which they are used to glory in, no where more than in their playhouses. Persons of high rank, and others of the very lowest, are present; and it seems as if the latter were determined to intimate that they were as good as the former.

The upper-gallery, which is occupied by the low part of the audience, will oftentimes govern the whole house, and the players are under a necessity to accommodate themselves to their whim, and to humour them.[40]

Most revealing are Lieutenant General John Burgoyne's comments on classes in the theatre in the last quarter of the century. Nicknamed "Gentleman Johnny," nephew of a baronet, son-in-law of an earl, much given to panache, Burgoyne might readily have fallen into the attitude that refined feelings are the property of the refined few. Arthur Sherbo feels Burgoyne betrayed this attitude, but he evidently read too hastily or too superficially.[41] Burgoyne's statement in the preface to his *Lord of the Manor* (1780) is no model of logic or consistency, but its bias is quite clear.

Continued interrupted scenes of tenderness and sensibility (*Comédie Larmoyante*) may please the very refined, but the bulk of an English audience, including many of the best understanding, go to a comic performance to laugh in some part of it at least. They claim a right to do so upon precedent of our most valued plays; and every author owes it to them, so long as the merriest among them shews he is equally capable of relishing and applauding what is elevated and affecting—an observation I have always seen hold good in an English gallery.

It might be assuming too much to quote any passages from the Lord of the Manor, as a test that every part of the house can relish refined sentiment; but were the fact ten times more apparent, I should still adhere to my former opinion, and intermix mirth: the censure of a critic

[40] Gebhard Friedrich August Wendeborn, *A View of England towards the Close of the Eighteenth Century*, II, 180.

[41] Arthur Sherbo, *English Sentimental Drama*, p. 84.

of fashion here and there in the boxes, who reckon every thing low
which is out of their own sphere, could never persuade me to turn Moll
Flagon out of my piece.

The force of the last remark may be missed by a modern reader
not familiar with the play and performance: Moll Flagon was
played by the popular low comedian Richard Suett—anticipating such performers as Dan Leno in modern Christmas pantomimes.

Burgoyne had already, even before his misadventures in America, ventured into playwriting. In the summer of 1774 he prepared
a *fête champêtre* to celebrate a wedding at his estate near Epsom,
a dramatic piece that appeared at Drury Lane in November as *The
Maid of the Oaks*. In the preface Burgoyne delivered himself of
what I take to be a most significant pronouncement on the English
audience of the day.

They who suppose an English audience, because used to plain entertainment, are incapable of relishing the most refined, are greatly mistaken. It is true, there will ever be spectators in the two extremes of
the house, who are tasteless and despicable—to the honour of the town
be it said, they are but few—and whether they bawl for a hornpipe
from the Upper Gallery, or yawn in the weariness of dissipation in the
Boxes, they equally betray stupidity, prejudice, or caprice: But the middle class and bulk of the assembly, like that of the kingdom at large,
will ever be on the side of nature, truth, and sense. Let the piece be
founded upon these principles and applause will follow every circumstance of elegance and decoration that can accompany them.

For the sake of emphasis I should like to call attention to two items
in this statement: first, the whole range is still there, the extremes
as well as the middle; second, the "middle class," which is said to
make up "the bulk of the assembly," quite clearly is meant to include all social and economic groups.[42] If only a few among the extremes deserve castigation, the remainder of even these extremes
must also be middle class in Burgoyne's sense of the term. In short,

[42] John Armstrong takes the same position—at any rate he uses the same
principle of classification—in "Taste" (1753), when he expresses scorn of "the
nobility, from the lowest to the highest" (reprinted version in *Miscellanies*, I,
125–142).

"middle class" as used here refers to an attitude, not to a station in the ranks of society. In this sense, Burgoyne's use is sound—even prophetic. If I may follow his lead and characterize the audience as made up largely of, in Eugene O'Neill's phrase, "the spiritual middle class,"[43] then the problem of describing its structure will be greatly simplified, because an important movement in English cultural history at this time is a great leveling, both upward and downward, in matters of morals and tastes. Wendeborn observed this leveling in his picture of the English audience: "Many of the gentlemen and ladies in the boxes, elegantly dressed and outwardly adorned as they are, resemble, notwithstanding, their very homely friends in the upper-gallery, who are more taken and pleased with the outward shew of the representation than with the intrinsic value of a good play."[44]

Three modern students of literary and cultural history lend considerable weight to this picture of eighteenth-century society. Alan McKillop suggests that, "instead of refining the bourgeois [in *Sir Charles Grandison*], as Defoe recommends in his *Compleat English Gentleman*, Richardson reverses the process and grafts bourgeois virtues and sentiments on the stock of the landed gentry."[45] F. C. Green stresses even further the blending of class taste.

Men of the delicacy of Bolingbroke, Chesterfield, and Horace Walpole were exceptions and, in general, the taste of the English nobility of the eighteenth century was not noticeably different from that of the lower classes, whose sports and diversions they often shared, and whose company, for political reasons, they were obliged to frequent. A French *seigneur* wintering in Paris could become really agitated about an infringement of the dramatic unities: his London *confrère* was much more likely to be exercised about rules of another sort, like those later

---

[43] Richard Findlater gives a much starker picture of the relationship between the English middle class and the theatre. In his account the bourgeoisie simply "ostracised" the theatre. "The middle classes did not go to the play"—evidently from the end of the sixteenth until the end of the nineteenth century (*The Unholy Trade*, pp. 18–19, 22, 24–25).

[44] Wendeborn, *View of England*, II, 182.

[45] Alan Dugald McKillop, *Samuel Richardson*, p. 207.

devised, for instance, by the ingenious and immortal Marquess of Queensberry.[46]

G. D. H. Cole confirms these assertions in his introduction to Defoe's *Tour thro' the Whole Island of Great Britain.*

Behind and underlying the world of Pope and Addison was a new world of *bourgeois* habits and culture, which, still insignificant politically even after 1688, was swiftly building itself up into the most powerful force in the nation. Fine Society had already recognized and largely assimilated Sir Josiah Child and the magnates of city commerce and finance. But behind these giants was the rising host of "complete trades-men" who, too numerous to be assimilated, were destined in time to assimilate society itself to their own habits and ideals.[47]

3

"For who can guess the effects of change," asks Samuel Johnson as he turns in his famous 1747 prologue from the past to the future. Growth in affluence and population combined with a fortuitous re-striction of the numbers of theatres to affect significant changes in the audience and, through the audience, in the drama. José Ortega y Gasset makes an interesting observation about this kind of growth in his *Revolt of the Masses*:

The history of the Roman Empire is also the history of the uprising of the Empire of the Masses, who absorb and annul the directing minorities and put themselves in their place. Then, also, is produced the phe-

---

[46] F. C. Green, *Minuet*, p. 5. *Town and Country Magazine* provides qualified support for Green's contention. In March 1772, in its "State of Europe" divi-sion, *Town and Country* studied English pastimes, first examining those of the gentry (foxhunting and the like), then those of the vulgar (boxing, cockfight-ing), and finally those "pursued in common by people of all ranks, such as stage plays, music meetings, tennis, fives, billiards, cards, riding, sailing, rowing, swimming, angling, fowling, and coursing." Some seventy-five years earlier B. L. de Muralt had made much the same observation, adding the emphasis of a surprised French visitor noting the ease with which high and low relaxed together (see especially Letter III in the English translation done a quarter of a century later, *Letters describing the Character and Customs of the English and French Nations*, pp. 32–49).

[47] George Douglas Howard Cole, Introduction to David Defoe, *Tour thro' the Whole Island of Great Britain*, I, x.

nomenon of agglomeration, of "the full." For that reason, as Spengler has very well observed, it was necessary, just as in our day, to construct enormous buildings. The epoch of the masses is the epoch of the colossal.[48]

Colossal is perhaps too strong a term to use in describing the theatres involved in the change that took place in the eighteenth century, but a qualifier only somewhat less gross would fit the structure that in 1794 replaced the small theatre designed by Sir Christopher Wren in 1674.

It is not easy to speak with certainty about the capacities of the various London theatres, at least not until the seventeen-eighties when detailed descriptions became available. Of the early Restoration houses very little is known. Since the population was still comparatively small and the audience less bourgeois than it was to become later, it is safe only to assume that no theatre used before 1700 could have seated as many as a thousand spectators in comfort; examples of theatre dimensions confirm this view. The earliest plan of which I am aware is the one reproduced by Richard Southern as most likely representing Wren's sketch for the Drury Lane house (1674–1791). Southern is persuaded that this house "could scarcely have held more than 500."[49] In *The London Stage* Avery and Scouten somewhat less conservatively suggest near twice that figure. The difficulty with their estimate is that it is arrived at largely from receipts, and receipts, even when available, can sometimes be hazardous as a basis for estimating effective capacity.[50]

[48] José Ortega y Gasset, *The Revolt of the Masses*, p. 21.

[49] Richard Southern, *The Georgian Playhouse*, p. 20.

[50] Their suggestion of a capacity of "about 1,000 spectators" appears on p. xliii of Part 1 of *The London Stage*. My cautionary note about using receipts for estimating the size of the house is not made in a spirit of ingratitude to the editors of this indispensable work. I wish simply to emphasize what they are themselves quite aware of, the various practices that make dependence on receipts hazardous: the overcrowding, especially in the pit; the issuing of numerous orders; the issuing of long-term "freedom of the theatre" to a variety of persons, especially writers and shareholders. This last item, the "free list," became in time quite formidable. A clipping in the Winston Collection, British Museum, discloses that Drury Lane under the prodigal R. B. Sheridan managed to forestall financial difficulties

Whatever its original size, Wren's house seems not to have been much changed in the seventy-five years following its construction. Colley Cibber talks about expansion under the elder Rich, but Rich's efforts must have been very modest. Changes during Garrick's quarter of a century, especially those at the beginning of his regime in 1747 and again in 1762, appear to have increased the size of the house to something like Stone's estimate of 1,800, which I should consider an absolute maximum.[51]

John Rich had meanwhile been involved in the management of two theatres. His first house, the second Lincoln's Inn Fields theatre, Avery judges to have been capable of holding 1,400 but this would appear to have been on a very crowded night.[52] Covent Garden,

_____

in 1786 by rescinding its list and resolving to "deal for ready money only." Another item in the same collection, dated 18 September 1795, informs the public that "the former free list of Drury Lane Theatre [consisting] of eight hundred names" will be suspended. In the same collection (December 1799) is a manuscript list by the Drury Lane treasurer, Peake, which specifies by groups the entire free list, the total having by then reached 775. And still another, a letter from a Mr. Mathias dated 24 August 1799 and addressed to Sheridan, asks if an enclosed note, dated 20 September 1776, in which Sheridan gives Mathias and Lady "free ticket before the curtain" is still good. It sounds like an accountant's nightmare.

[51] *London Stage*, pt. 4, p. xl. Pedicord gives a wealth of figures, but I find it hard to place much confidence either in his method or in his results. One sample should suffice. Beginning with an estimate of 1,335 for the new Covent Garden, an estimate based on a doubtful method, he reads Aaron Hill's casual and equivocal statement that Covent Garden is larger than Drury Lane "by one part in three" to mean that Drury Lane is "three fourths the size of its competitor," though Hill's vague statement might just as easily be taken to mean two thirds. By using these shaky approximations he eventually derives a figure of 2,362 for Drury Lane in 1762, a figure with the double defect of being much too large and misleadingly precise looking. Wendeborn, who was attending the theatres in the mid-eighties after the enlargement of Covent Garden in 1782, reports what might be termed received estimates, estimates that perhaps sin in the opposite direction of being too small: "The house in Covent Garden is said to hold, when it is full, about fifteen hundred people, and that in Drury Lane about thirteen hundred, because it is somewhat smaller" (*View of England*, II, 178).

[52] *London Stage*, pt. 2, p. xxxiv. *The British Stage: or, The Exploits of Harlequin*, has Windmill, who presumably represents Spiller, one of Rich's comedians, boast that "every night of our celebrated representation [of the Faustus pantomime], we are honoured with an audience of fifteen hundred persons" (p. 3).

which from the start seems to have been sizably larger than its rival nearby, Scouten estimates at 1,400 also.[53] If Rich had been impelled by recent successes to aim at something nearer the colossal in 1732 he might well have been deterred by the appearance in this premonopoly period of smaller rivals in the Haymarket and at Goodman's Fields. It was not until some twenty years after his death and with the expiration of the original fifty-year lease that Covent Garden was greatly expanded. Since the architect was confined within the original walls the most he could achieve in 1782 was a capacity of 2,170.[54]

Prior to the seventeen-nineties, the sizes of two other houses are important. Though John Palmer's Royalty Theatre was eventually not allowed to compete with the patent houses, it was built as their competitor and its size has some significance. *Gentleman's Magazine* for June 1787 gives a detailed account of the new house; with a lower gallery that probably held more people than Wren's original Drury Lane, the theatre had a capacity of 2,594. Sir John Vanbrugh's baroque house in the Haymarket, opened in 1705, was designed as an opera house and, even though it served in its early years as a rival to Drury Lane, it proved for a variety of reasons acoustically unsuited for plays. It seems difficult now to discover what its seating capacity was. Scouten estimates that it would seat "not much over 1400" though he reports the use in 1735 of "a contrivance . . . to accommodate 2,000 people."[55] Better information on the size of the replacement for this house after it burned in 1789 is also unavailable. Surely the figure given by more than one witness in 1791 is not acceptable as the actual capacity. Horace Walpole, reporting to Mary Berry on 11 March concerning the opening, gives the results of offering an opera gratis:

[53] *London Stage*, pt. 3, p. xxxii.

[54] George Saunders, *A Treatise on Theatres*, p. 87. This count is obviously reliable, though Saunders does err in saying the rebuilding occurred in 1784. Stone, who makes an insignificant error in adding up the total, somehow gets the notion that this figure applies to Covent Garden "before its enlargement in 1782" (*London Stage*, pt. 4, p. xxx).

[55] *London Stage*, pt. 3, p. xx.

"It is computed that four thousand people accepted the favour."[56] An even more amazing account in a contemporary newspaper states that a similar throng gathered six months later when the Drury Lane company opened its fall season at the Haymarket, which it occupied while its new house was being constructed: "It is a fact, however extraordinary it may seem, that so great was the public avidity for seeing the new Haymarket Theatre, nearly eight thousand people applied for admittance on Thursday evening, of whom upwards of four thousand actually procured admission in the house."[57] It would appear that the mysterious contrivance had somehow survived the flames.

Though the precise size of the rebuilt Haymarket opera house is unknown, George Kearsley's *Stranger's Guide* [c. 1793?] states that it was the largest of the existing theatres, larger even than Covent Garden, which had again been rebuilt in 1792 and about which some facts are extant. I am not at all sure I should classify as fact the publicity release given by James Harris to the newspapers. In it he claims that the whole effect is that of "a small theatre and it is not calculated to hold many more than the old one." The actual capacity of Covent Garden seems to have been 2,652 on opening night, hardly a small theatre. When Harris lost his battle with the gods and was obliged to restore the missing upper gallery, the count went up to 3,013. Theatres begin now to approach the colossal.[58]

During the spring of 1791 the managers of Drury Lane had

[56] Horace Walpole, *Horace Walpole's Correspondence*, edited by Wilmarth Sheldon Lewis, XI, 218–219.

[57] Clipping in Winston Collection, British Museum, 24 September 1791.

[58] The publicity release, which gives very full details but no figures for capacity, was reproduced by the newspapers. My check of the *Public Advertiser*, the *Morning Chronicle*, and the *Diary: or, Woodfall's Register* suggests a reasonably faithful rendering. The *Monthly Mirror* cut at some places, perhaps most misleadingly removing the *many* from the comment on the size of the new house. *Gentleman's Magazine* cut three paragraphs completely, among them the one in which this sentence appeared. Thomas Gilliland reproduces this description in

finally made the momentous decision to tear down the venerable house that had stood on the same site for almost a century and a quarter. Their temporary occupancy of the opera house in the Haymarket gave rise to protest from some members of the company, who felt the house was too large. Occasional preludes serve as an omen of what was bound to happen as theatres increased in size. James Cobb's *Poor Old Drury*, with which the company opened the 1791–1792 season, is intended only as a whimsical observation on the new location. George Colman's *Poor Old Haymarket*, with which the manager of the summer company opened his new season at the Little Haymarket the following June, is less mild. The central figure, a Mr. Project, is intent on tearing down their small house and, now that gigantic theatres are the rage, building "a long Salisbury-Plain of a stage all across Suffolk Street."

Something of the sort Mr. Project had in mind was opened by the Drury Lane company on 12 March 1794. The newspapers and periodicals of the time are full of details that leave no room for doubt: the age of the colossal had arrived. Three seasons later, in July 1797, the *Monthly Mirror* gives the actual capacity: 3,611. This, it will be observed, is some four times the size of the 1674 house or even larger if the more conservative estimate of Wren's house is accepted.[59]

The results of this expansion, to the detriment of seeing and hearing, are predictable. English drama moved farther and farther in the direction of the loud and the spectacular. Melodrama had al-

---

the *Dramatic Mirror* (1808) making minor revisions and adding dimensions and capacities—just before the house was destroyed by fire. *The Microcosm of London* (1808–1811) reproduces Gilliland's version with proper acknowledgement— the so-called reprint of 1904 misprints 1792 as 1799. Brayley also reproduces it in his 1826 account, though he is characteristically silent about his indebtedness.

[59] The *Thespian Magazine* devotes several pages in the issues from February through April to describing this theatre. Perhaps more accessible to the general reader and more graphic would be a comparison provided by two plates in Southern's excellent little book: Plates 2 and 5 face each other and give the reader an opportunity of comparing Wren's 1674 interior with Holland's 1794 one.

ready appeared before the age of gigantism. Richard Cumberland's *Brothers* (1769), though usually classified as sentimental comedy, contains most of the ingredients of melodrama from its opening scene of storm and shipwreck to the closing one of villainy exposed and virtue rewarded. Or take *Richard Coeur de Lion* (1786), adapted from Sedaine by that stout champion of the middle class, General Burgoyne. With the enlarged theatres of the seventeen-nineties and their greatly increased capabilities for the spectacular, the trickle of melodrama became a flood. Cumberland's *Wheel of Fortune* (1795), Colman's *Iron Chest* (1796), Monk Lewis's *Castle Spectre* (1797), Thompson's *Stranger* (1798)—these representative pieces indicate clearly where the theatre is headed.

How much the increased size of the theatre buildings is cause and how much mere effect is impossible to say. There is doubtless a great deal of the phenomenon called reinforcement at work here with an increased effect operating in turn as a cause. Ortega y Gasset sees the problem as a simple one: "Romanticism was the prototype of a popular style. First-born of democracy, it was coddled by the masses."[60] Possibly so. To persons of cloudier vision the problem is more complex. In the present instance, the increase in affluence, the increase in the numbers of the less "cultivated" people in the audience would tend to increase the demand for coarser emotional effects, scenic display, and the like. But there is much of the sheer mechanical here. Increased distances call for starker effects. The development of the machinery for such effects would lead to still greater use of the very thing the machinery was designed for. The practice of giving credit in the playbills to those responsible for scenery or costume begins, by no accident, about this time.

An even more graphic illustration of this point concerning the effects of new machinery is to be found in the accounts of the first play given at the new Drury Lane theatre, the performance of *Macbeth* on 21 April 1794. The newspapers of the day are filled with items concerning the new house and the crowd that had jammed

---

[60] José Ortega y Gasset, *The Dehumanization of Art*, p. 5.

the theatre long before the curtain rose. Miss Farren spoke an occasional epilogue designed to call attention to the most novel features. With so long a history of freedom from fire it might seem that the company would have been content to stand on its record, but the recent disasters at the Haymarket Opera House and the Pantheon had made everyone fire-conscious. Several of the lines spoken by the charming actress were devoted to the theme of fire, or to the elaborate precautions: the plating, the iron curtain soon to be installed, the reservoir of water.[61] To dramatize the management's concern for public safety, "a boy was introduced rowing a boat on a canal of real water,"[62] or, as another account gives it, "a lake of real water."[63] The introduction of canals and lakes may initially have been in the interest of safety. Eventually they were to be exploited for scenic display. Soon sea fights and cascades—and earthquakes and volcanoes as well—were mounted.

A final example of the increase in the spectacular is found in the "grand heroic pantomime entitled *Alexander the Great: or, The Conquest of Persia,* which ran at Drury Lane from 12 February 1795 on through March and into April. This procession to end all processions, which would have made the late John Rich envious, attained its climax with the entry of Alexander's car, drawn by two elephants: Colley Cibber remembers that old Christopher Rich at the other end of the century had to be dissuaded from putting elephants on the stage, but by 1795 the theatre was seriously engaged with the colossal.

It is hard not to wonder how Richard Steele might have reacted to these developments. Many of the demands he expressed in peri-

---

[61] Some of the precautions may have had greater psychological value than useful physical effect. David Hartley's *Proposals for the Security of Spectators in Any Public Theatre against Fire* (1792), to a nonexpert a very careful study of such matters, states that the plating—installed originally in the burned-out Pantheon—was a snare and a delusion.

[62] Unidentified newspaper clipping, 21 April 1794, Winston Collection, British Museum.

[63] Walley Chamberlain Oulton, *The History of the Theatres of London,* II, 150.

odical and preface had been filled: the moral tone of the drama had become more bourgeois, the public behavior of the audience, though sometimes still rowdy, resembled his prescription. There were to be sure side effects that Steele could not have foreseen and possibly would not have approved. Since, however, they mostly involved scale and since his own objective was an ever wider spread of what had been the moral and esthetic traits of the few, he would as a reasonable man have been forced to accept the changes. Perhaps he would have chosen the latter end of the century, especially if he could still claim credit for having wrought much of what it represented.

WORKS CITED

THEATRICAL COLLECTIONS

London. British Museum.
  Charles Burney collection of notebooks [on] actors.
  Charles Burney collection of notebooks [on] the history of the stage.
  Charles Burney collection of notebooks [on] David Garrick.
  Charles Burney press cuttings and MS notes [on] David Garrick.
  Charles Burney, "Theatrical Register."
  Collection of memoranda etc. [on] Drury Lane.
  Collection of newspaper cuttings [on] Drury Lane.
  Collection of playbills.
  R. J. Smith Collection.
  Theatre Collection.
  Winston Collection.
London. Victoria and Albert Museum.
  Enthoven Theatrical Collection.
New York. Public Library.
  Theatre Collection.
San Marino, California. Henry E. Huntington Library.
  Larpent MS play collection (includes *Covent Garden Theatre* [1752], *A Lick at the Town* [1751]).
Washington, D.C. Folger Shakespeare Library.
  Richard Cross MS diary.
  William Hopkins MS diary.
  Various theatrical clippings.
  Winston Collection.

BOOKS

Abrams, Meyer Howard. *The Mirror and the Lamp*. New York: Oxford University Press, 1953.
Addison, Joseph, and Richard Steele. *The Spectator*. Edited by Donald Frederick Bond. 5 vols. Oxford: Clarendon Press, 1965.

Appleton, William Worthen. *Charles Macklin*. Cambridge, Mass.: Harvard University Press, 1960.

Armstrong, John. "Taste." In *Miscellanies*. 2 vols. London, 1770.

Austen, Jane. *Jane Austen's Letters*. Edited by Robert William Chapman. 2nd ed. Oxford: Clarendon Press, 1952.

Baker, Thomas. *The Humour of the Age*. London, 1701.

Belden, Mary Megie. *The Dramatic Works of Samuel Foote*. New Haven: Yale University Press, 1929.

Beljame, Alexandre. *Men of Letters and the English Public in the Eighteenth Century, 1660–1744*. London: Kegan Paul, et al., 1948.

Bernbaum, Ernest. *The Drama of Sensibility*. Boston and London: Ginn, 1915.

Boswell, James. *Boswell: The Ominous Years 1774–1776*. Edited by Charles Ryskamp and Frederick Albert Pottle. New York: McGraw-Hill, 1963.

———. *Boswell in Search of a Wife, 1766–1769*. Edited by Frank Brady and Frederick Albert Pottle. London: Heinemann, 1957.

———. *Boswell's Journal of a Tour to the Hebrides*. Edited by Frederick Albert Pottle and Charles Hodges Bennett. New York: Viking, 1936.

———. *Boswell's Life of Johnson*. Edited by George Birkbeck Hill and Lawrence Fitzroy Powell. 6 vols. Oxford: Clarendon Press, 1934–1950.

———. *Boswell's London Journal 1762–63*. Edited by Frederick Albert Pottle. New York: McGraw-Hill, 1950.

The Bow Street Opera. London, 1773.

The British Stage: or, The Exploits of Harlequin. London, 1724.

Brown, John. *An Estimate of the Manners and Principles of the Times*. London, 1757.

Brownsmith, J. *Dramatic Time-piece. London,* 1767.

Burgoyne, John. *The Lord of the Manor*. London, 1781.

Burke, Edmund. *Reflections on the Revolution in France*. Edited by Thomas H. D. Mahoney. Indianapolis: Bobbs-Merrill, 1955.

Burney, Fanny. *Evelina*. 4th ed. 3 vols. London, 1779.

Byrd, William. *The London Diary, 1717–1721, and Other Writings*. Edited by Louis Booker Wright and Marion Tinling. New York: Oxford University Press, 1958.

Campbell, Thomas. *Dr. Campbell's Diary of a Visit to England in 1775*. Edited by James Lowry Clifford. Cambridge: Cambridge University Press, 1947.

The Case of Our Present Theatrical Disputes. London, 1743.

Cazamian, Louis. *A History of French Literature.* Oxford: Clarendon Press, 1955.

Chaucer, Geoffrey. *The Canterbury Tales.* Edited by F. N. Robinson. Boston: Houghton, Mifflin, 1957.

Cibber, Colley. *An Apology for the Life of Mr. Colley Cibber.* Edited by Robert William Lowe. 2 vols. London: J. C. Nimmo, 1889.

———. *The Lady's Last Stake.* London, [1708].

Cibber, Theophilus. *An Epistle from Theophilus Cibber to David Garrick Esq.* London, 1755.

———. *The Lives and Characters of the Most Eminent Actors and Actresses.* London, 1753.

Clifford, James Lowry. *Hester Lynch Piozzi.* Oxford: Clarendon Press, 1941.

The Conduct of the Four Managers of Covent-Garden Theatre. London, 1768.

Congreve, William. *Love for Love.* London, 1695.

Cooke, Alistair. *One Man's America.* New York: Knopf, 1952.

Cooke, Thomas. *The Mournful Nuptials.* London, 1739.

The Country Gentleman's Vade Mecum. London, 1699.

Cradock, Joseph. *Literary and Miscellaneous Memoirs.* 4 vols. London: John Bowyer Nichols, 1828.

Cumberland, Richard. *Memoirs of Richard Cumberland.* 2 vols. London: Lackington & Allen, 1807.

Davies, Thomas. *Memoirs of the Life of David Garrick.* 2 vols. Dublin, 1780.

Defoe, David. *A Tour thro' the Whole Island of Great Britain.* Edited by George Douglas Howard Cole. 2 vols. London: Peter Davies, 1927.

Dennis, John. *The Critical Works of John Dennis.* Edited by Edward Niles Hooker. 2 vols. Baltimore: Johns Hopkins Press, 1939–1943.

A Dialogue in the Green-room upon a Disturbance in the Pit. London, 1763.

The Dictionary of National Biography. Edited by Leslie Stephen and Sidney Lee. 66 vols. London: Smith, Elder, & Co., 1885–1901.

The Disputes between the Managers of the Theatres and Their Actors Adjusted. London, 1744.

D–ry-L–ne P–yh–se broke open. London, 1748.

Dryden, John. *Conquest of Granada by the Spaniards: In Two Parts.* London, 1672.

———. *Essays of John Dryden.* Edited by William Paton Ker. 2 vols. Oxford: Clarendon Press, 1926.

———. *The Kind Keeper: or, Mr. Limberham.* London, 1680.

————. *The Vindication of the Duke of Guise*. London, 1683.

————. *The Wild Gallant*. London, 1669.

D'Urfey, Thomas. *The Old Mode & the New*. London, 1703.

Etherege, George. *She Wou'd if She Cou'd*. London, 1668.

Farington, Joseph. *The Farington Diary*. Edited by James Greig. 7 vols. London: Hutchinson, n.d.

Farquhar, George. *A Discourse on Comedy*. Edited by Louis A. Strauss. Boston: D. C. Heath, [1914].

————. *The Twin-rivals*. London, 1703.

Fielding, Henry. *The Author's Farce*. London, 1734.

————. *The History of Tom Jones, a Foundling*. 2nd ed. 6 vols. London, 1749.

————. *Miss Lucy in Town*. London, 1742.

————. *The Universal Gallant*. London, 1735.

Findlater, Richard. *The Unholy Trade*. London: Gollancz, 1952.

Garrick, David. *The Diary of David Garrick, Being a Record of His Memorable Trip to Paris in 1751*. Edited by Ryllis Clair Alexander. New York: Oxford University Press, 1928.

————. Epilogue to *The Maid of the Oaks*, by John Burgoyne. London, 1774.

————. *Lethe: or, Esop in the Shades*. London, 1745.

————. *Letters*. Edited by David Mason Little and George Morrow Kahrl. 3 vols. Cambridge, Mass.: Belknap Press of Harvard University Press, 1963.

————. *The Poetical Works of David Garrick, Esq*. Edited by George Kearsley. 2 vols. London, 1785.

————. *The Private Correspondence of David Garrick*. Edited by James Boaden. 2 vols. London: H. Colburn and R. Bentley, 1831–1832.

The Genuine Arguments of the Council, with the Opinion of the Court of Kings' Bench. London, 1774.

George, Mary Dorothy. *Catalogue of Political and Personal Satires Preserved in the Department of Prints and Drawings in the British Museum*. Vol. VII. London: Trustees of the British Museum, 1942.

Gibbon, Edward. *Gibbon's Journal to January 28th, 1763*. Edited by David Morrice Low. New York: Norton, [1929].

Goldsmith, Oliver. *Collected Works*. Edited by Arthur Friedman. 5 vols. Oxford: Clarendon Press, 1966.

Green, F. C. *Minuet*. London: J. M. Dent, 1935.

Grosley, Pierre Jean. *A Tour to London*. Translated by T. Nugent. 2 vols. London, 1772.

A Guide to the Stage: or, Select Instructions and Precedents from the

Best Authorities towards Forming a Polite Audience. 2nd ed. London, 1751.

Hartley, David. *Proposals for the Security of Spectators in Any Public Theatre against Fire*. London, 1792.

Hawkins, John. *The Life of Samuel Johnson, LL.D*. London, 1787.

Hemlow, Joyce. *The History of Fanny Burney*. Oxford: Clarendon Press, 1958.

Hill, Aaron. *The Works of the Late Aaron Hill*. 4 vols. London, 1753.

Historia Histrionica, 1699. Reprinted in *An Apology for the Life of Mr. Colley Cibber*. Edited by Robert William Lowe. 2 vols. London: J. C. Nimmo, 1889.

Holcroft, Thomas. *Rival Queens*. London. 1794.

Horace. *Q. Horatii Flacci: Epistolae ad Pisones et Augustum*. Edited by Richard Hurd. London, 1753.

Hotson, Leslie. *The Commonwealth and Restoration Stage*. Cambridge, Mass.: Harvard University Press, 1928.

Hughes, Edward. *North Country Life in the Eighteenth Century*. 2 vols. London and New York: Oxford University Press, 1952–1965.

Hughes, Leo. *A Century of English Farce*. Princeton: Princeton University Press, 1956.

The Intimate Letters of Hester Piozzi and Penelope Pennington, 1788–1821. Edited by Oswald Greenways Knapp. London and New York: John Lane, 1914.

Ireland, Samuel. *Mr. Ireland's Vindication of His Conduct*. London, 1796.

Jackman, Isaac. *Royal and Royalty Theatres*. London, 1787.

Jacob, Hildebrand. *A Nest of Plays*. London, 1738.

Johnson, Samuel. *Lives of the English Poets*. Edited by George Birkbeck Hill. 3 vols. Oxford: Clarendon Press, 1952.

———. *The Works of Samuel Johnson*. Edited by E. L. McAdam, Jr. New Haven and London: Yale University Press, 1958–. Vol. II, *The Idler and The Adventurer*, edited by Walter Jackson Bate, 1963; Vol. VI, *Poems*, 1964.

Kitchin, Laurence. *Mid-Century Drama*. London: Faber and Faber, 1960.

Krutch, Joseph Wood. *Comedy and Conscience after the Restoration*. New York: Columbia University Press, 1924.

Lancaster, Henry Carrington. *A History of French Dramatic Literature in the Seventeenth Century*. 5 vols. Baltimore: The Johns Hopkins Press, 1929–1942.

Latter, Mary. *Siege of Jerusalem*. London, 1763.

LeBlanc, Jean Bernard. *Letters on the English and French Nations.* 2 vols. London, 1747.

A Letter to Mr. Garrick on the Opening of the Theatre. London, 1758.

A Letter to Mr. G. K., Relative to His Treble Capacity of Manager, Actor, and Author; with Some Remarks on Lethe. London, 1749.

A Letter to My Lord . . . on the Present Diversions of the Town. London, 1725.

Lichtenberg, Georg Christoph. *Lichtenberg's Visits to England.* Edited by Margaret Laura Mare and William Henry Quarrell. Oxford: Clarendon Press, 1938.

Lillo, George. *The London Merchant: or, The History of George Barnwell, and Fatal Curiosity.* Edited by Adolphus William Ward. Boston and London: D. C. Heath, 1906.

Loftis, John. *The Politics of Drama in Augustan England.* Oxford: Clarendon Press, 1963.

————. *Steele at Drury Lane.* Berkeley: University of California Press, 1952.

The London Stage. Edited by William Van Lennep, Emmett L. Avery, Arthur H. Scouten, George Winchester Stone, Charles Beecher Hogan. 5 parts. Carbondale: Southern Illinois University Press, 1960–.

Lough, John. *Paris Theatre Audiences in the Seventeenth and Eighteenth Centuries.* London: Oxford University Press, 1957.

Lynch, James Jeremiah. *Box, Pit, and Gallery.* Berkeley: University of California Press, 1953.

McKillop, Alan Dugald. *Samuel Richardson.* Chapel Hill: University of North Carolina Press, 1936.

Mélèse, Pierre. *Le théâtre et le public à Paris sous Louis XIV, 1659–1715.* Paris: E. Droz, 1934.

The Microcosm of London. 3 vols. London: T. Brensley, [1808–1811].

Miller, James. *The Coffee House.* London, 1737.

Misson, Henri. *Mr. Misson's Memoirs and Observations.* Translated by John Ozell. London, 1719.

Molière. *Plays by Molière.* Edited by Francis Ferguson. Modern Library Edition. New York: Random House, 1950.

Molloy, Charles. *The Coquet.* London, 1718.

Morgan, Macnamara. *Philoclea.* London, 1754.

Morley, Christopher. Preface to *Boswell's London Journal 1762–63.* Edited by Frederick Albert Pottle. New York: McGraw-Hill, 1950.

Motteux, Peter Anthony. *Farewel Folly.* London, 1707.

Muralt, B. L. de. *Letters Describing the Character and Customs of the English and French Nations.* London, 1726.

Neville, Sylas. *Diary, 1767–1788*. Edited by Basil Cozens-Hardy. London: Oxford University Press, 1950.

Nicholson, Watson. *The Struggle for a Free Stage in London*. Boston and New York: Houghton, Mifflin, 1906.

Nicoll, Allardyce. *A History of English Drama, 1660–1900*. 6 vols. Cambridge University Press, 1955–1961.

Le nouveau théâtre anglois. Edited by Marie Jeanne Riccoboni. 2 vols. Paris, 1769.

Observations on the Importance and Use of Theatres. London, 1759.

Ortega y Gasset, José. *The Dehumanization of Art*. Princeton: Princeton University Press, 1948.

———. *The Revolt of the Masses*. New York: W. W. Norton, 1958.

Oulton, Walley Chamberlain. *The History of the Theatres of London*. 2 vols. London, 1796.

Palmer, Joseph. *A Four Months Tour through France*. Dublin, 1776.

Paston, George. *Social Caricature in the Eighteenth Century*. London: Methuen, 1906.

Pedicord, Harry William. *The Theatrical Public in the Time of Garrick*. New York: King's Crown Press, 1954.

Pepys, Samuel. *The Diary of Samuel Pepys*. Edited by Henry B. Wheatley. 8 vols. London: G. Bell & Sons, 1923.

The Playhouse Pocket-companion, or Theatrical Vade-mecum. London, 1779.

Pope, Alexander. *Correspondence*. Edited by George Sherburn. 5 vols. Oxford: Clarendon Press, 1956.

———. *The Poems of Alexander Pope*. Edited by John Butt. 10 vols. London: Methuen, 1939–1967.

———. *The Works of Alexander Pope Esq*. Edited by William Warburton. 9 vols. London, 1751.

Pottle, Frederick Albert. *James Boswell: The Earlier Years, 1740–1769*. New York: McGraw-Hill, 1966.

Ralph, James. *The Touch-Stone*. London, 1728.

Reed, Joseph. *Retort Courteous*. London, 1787.

Reflections Upon Theatrical Expression in Tragedy. London, 1755.

Rennel, Gabriel. *Tragi-Comical Reflections*. London, 1755.

Reynolds, Frederick. *The Life and Times of Frederick Reynolds*. 2 vols. London: Henry Colburn, 1826.

Richardson, Samuel. *Clarissa*. 7 vols. London, 1747–1748.

———. *Clarissa: Preface, Hints of Prefaces, and Postscript*. Augustan Reprint Society No. 103, edited by R. F. Brissenden. Los Angeles: University of California at Los Angeles, 1964.

————. *Familiar Letters on Important Occasions.* Edited by Brian W. Downs. London: G. Routledge and Sons, 1928.

Rowe, Nicholas. *The Ambitious Step-Mother.* London, 1701.

Ryder, Dudley. *The Diary of Dudley Ryder, 1715–1716.* Edited by William Matthews. London: Methuen, 1939.

Saunders, George. *A Treatise on Theatres.* London, 1790.

Saussure, César de. *Lettres et voyages en Allemagne, en Hollande et en Angleterre (1725–1729).* Edited by B. Van Muyden. Lausanne: n.p., 1903.

Schultz, William Eben. *Gay's Beggar's Opera.* New Haven: Yale University Press, 1923.

A Seasonable Examination of the Pleas and Pretensions of the Proprietors of, and Subscribers to, Play-houses, Erected in Defiance of the Royal Licence. London, 1735.

Shadwell, Charles. *The Fair Quaker of Deal: or, The Humours of the Navy.* London, 1710.

————. *The Humours of the Army.* London, 1713.

Shadwell, Thomas. *The Sullen Lovers: or, The Impertinents.* 2nd ed. London, 1670.

Shenstone, William. "Essays on Men, Manners, and Things." In *The Works in Verse and Prose,* edited by Robert Dodsley. 2 vols. London, 1764.

————. *The Letters of William Shenstone.* Edited by Marjorie Williams. Oxford: B. Blackwell, 1939.

Sherbo, Arthur. *English Sentimental Drama.* East Lansing: Michigan State University Press, 1957.

Sheridan, Richard Brinsley. *Critic.* London, 1779.

Smith, Dane Farnsworth. *The Critics in the Audience of the London Theatres from Buckingham to Sheridan.* Albuquerque: New Mexico University Press, 1953.

Some Considerations on the Establishment of the French Strolers. London, 1749.

Southern, Richard. *The Georgian Playhouse.* London: Pleiades Books, 1948.

Southerne, Thomas. *The Wives Excuse: or, Cuckholds Make Themselves.* London, 1692.

The Spleen: or, The Offspring of Folly. London, 1776.

Stamper, Francis. *A Modern Character, Introduc'd in the Scenes of Vanbrugh's Aesop.* London, 1751.

Steele, Richard. *The Conscious Lovers.* London, 1723.

————. *The Lying Lover.* London, 1704.

————. *Mr. Steele's Apology for Himself and His Writings.* London, 1714.

————. *The Theatre, 1720.* Edited by John Loftis. Oxford: Clarendon Press, 1962.

Summers, Montague. *The Restoration Theatre.* London: Kegan Paul et al., 1934.

Theatrical Disquisitions. London, 1763.

Thomson, James. *Letters and Documents.* Edited by Alan Dugald McKillop. Lawrence: University of Kansas Press, 1958.

Three Original Letters to a Friend in the Country. London, 1763.

Tocqueville, Alexis de. *Democracy in America.* 2 vols. New York: Knopf, 1945.

Tricks of the Town. Edited by Ralph Straus. London: Chapman and Hall, 1927. [Reprints *The Country Gentleman's Vade-mecum.* London, 1699.]

Uffenbach, Zacharias Konrad von. *London in 1710.* Edited by William Henry Quarrell and Margaret Mare. London: Faber and Faber, 1934.

Victor, Benjamin. *An Epistle to Sir Richard Steele, on His Play, Call'd, The Conscious Lovers.* 2nd ed. London, 1722.

————. *The History of the Theatres of London and Dublin.* 3 vols. London, 1761.

————. *Original Letters, Dramatic Pieces, and Poems.* 3 vols. London, 1776.

Walpole, Horace. *Horace Walpole's Correspondence.* Edited by Wilmarth Sheldon Lewis. 34 vols. New Haven: Yale University Press, 1937–1965.

Warton, Thomas. *The Pleasures of Melancholy.* London, 1747.

Wendeborn, Gebhard Friedrich August. *A View of England towards the Close of the Eighteenth Century.* London, 1791.

The Wentworth Papers, 1705–1739. Edited by James Joel Cartwright. London: Wyman and Sons, 1883.

Whincop, Thomas. *Scanderbeg. . . . To which are added, a Compleat List of All the Dramatick Authors.* London, 1747.

Whitney, Lois. *Primitivism and the Idea of Progress.* Baltimore: Johns Hopkins Press, 1934.

Wilkinson, Tate. *Memoirs of His Own Life.* 4 vols. York, 1790.

Wright, Thomas. *The Female Vertuoso's.* London, 1693.

Wycherley, William. *The Country Wife.* London, 1675.

Wyndham, Henry Saxe. *The Annals of Covent Garden Theatre from 1732–1897.* 2 vols. London: Chatto and Windus, 1906.

198 *Works Cited*

ARTICLES

Avery, Emmett L. "The *Plain Dealer* in the Eighteenth Century." *Research Studies of the State College of Washington*, 12 (1944), 234–256.

———. "The Reputation of Wycherley's Comedies as Stage Plays in the Eighteenth Century." *Research Studies of the State College of Washington*, 12 (1944), 129–137.

Beaumont, Elie de. "Un voyageur français en Angleterre en 1764." *Revue Britannique*, 5 (September–October 1895).

Chapman, Robert William, and Allen T. Hazen. "Johnsonian Bibliography: A Supplement to Courtney." *Oxford Bibliographical Society Proceedings and Papers*, 5 (1938), 117–166.

Crean, P. J. "The Stage Licensing Act of 1737." *Modern Philology*, 35 (August 1937–May 1938), 239–255.

Jackson, Alfred. "Play Notices in the Burney Newspapers." *PMLA*, 48 (1933), 815–849.

Scouten, Arthur H. Review of *All Right on the Night* by V. C. Clinton-Baddeley. *Philological Quarterly*, 34 (1955), 256.

Tynan, Kenneth. "An Audience of Critics." *Holiday*, 36, no. 4 (October 1964), 111–119.

Woods, C. B. "Captain B——'s Play." *Harvard Studies and Notes*, 15 (1933), 243–255.

PERIODICALS AND NEWSPAPERS

Bingley's Journal, 1770–1790.
Censor, 1715–1717.
Champion, 1739–1743.
Common Sense, 1737–1743.
Connoisseur, 1754–1756.
Courier and Evening Gazette, 1798.
Covent-Garden Journal, 1752.
Craftsman, 1726–1750.
Critical Review, 1773.
Critick, 1718.
Daily Journal, 1720–1737. Especially the "Occasional Prompter" articles.
Daily Post, 1719–1746.
Diary: or, Woodfall's Register, 1789–1793.
Female Tatler, 1709–1710.
Gazetteer and London Daily Advertiser, 1735–1796.
General Advertiser, 1744–1752.

Gentleman's Magazine, 1731–1800.

Grub-Street Journal, The, 1730–1737.

Guardian, 1713.

Inspector, 1751.

Lloyd's Evening Post, 1757–1790 *passim.*

London Daily Post, 1734–1744. (Started in 1734 as *London Daily Post and General Advertiser,* changed in March 1744 to plain *General Advertiser,* again changed in December 1752 to *Public Advertiser,* again in March 1794 to *Oracle and Public Advertiser,* and finally in 1798 was absorbed by the *Daily Advertiser.*)

London Evening Post, 1727–1800.

London Magazine, 1732–1785.

Midwife: or, Old Woman's Magazine, 1752–1753.

Mist's Weekly Journal, 1717–1737.

Monthly Mirror, The, 1795–1800.

Morning Chronicle, 1769–1800.

Morning Post, 1772–1800.

Oxford Magazine, 1768–1776.

Parker's Penny Post, 1718 [?]–1733 [?].

Prater, 1756.

Prompter, 1734–1736.

Prompter, 1789.

Public Advertiser, 1752–1794.

Rambler, 1750–1752.

Read's Weekly Journal, 1715–1761.

Spectator, 1711–1712, 1714.

Sunday Chronicle, 1788–1790.

Tatler, 1709–1711.

Theatre, 1720.

Theatrical Guardian, 1791.

Theatrical Review, The, 1758, 1763, 1772.

Thespian Magazine, The, 1792–1794.

Town and Country Magazine, 1769–1796.

Universal Magazine, 1747–1803.

Universal Spectator, 1728–1746.

Westminster Magazine, 1773–1785.

INDEX